The Population of Britain in the 1990s

All the authors were members of the Geography Department at the University of Newcastle upon Tyne during the main stages of the preparation of this atlas, working within or in association with the NorthEast Regional Research Laboratory, the Centre for Urban and Regional Development Studies, and the Spatial Data Group of the University's Institute for Urban and Rural Research.

Individual authors

TONY CHAMPION is Professor of Population Geography at Newcastle University. His principal interests are in the monitoring and analysis of population and social change in Britain, particularly their regional and local dimensions. He was Chair of the Institute of British Geographers Population Geography Study Group, 1992–5, and Council member of the British Society for Population Studies, 1991–5. He chaired the IBG Working Party on Migration in Britain and was co-director of the ESRC-funded Census Analysis Group. Previous publications include *Counterurbanization* (Edward Arnold, 1989), *Contemporary Britain: A Geographical Perspective* (Edward Arnold, 1990), *People in the Countryside* (Paul Chapman, 1991), *Migration Processes and Patterns* (Belhaven, 1992), and *Population Matters: The Local Dimension* (Paul Chapman, 1993).

CECILIA WONG is Lecturer in the Department of Planning and Landscape at Manchester University. After a Master's degree in Town and Country Planning, she worked as a planner in Cleveland County Council and then as a full-time researcher in the Centre for Urban and Regional Development Studies at Newcastle University. Her research interests are in the development of quantitative methods for resource allocation and policy evaluation, and in the application for information technology in planning. She is co-author of *Developing indicators to assess the potential for urban regeneration* (HMSO, 1991).

ANN ROOKE is cartographer at the Geography Department at Newcastle University. She is a B.Sc. Geography graduate from University College of Swansea and took the Higher National Certificate in Cartography and Mathematics at the former Kingston Polytechnic. She also undertakes freelance cartographic work for the tourist industry, including Northumberland National Park.

DANIEL DORLING is Lecturer in Geography at the University of Bristol. He graduated from Newcastle University in Geography, Mathematics, and Statistics in 1989 and completed his Ph.D. on the visualization of spatial social structure in 1991. He then held a 2-year Joseph Rowntree Fellowship awarded to Newcastle University's Housing and Society Research Group and subsequently was British Academy Fellow in the Geography Department. His research interests include studying the geography of society, politics, and housing, notably through the computer mapping and analysis of census data.

MIKE COOMBES is Principal Research Associate in the Centre for Urban and Regional Development Studies. A graduate in philosophy, he has been a full-time researcher for over 15 years. He is on the national executive of the Labour Market Statistics Users Group, and has led the research to define the government's Travel-to-Work Areas. He has a particular interest in creating statistical 'profiles' of cities and regions, including measures of deprivation. He is co-author of *Developing indicators to assess the potential for urban regeneration* (HMSO, 1991).

CHRIS BRUNSDON is Lecturer in the Department of Town and Country Planning at Newcastle University. He holds M.Sc. (with Distinction) in Medical Statistics from Newcastle University, 1985, and his Ph.D. work was in the analysis of crime patterns, also at Newcastle. Subsequently, he has researched on the UK housing market and various techniques in spatial analysis and Geographical Information Systems.

The Population of Britain in the 1990s

A Social and Economic Atlas

Tony Champion, Cecilia Wong, Ann Rooke, Daniel Dorling,
Mike Coombes, and Chris Brunsdon

CLARENDON PRESS · OXFORD
1996

Oxford University Press, Walton Street, Oxford OX2 6DP

Oxford New York
Athens Auckland Bangkok Bogota Bombay
Buenos Aires Calcutta Cape Town Dar es Salaam
Delhi Florence Hong Kong Istanbul Karachi
Kuala Lumpur Madras Madrid Melbourne
Mexico City Nairobi Paris Singapore
Taipei Tokyo Toronto
and associated companies in
Berlin Ibadan

Oxford is a trade mark of Oxford University Press

Published in the United States
by Oxford University Press Inc., New York

British Library Cataloguing in Publication Data
Data available

Library of Congress Cataloging in Publication Data
Champion, A. G. (Anthony Gerard)
The population of Britain in the 1990s: a social and economic atlas /
Tony Champion . . . [et al.]
1. Great Britain—Population.   2. Great Britain—Population—Maps.
I. Title.   G1812.21.E2C4   1996 ⟨G&M⟩   304.6′0941′022—dc20   96–1647
ISBN 0–19–874174–X
ISBN 0–19–874175–8 (Pbk)

Typeset by Hope Services (Abingdon) Ltd.
Printed in Great Britain
on acid-free paper by
The Bath Press

Preface

This atlas aims to portray key features of the human geography of Britain in the 1990s. It covers a wide range of topics which we have grouped under seven broad headings relating, in turn, to population distribution and composition, birthplace and ethnicity, employment and education, life chances, housing, transport and facilities, and political geography. In addition, the atlas has the secondary objective of illustrating how different types of maps and measures can portray a variety of different topics. In other words, it is hoped that the reader will remember that the map-maker was able to choose from many options when compiling any one map. In this introductory discussion we set out our justification for taking this new look at Britain at this time and highlight the types of decisions which we needed to take in planning the atlas.

In terms of presenting the case for this volume, the principal rationale lies in the pace and nature of the changes which have been affecting people in Britain over the past decade. Some of these changes constitute reversals of earlier trends, such as the shift from the substantial population growth and overall economic expansion of the early post-war decades to slower growth and recession more recently. Other changes represent an extension, and in some cases a reinforcement, of established trends which continue to alter the complexion of localities across Britain, such as the movement of people away from the larger cities to smaller settlements and more rural areas, and the shift of employment out of production sectors into services.

This is also an opportune time to carry out such an updating of Britain's human geography because of the wealth of fresh data available to us. While a range of official statistics are published on an annual basis, most of these derive from sample surveys which cannot provide reliable country-wide information below the scale of the standard region (e.g. East Anglia, South West). For more local information, the primary source is the Census of Population which is undertaken only once every ten years. The most recent Census took place in 1991, and the results of this nearly complete enumeration of people in Britain have been appearing steadily over the past four years, ending up with the special datasets on commuting and migration. We therefore now have available to us the full range of output from the 1991 Census and have been able to identify what we consider to be the major findings to be drawn from it. These make up about two-thirds of the contents of this atlas, with the remaining one-third using statistics drawn from other sources which complement or update the Census material.

In setting about the task of producing this volume, we have had to make a number of decisions about what to include and how the material should be presented. This approach is outlined in the next few paragraphs with the dual purposes of providing guidance on the way that information in the atlas should be interpreted and of trying to provoke critical thought about alternative methods of presentation. The key point is that we faced many choices, and it is quite likely that we opted for methods of presentation which either fitted most closely to our expectations or showed things in what we considered to be a novel or interesting light.

The first decision to make is, of course, what topics should comprise the contents of the atlas. It is not really necessary here to emphasize that the range of issues which could be covered by an atlas of human geography is dauntingly wide and varied. The selection made here is unashamedly influenced by the personal interests of the authors, but it is even more influenced by data availability. For example, no map of average incomes by area is included here because there are no official statistics for this most fundamental issue below the county level. Maps of 'poverty' or 'affluence' have to rely on indirect, or 'proxy', measures. Among other basic issues which are not included here—because there are not even any plausible proxy measures which can be mapped—are, for instance, area averages of people's height, of their membership of religious or other organizations, of their first language, or of their leisure interests. The atlas seeks to compensate for some of these omissions with a diverse selection of measures which include some complex or unfamiliar statistics.

The next decision to be made by the map-maker involves choosing how to analyse the chosen dataset to produce a measurement, or other form of information, which can then be mapped. For those datasets where data availability is less of a problem, straightforward counts, ratios, percentages, and trend analyses are usually presented here to help the reader by choosing easy-to-understand measures wherever they would be appropriate. In some cases, however, one or more datasets have to be analysed in non-standard ways in order to provide the most meaningful measure—perhaps as a proxy for a 'missing' dataset, perhaps because the aim is to represent a rather abstract issue.

For any one topic which the map-maker has selected as the primary feature, there is often another issue which provides the context within which it can best be understood. Glancing through this atlas, it may seem that only one or two of the maps—such as

Information cities—deal with more than a single topic at the same time. Yet this is to forget how a map is read. How many people look at a map of Britain without the knowledge that London is in the southeast while the least populated regions are in the northern and western periphery? Most readers will also know that the central areas of the country are largely characterized by the effects of industrialization, and so will see in many maps the influence of industrial traditions or long-term economic decline. In other words, the map may feature only one topic explicitly, but can be presented in a way which allows most people to 'read into it' a more considered underlying pattern. Of course, the reader needs to be careful not to read patterns into maps in which the evidence is more ambiguous or, indeed, may be presented by the map-maker in such a way as to exaggerate the strength of the evidence for one interpretation of the data rather than another.

How can one 'reading' of a map pattern be promoted at the expense of other alternatives? Quite apart from the commentary provided in the accompanying text, the other nearby material can stimulate a particular way of looking at the map. For example, there may be one or more adjacent maps in which, say, a North–South divide of the country is starkly evident. It will then be instinctive for the reader to check all other maps nearby to see if they echo this pattern. Adjacent diagrams or graphs may also raise spatial contrasts (e.g. between metropolitan and rural areas) which are then likely to be uppermost in the mind when the nearby map is being examined.

The overall impression given by a map itself is largely the product of a series of technical map-making decisions which will have been taken to emphasize that aspect of the input data which is considered to be of most interest. On its own, Britain covers quite a small area of the globe so the choice of projection (e.g. Mercator) is not very influential in shaping most maps of this country. Two of the maps in this atlas (see *Voters' apathy* and *Election results 1992*, as well as the key map in Appendix 2), however, show that there is a still more fundamental question of how to present a 'human geography' map. This option is a cartogram, which serves as a reminder of one of the assumptions usually made when reading a map. This assumption is that a certain-sized area of map surface represents a certain-sized area of land surface (subject to any distortion caused by the projection). On the cartogram, however, the map is scaled so that a constant area of map covers a constant number of people. This is one, particularly dramatic, example of the map-maker's key technical decisions radically affecting the way the maps in this atlas appear. The cartogram is an option which presents itself when the map-maker needs a secondary issue (in this case, population distribution)

to be a very evident part of the background to the primary topic of the map.

The way in which population distribution shapes the cartogram acts as a reminder of how 'area distribution' forms the background to the more familiarly shaped maps. As a result, the conventional map can tend to draw attention to the parts of the country where few people live, simply because areas such as the Highlands of Scotland take up a large proportion of the land—and hence map—surface. For an atlas of human geography, it is a relevant question whether the maps should be emphasizing those areas where there are more sheep than people! The 'trade-off' which the map-maker faces is between, on the one hand, the problem of conventional maps over-emphasizing rural areas and, on the other hand, the cartogram's unfamiliarity which makes it harder for readers to recognize and interpret the patterns by using their prior knowledge and understanding in the way discussed earlier. One reason why the cartogram's pattern tends to be harder to interpret is that the coastline of Britain provides the usual link between the reader's prior information and the data on the new map: for example, the pattern of values in and around most of Britain's largest conurbations can soon be identified by the many people who know their location near to the coastline and the recognizable estuaries such as the Thames, Mersey, and Clyde in particular. The cartogram doesn't provide the conventional coastline by which the reader tends to orientate.

Whether drawing a cartogram or a conventional map, the next key decision is usually the level of detail which will be employed to reveal the contrasting spatial pattern of that topic. For most maps in human geography, this decision boils down to the choice of areal units—the 'building block' of the map. There will be purely technical constraints, with the size of the eventual printed image preventing too detailed a breakdown of the country. Often, the available data provides the limit to the detail which could be presented. At the same time, there can be good arguments to counter the natural presumption that showing the fullest possible detail is the ideal choice. Readers may well find it harder to interpret a pattern which is hugely fragmented, and be less able to compare it with, and add it to, the knowledge they already have about Britain's geography. A complex image can contain a huge volume of information, yet it may be far less intelligible than a simpler one.

A more abstract issue arises at this point—the so-called 'modifiable areal unit problem'. Put simply, the same basic data can present very different patterns when it is grouped and presented for different sets of areas. For example, Glasgow's tenement districts include some of the most densely populated areas of the country, but if the city's statistics are grouped with the other districts in the region of

Strathclyde then this region is seen to have a lower population density than any of the English metropolitan counties with which it would normally be compared. This particular example may be explained by the inclusion within Strathclyde of some very sparsely populated rural areas which lower the region's overall density value, but it still serves to demonstrate the fundamental sensitivity of the analysis to the areal units used.

This modifiable areal unit problem can thus be seen as something which should force map-makers to consider which areal units are *appropriate* for presenting each particular measure they have chosen to map. In many cases, the problem revolves around the question of whether cities are over- or under-bounded (where Glasgow is hugely over-bounded when represented by Strathclyde). Any 'given' set of areal units, such as counties and Scottish regions, can lead to misleading comparisons between cities because some are more generously bounded than others. Even if each set of areas was consistent in its treatment of all cities, there would still remain the question, for any particular map, of whether it would be more appropriate to have generously or narrowly bounded cities. For many socio-economic issues, it has long been recognized that city regions, or labour-market areas, are the appropriate units of analysis because they will include both the inner-city residents and the rural commuters who live within the same urban system, and who depend on the same economic prospects. Unfortunately, Census data is not published for any set of areas of this kind. For this atlas, therefore, a special set of areas has been devised to divide Britain into a meaningful and comparable set of 'places' (see the notes to *Ethnicity and opportunity*).

For maps which are not labour-market related topics, standard administrative areas are often used because in these cases the 'trade-off' tips in favour of the greater familiarity of these units, and of recognizable boundaries such as the counties along much of England's south coast. To aid the reader, a set of key maps showing counties and Scottish regions, local government districts, 'places', and political constituencies (on their cartogram basis) is provided at the end of the atlas in order to identify individual areas and localities.

Having decided on the topic(s), measure(s), and areal units for the map, the remaining choices are more cartographic in nature. Would the values be more intelligible if the map plotted, in each area of the country, a device such as columns or proportionally sized circles (as for *Born outside marriage* or *Wealth*)? The column could perhaps itself take the form of a bar chart (as for *House prices and negative equity*), while the circle could take the form of a divided pie chart (as for *Exam results and qualifications*). Other options include flow maps using arrows or lines of linkage proportional to the amount of interaction between areas (as for *Migration between regions* and *Patterns of commuting*).

The most familiar form of map in human geography, however, is the shaded or 'choropleth' map. The distribution of a particular population subgroup (such as *The elderly*), say, or the intensity of a problem such as unemployment relative to that of other areas (as for *Men without work*), is readily shown and understood as the intensity of the shading within that area's boundary. The use of colour clearly increases the options available, which can be particularly valuable if the map is of trends over time, and some values can be positive and others negative (as for *Patterns of population change*). The map's shading may be presented solely by colouring of different intensity, or by different forms of hatching—or indeed by some combination of these (as in *Ethnicity and opportunity*). Such decisions may appear quite technical, but do starkly affect the image which is presented and hence the way the map will be read.

There is a less obvious, but at least as influential, set of decisions on the shading categories for the map. Choosing how many different categories will be shown, and where in the distribution of values to split one category from the next, affects greatly the clarity of the final map by determining whether, for example, many small areas will be shaded similarly and strongly. Equally obviously, the setting of the class limits—the values at which one category is split from the next—directly controls whether 'extreme' values appear to be widespread or to be concentrated in only certain parts of the country.

A few maps in this atlas (for example, *Railways and motorways*) appear to be closer to the 'topographic' style of a road map than to the shaded 'polygon' map which has been the focus for much of the discussion here so far. Yet these apparently simple maps clearly also involve fundamental decisions on what information to include, and how to present it. For example, the map of *Major tourist attractions* was just as much the product of technical decisions on which categories to present, what class limits to use, and what areas to show as background, as were the choropleth maps in the atlas.

A map reader might feel that all these subjective decisions mean that the cliché of 'lies, damned lies, and statistics' can be applied to the eventual map, because it is essentially an artefact of the map-maker's own point of view. It is inevitably true that the map-maker will highlight one particular aspect of the topic: the justification has to be that this aspect is arguably the most significant or interesting. In this atlas, the accompanying text to the maps makes no claim that there is only a single possible 'reading' of the data; the aim here is the simpler one of providing some initial material and ideas to prompt further thought and examination of a wide range of topics. This introductory discussion, of the decisions lying behind the maps which are presented in this atlas, explicitly recognizes that many very different atlases of Britain's human geography could have been produced from the range of data which has been drawn upon here. Hopefully, what we have presented in this atlas will inspire—or provoke—readers to develop their own alternative perspectives and to go on to examine a wider range of topics from the types of sources which we have used here.

In terms of using the atlas, we have contrived to make the atlas as user-friendly and informative as possible. Each of the sixty-four topics has been designed as a self-contained double-page spread, with its own commentary. Any cross-referencing between topics is done by showing a topic heading highlighted in italic type. The sources of the data for each topic are given in separate notes at the back of the atlas, along with any more technical information about methods of calculation and guidance as to how to interpret the data shown. Also included at the end, as mentioned above, are key maps for all the main map bases which we have used.

As suggested by the multiple authorship listed on the title page, this atlas results from a team effort involving regular meetings to plan the atlas and discuss the draft material. As in all good teams, however, division of labour was the order of the day. Ann Rooke handled all the final cartography, constantly impressing the rest of the team with her dexterity on her AppleMac, and devising eye-catching icons in her attempts to diversify away from the standard choropleth map. Daniel Dorling set up the digital boundaries and data aggregation programs as the basis for data analysis and mapping. In terms of taking the lead on individual topics, Chris Brunsdon was primarily responsible for *Projecting future employment patterns*, *Contrasting employment sectors*, *Offenders and crimes*, *The future of private housing*, *Projecting voting patterns*, and *Tactical voting and a future political map*. Daniel Dorling took the lead on *Exam results and qualifications*, *Wealth*, *Death chances*, *House prices and negative equity*, *Voters' apathy*, and *Election results 1992*. Mike Coombes contributed *New and old universities*, *Patterns of commuting*, *Railways and motorways*, *International gateways*, *Major tourist attractions*, *Information cities*, and *Sporting cities*. Cecilia Wong and Mike Coombes worked together on *Ethnicity and opportunity*, *Men without work*, *Lacking skills and jobs*, *Staying on at school*, *Matching ability to responsibility*, *New enterprise*, *Waged and unwaged*, *Growing up in poverty*, *Housing choice*, *Leaving the car at home*, and *Places to visit*. Tony Champion prepared the other thirty-four topics and had overall editorial responsibility for the atlas.

The team also drew on the resources and expertise available more widely in the NorthEast Regional Research Laboratory at Newcastle University. Stan Openshaw and Martin Charlton participated in the early discussions about the form that the atlas should take. Martin Charlton, David Atkins, and Simon Raybould helped to prepare the data for some of the topics. Much of the Census data was extracted from files compiled on the Newcastle University computer by Colin Wymer. Amanda Stonehouse typed Mike Coombes's drafts. The team is very grateful to these people for their support, as it is too to the Head of the Geography Department, Tony Stevenson, for encouraging this work and for allowing Ann Rooke to spend so much time on it.

Beyond the University, thanks go to Andrew Goudie for the original invitation to undertake this work, made in his capacity as President of the Geographical Association. This atlas is a companion to *The Environment of the British Isles: An Atlas*, prepared by Andrew Goudie and Denys Brunsden as part of the Association's centenary celebrations and also published by Oxford University Press. We are very grateful for the support of Oxford University Press, notably to Andrew Schuller for seeing the proposal successfully through the Delegates, and to his successor as Senior Editor, Andrew Lockett, and most particularly to Enid Barker who has been very helpful as our point of contact from the earliest trials of the computer mapping and reproduction procedures through to the final stages. Lastly, we acknowledge the copyright permissions granted by the Ordnance Survey and the Office of Population Censuses and Surveys and the other sources listed in the separate Acknowledgements section and in the notes on each topic.

Mike Coombes, Tony Champion

Newcastle upon Tyne
October 1995

Acknowledgements

The authors gratefully acknowledge permission granted to use and reproduce material, as follows. The boundary data used is derived from Crown Copyright material but its free use for this educational purpose was permitted by Ordnance Survey. The Census data used in this publication is also Crown Copyright. Derived from the 1991 Census and earlier Censuses, the Census data is reproduced with the permission of the Controller of Her Majesty's Stationery Office. The Census data has been extracted from the ESRC/JISC purchase held and maintained by Manchester Computing. The data used to map non-registration of voters was provided by Steve Simpson. Barry Bissett, of Nationwide Building Society, provided the data used to calculate the geography of house prices. The sources for each topic are detailed in the notes in Appendix 1.

Contents

People and Places

Where people live

People are extremely unevenly distributed across Britain, but there is no one method for showing this. Plotting each person as a separate dot on a map is laborious and it does not yield any summary statistics. One alternative is to use a cartogram with symbols proportional to the population under study, as used later (see *Voters' apathy*). More common approaches are to show the proportion of people in each place or to calculate the density of population in an area.

The table shows that London accounts for one in eight (12.3%) of people in Britain, even though it comprises under 1% of national land area. At the other extreme, districts classified as 'Remoter mainly rural' contain fewer people but make up over half the land area. The range of densities is huge: from only 52 per km² for the latter—barely a fifth of the national level—to over 8,200 for Inner London, thirty-three times the average.

Population density, by district type, 1991

District type	Population		Area		Density
	000s	%GB	km²	%GB	persons/km²
Great Britain (GB)	56,206	100.0	228,320	100.0	246
Greater London	6,890	12.3	1,579	0.7	4,364
Inner London	2,627	4.7	320	0.1	8,209
Outer London	4,263	7.6	1,259	0.6	3,386
Metropolitan	12,729	22.7	8,568	3.8	1,486
Principal cities	4,139	7.4	1,732	0.8	2,389
Other districts	8,590	15.3	6,836	3.0	1,257
Non-metropolitan	36,587	65.1	218,173	95.6	168
Cities	5,647	10.0	7,708	3.4	1,365
Industrial areas	7,568	13.5	24,564	10.8	308
New towns	2,880	5.1	6,697	2.9	430
Resort, port, and retirement	3,626	6.5	10,496	4.6	346
Urban and mixed urban–rural	10,364	18.4	43,544	19.1	238
Remoter mainly rural	6,503	11.6	125,164	54.8	52

The map on this page shows the broad pattern of population distribution. It emphasizes the large conurbations of West Midlands county, Merseyside, Greater Manchester, and Tyne and Wear, as well as London, and shows the most sparsely populated areas to be the most rural parts of Wales and Scotland, with Highland region lowest at only 8 per km². The main zone of concentration stretches from north-west England through the Midlands to the south coast and is known variously as 'the coffin' and 'the hour glass' because of its shape, sometimes as 'the English Megalopolis'.

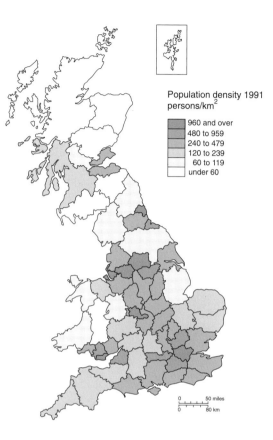

Population density 1991
persons/km²

- 960 and over
- 480 to 959
- 240 to 479
- 120 to 239
- 60 to 119
- under 60

0 50 miles
0 80 km

Population-weighted density

Conventional density calculations are very dependent on where boundaries of areas are drawn, accounting for the prominence on this map of South Glamorgan (a small area dominated by Cardiff) and the low profile of Glasgow (located within the huge Strathclyde region). Therefore the map opposite not only uses the finer-grained district level but is based on the density of the census ward in which people live. Where more people in a district live in the main town, this can give a very different density reading; for instance, for Cleethorpes district one of 1,471 per km², much higher than the overall average of 421.

Locally just as at the national scale, people are clustered on the ground, reflecting past patterns of urban development and the effect of land-use planning controls. But in recent decades some of these knots have begun to loosen.

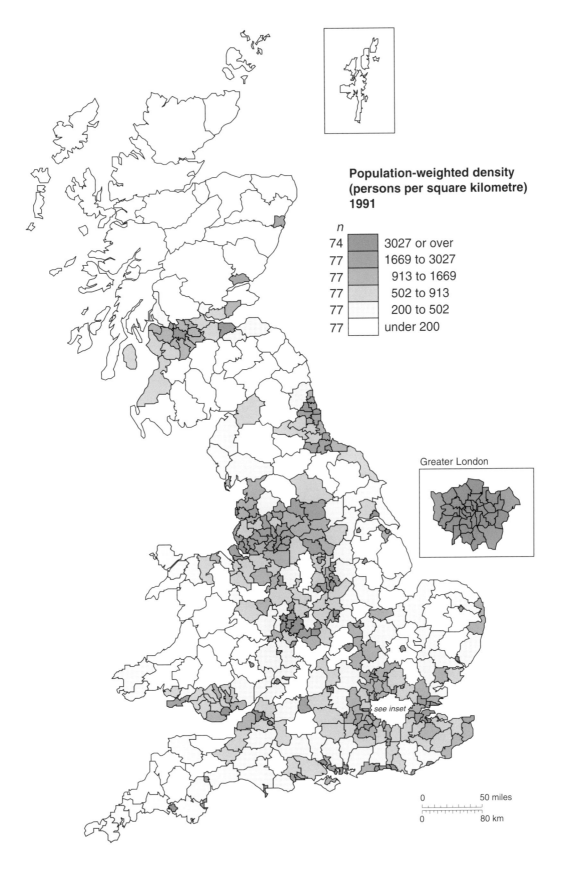

**Population-weighted density
(persons per square kilometre)
1991**

n		
74		3027 or over
77		1669 to 3027
77		913 to 1669
77		502 to 913
77		200 to 502
77		under 200

Greater London

see inset

| 0 | | | | | 50 miles |
| 0 | | | | | 80 km |

Patterns of population change

According to the table, East Anglia gained population fastest between 1981 and 1991. Higher than average rates were also recorded by the other three regions of the South and by Wales. Three northern regions lost population during the decade, while in between the populations of the West Midlands and Yorkshire and Humberside grew in absolute terms, but at a slower rate than nationally.

The bar graph presents this information in such a way that the volume of each bar is proportional to the absolute amounts of population change shown in the table. Reference to the Great Britain rate (shown by the pecked line) shows clearly which regions increased their share of the national population and which lost out. The North–South divide was clearly operating strongly during the 1980s.

English metropolitan counties contained fewer people in 1991 than ten years before. So too did some of the counties with legacies of mining and heavy industry in north-east England, south Wales, and central Scotland. The highest rates of growth are found in the less populated areas of the South, notably in the belt of counties stretching from Cornwall to East Anglia and Lincolnshire.

Map (b) provides an alternative perspective on the same period by focusing on the change in numbers of people per unit of land area. By definition, the areas of population decline remain the same, but the geography of growth presents a rather different picture from map (a), revealing that the largest absolute gains in population are concentrated in a pound-sign pattern of counties in the South.

Shift in patterns since the 1970s

As shown in the table and map (c), the North–South and urban–rural dimensions were already evident in the 1970s. The main change in the 1980s was the strengthening of the former at the expense of the latter. The area gaining most benefit from these changes was the South East region, with an upward shift of 4.4 percentage points in growth rate. All other regions performed more poorly in 1981–91 relative to the national rate of +1.7% points (see final column of the table).

These shifts in change rate between the two decades are shown at county level in map (d), revealing the impressive recovery of London from severe loss in the 1970s and showing the cutbacks recorded by the less urbanized counties of East Anglia, West Midlands, Wales, and Scotland.

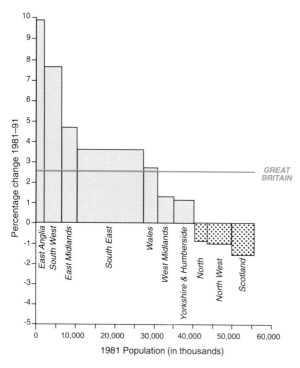

County patterns 1981–1991

The greater detail provided by the counties and Scottish regions in map (a), opposite, reveals an urban–rural shift working alongside the North–South drift. Strathclyde and all but one of the six

Population change, by region

Region (in order of 1981–91 change rate)	1981 population (000s)	1981–91 change (000s)	1981–91 change (%)	1971–81 change (%)	Shift (% point)
East Anglia	1,894	187	9.9	12.2	−2.3
South West	4,381	336	7.7	6.6	+1.1
East Midlands	3,853	183	4.7	5.5	−0.8
South East	17,011	626	3.7	−0.7	+4.4
Wales	2,814	78	2.8	2.7	+0.1
West Midlands	5,187	79	1.5	0.8	+0.7
Yorks. and Humb.	4,918	64	1.3	0.3	+1.0
North	3,117	−26	−0.8	−1.1	+0.3
North West	6,459	−63	−1.0	−2.6	+1.6
Scotland	5,180	−73	−1.4	−1.1	+0.3
Great Britain	54,814	1,392	2.5	0.8	+1.7

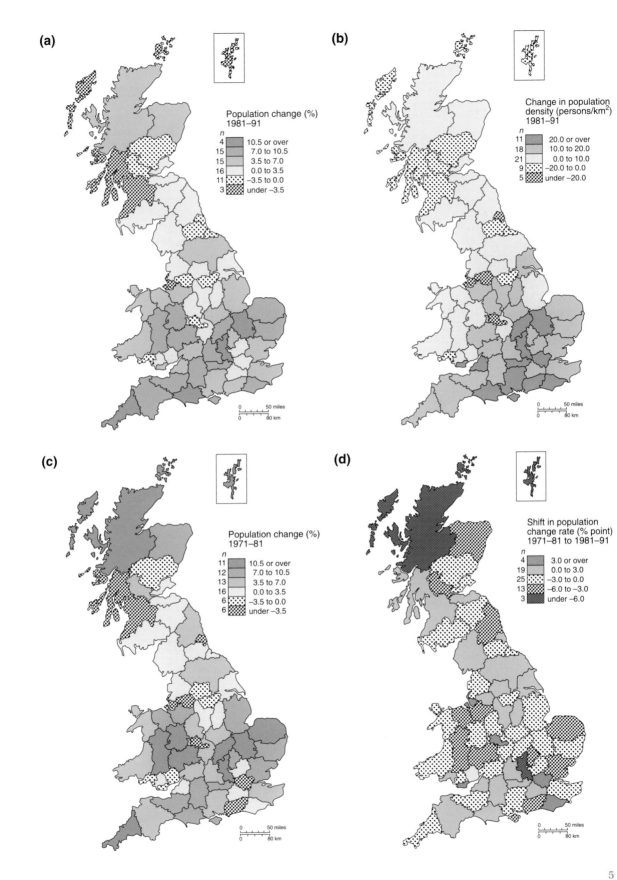

5

Births, deaths, and migration

Overall population changes can be decomposed into two main components—natural change and migration. The rates for 1981–91 are shown for these in maps (a) and (b). Natural change refers to the surplus of births over deaths. Maps (c) and (d) show the 'crude' birth and death rates for the last full year of the 1981–91 decade.

Birth, death, and natural change rates, when calculated with respect to the total population as they are here, are strongly influenced by age structure. Natural change rates tend to be higher in areas with fewer elderly people, because crude death rates are lower there and the proportion of women of child-bearing age is greater. Hence the high rates in the block of counties stretching from Berkshire to Leicestershire and Cambridgeshire, with very low death rates and generally high birth rates. At the other extreme, many of the more peripheral (i.e. coastal) and rural counties record low levels of natural change, with low birth rates and high death rates reflecting their older age structure (see *Age structure*).

Migration is the more important component of population change at county level. This is shown by the wider range of shading in map (b), which uses the same class intervals as in map (a) to allow direct comparison. The urban–rural shift is very clear at this level, with the net migration losses from the areas with major conurbations and traditions of mining and heavy industry. Above-average gain rates dominate in the less heavily urbanized areas, with the highest rates being for traditional retirement areas along the south coast.

The greater importance of migration is reflected in the rectangular shape of the graph which plots the

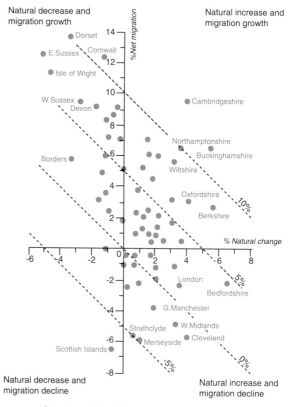

------- Overall population change rate

data from maps (a) and (b). Note the 'retirement counties' in the top left-hand corner, with their strong migration gains and natural decrease. Top-right are counties which have proved very attractive to younger people and have high rates of natural increase as well as of migration gain. Lower-right are counties which record strong natural increase despite heavy migration losses, reflecting the high birth rate shown in map (c).

The table of district types shows how strong migration gain enables the retirement districts to head the league of overall change despite their marked natural decrease. The remoter mainly rural districts are similar, though with less extreme rates. The new towns are the third fastest-growing type, thanks to their very high rate of natural increase, resulting in large part from their youthful age structure. London's high rate of natural increase is offset by net migration losses, but it is the metropolitan districts that recorded the highest rate of migration loss over the decade.

Population change, by district type, 1981–1991

District type	Population 1981 (000s)	Overall change 1981–91 000s	Overall change 1981–91 %	Natural change (%)	Net migration (%)
Great Britain	54,814	1,392	2.5	1.7	0.9
Greater London					
Inner London	2,550	77	3.0	4.4	−1.4
Outer London	4,256	7	0.2	3.0	−2.9
Metropolitan					
Principal cities	4,324	−185	−4.4	1.2	−5.5
Other districts	8,702	−112	−1.3	2.0	−3.3
Non-metropolitan					
Cities	5,598	49	0.9	1.7	−0.8
Industrial areas	7,440	128	1.7	2.4	−0.7
New towns	2,686	194	7.2	4.8	2.4
Resort, port, and retirement	3,368	258	7.7	−4.7	12.4
Urban and mixed urban–rural	9,840	524	5.3	2.4	2.9
Remoter mainly rural	6,051	452	7.5	−0.6	8.0

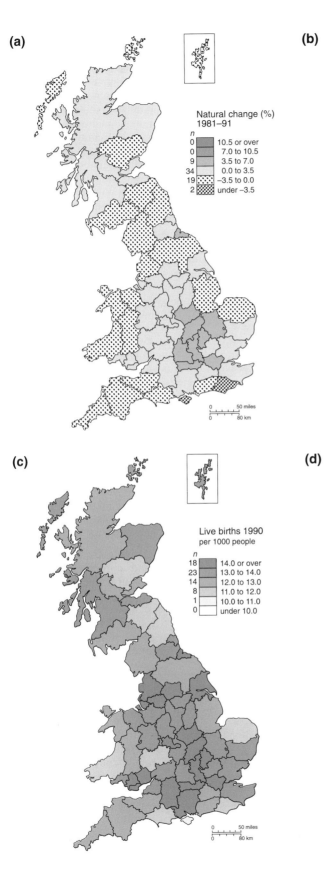

(a)

Natural change (%)
1981–91

n	
0	10.5 or over
0	7.0 to 10.5
9	3.5 to 7.0
34	0.0 to 3.5
19	–3.5 to 0.0
2	under –3.5

0   50 miles
0   80 km

(b)

Migration and
other changes (%)
1981–91

n	
4	10.5 or over
9	7.0 to 10.5
13	3.5 to 7.0
19	0.0 to 3.5.
12	–3.5 to 0.0
7	under –3.5

0   50 miles
0   80 km

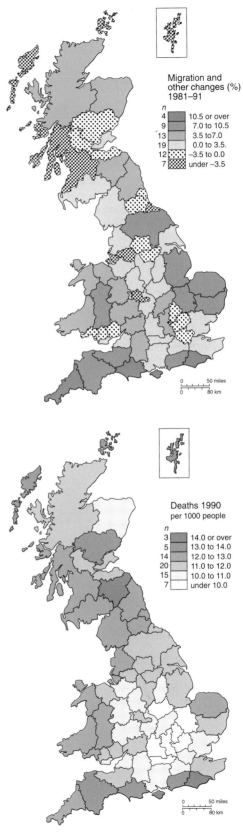

(c)

Live births 1990
per 1000 people

n	
18	14.0 or over
23	13.0 to 14.0
14	12.0 to 13.0
8	11.0 to 12.0
1	10.0 to 11.0
0	under 10.0

0   50 miles
0   80 km

(d)

Deaths 1990
per 1000 people

n	
3	14.0 or over
5	13.0 to 14.0
14	12.0 to 13.0
20	11.0 to 12.0
15	10.0 to 11.0
7	under 10.0

0   50 miles
0   80 km

People on the move

While migration is clearly a major component of overall population change, the net changes shown on the previous two pages represent only the 'tip of the iceberg' compared with the total numbers of people who move house every year. These two pages use 1991 Census data about people who said that their normal address was different from that of twelve months before. They show that most people moved house over relatively short distances, often staying within the same broad area and therefore not altering the size of its population. Where people did cross a boundary and enter a different area, they were to a large extent taking the place of people leaving it.

According to the 1991 Census, 5.35 million people had migrated in the twelve-month period before Census night, virtually one in every ten people. Truly, Britain can be considered a 'nation on the move'. Yet even this large figure is known to be an underestimate of the total number of moves made during that period; see the technical appendix to check whether you have thought of all the reasons why this should be so.

The importance of such 'one-year migrants' in the population varies across the country. In Oxfordshire the proportion of people living at a different address compared to a year before was 13.2%, while at the other extreme the figure was only 7.1% for Mid Glamorgan. The full picture in map (a), opposite,

Migration within Britain 1990–1991, by distance of move

Type of person	Proportion (%) by distance of move (km)			
	0–4	5–9	10–79	80+
All persons	55.9	12.7	17.6	13.7
Males	55.1	12.7	17.9	14.3
Females	56.8	12.7	17.5	13.1
Persons aged:				
1–4	62.6	12.1	14.2	11.1
18–19	54.3	12.4	17.3	16.0
20–29	53.3	13.6	18.9	14.1
45–64	54.8	12.2	18.6	14.5
75+	61.3	13.1	16.6	8.9

shows the highest proportions of one-year migrants to be concentrated in southern England (bar Essex) and northern Scotland.

Local residential turnover accounts for a large part of this migration and of its variation across Britain. Map (b) is based on the 72% of one-year migrants that had moved home but had not changed their county or Scottish region. On average, 7.1% of all residents fell into this category that year, but the proportion ranges from 5.4% for Warwickshire to 9.2% for Tayside.

The predominance of short-distance moves is confirmed by the table. Well over half of the people moving within Britain have a new address that is under 5 km from their previous one, with over two-thirds moving less than 10 km. Men and women are very similar in behaviour, but the very young and the elderly tend to move over much shorter distances than average.

Rates of in-migration, shown in map (c), present a pretty familiar picture of contrast between urban–industrial and more rural parts of the country—similar to the net change patterns shown in map (b) on the previous page. Less expected, perhaps, is that the pattern of gross out-migration rates is not so different from this. As seen from map (d), the highest rates of exodus feature some of the wealthiest and fastest-growing counties in southern England, while the northern conurbations have amongst the lowest rates of people moving away.

The close link between rates of gross in- and out-migration is clear from the graph and is, in fact, a well-documented phenomenon related to regional differences in the distribution of the most mobile people.

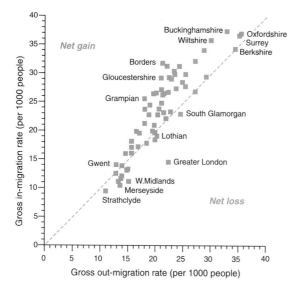

(a)

Migrants as proportion
of all residents (%)
1990–91

n
11   11.5 or over
13   10.5 to 11.5
12   9.5 to 10.5
17   8.5 to 9.5
11   under 8.5

0   50 miles
0   80 km

(b)

Migrants within area
as proportion of all
residents (%)
1990–91

n
9   7.9 or over
20   7.2 to 7.9
10   6.6 to 7.2
15   6.1 to 6.6
10   under 6.1

0   50 miles
0   80 km

(c)

In-migration from
rest of Great Britain
(per 1000 people)
1990–91

n
13   30.0 or over
15   25.0 to 29.9
14   20.0 to 24.9
10   15.0 to 19.9
12   under 15.0

0   50 miles
0   80 km

(d)

Out-migration to
rest of Great Britain
(per 1000 people)
1990–91

n
5   30.0 or over
7   25.0 to 29.9
26   20.0 to 24.9
17   15.0 to 19.9
9   under 15.0

0   50 miles
0   80 km

Migration between regions

While most migration takes place over short distances, it is the longer-distance moves that tend to attract most attention. This was particularly true of the 1980s when the widening of the North–South divide became a major political issue. These two pages use data from the National Health Service Central Register, a source which—unlike the Census—provides a continuous record of longer-distance moves within Britain.

The main lesson to be learnt from the graph showing the annual net movement of people between the North and South of Britain is that the rate of such movement, and even its direction, varies over time and can vary quite suddenly. The level of net gains for the South rose steeply during the mid-1970s to the 50,000-a-year mark, around which it fluctuated somewhat for about a decade. Between 1986 and 1988 the relative attractiveness of the South plummeted, to the extent that in 1989 and 1991 slight net transfers from South to North were recorded. These trends are mirrored in the trends in house prices (see *House prices and negative equity*) and are related to regional differences in the rate of recovery from the 1979–83 recession and in the onset of the major economic depression of the late 1980s.

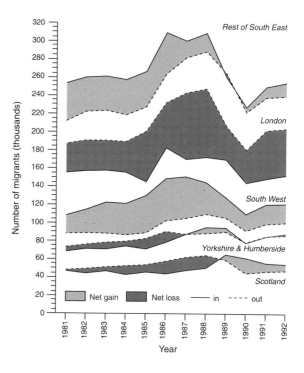

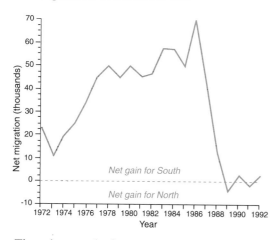

The other graph gives more detail about the complexity of these trends over time, showing the experience of different regions since 1980 in terms of gross as well as net movements. Most notable is the way in which out-migration from Scotland to the rest of Britain slowed down near the end of the 1980s and in-migration was running at a higher level than previously, giving several recent years of migration gains. The pattern for Yorkshire and Humberside was similar, though here the change took place a couple of years earlier and was less pronounced.

The direction of net migration in southern England was more robust over this twelve-year period, with the South West region being a consistent net gainer and London a substantial net loser, but in both cases the scale of movement diminished at the end of the decade. The South East region outside London, traditionally a major recipient of migration from London and northern Britain, saw a big departure from past trends at this time.

The maps opposite show gross flows for 1991. Each region sent to every other region at least 1,000 people that year and received at least 1,000 from every other region. The biggest flows are generally between adjacent regions as shown in map (b) and between London and the Rest of the South East in map (a). But also very impressive is the way in which the remainder of the larger flows are dominated by moves which had either origin or destination in London (map (a)) and in the rest of the South East (map (c)). Only the South West comes anywhere near these two in degree of inter-regional migration linkages.

Patterns of gross flows between regions are pretty stable, but relatively small changes in these can produce quite large shifts in net migration levels. These pose a great challenge for regional and local population forecasting.

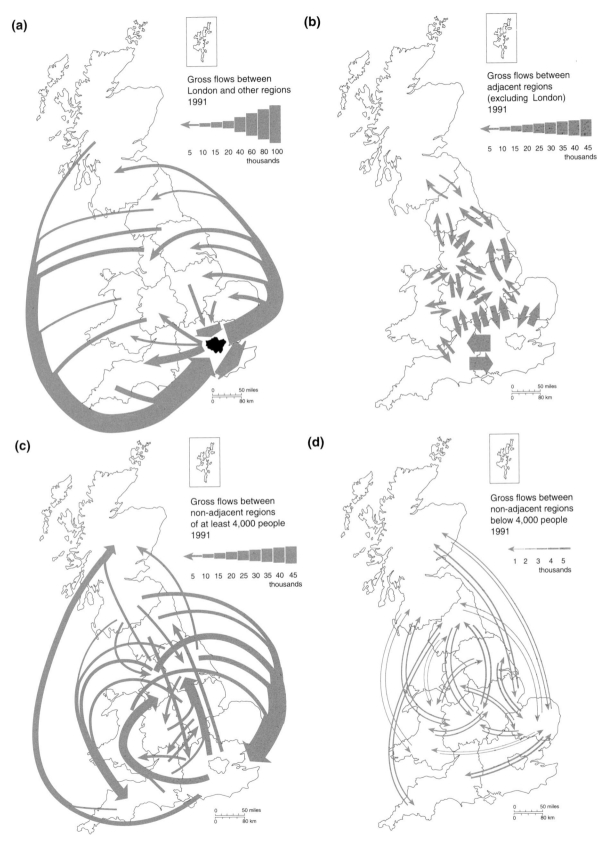

(a)

Gross flows between London and other regions 1991

5 10 15 20 40 60 80 100
thousands

0   50 miles
0   80 km

(b)

Gross flows between adjacent regions (excluding London) 1991

5 10 15 20 25 30 35 40 45
thousands

0   50 miles
0   80 km

(c)

Gross flows between non-adjacent regions of at least 4,000 people 1991

5 10 15 20 25 30 35 40 45
thousands

0   50 miles
0   80 km

(d)

Gross flows between non-adjacent regions below 4,000 people 1991

1 2 3 4 5
thousands

0   50 miles
0   80 km

11

Age of newcomers

Another very well-documented aspect of migration is that there are very regular and significant age variations in people's tendency to move house. This is demonstrated here by reference to the Population Census data on change of address over the previous twelve months.

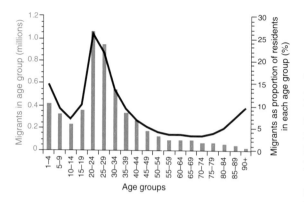

The bar graph on this page shows the number of people in each age group who were recorded as resident in Britain at the Census in April 1991 but who had been living at a different address a year before. Migration is clearly dominated by younger adults, with considerably fewer children and much smaller numbers of people aged 45 and over. Most impressive is the peaking in numbers for the 20–24 and 25–29 year-olds, who together account for over 2 million of the 5.35 million migrants identified by the Census, i.e. 38% of all migrants.

Obviously, part of the variation between the bars in this graph arises because of differences in the total population of each age, but even when allowance is made for this by calculating the proportion of one-year migrants in each age group (shown by the line and the right-hand scale), the general pattern is quite similar, with around one in four young adults being migrants but less than one in twenty of those aged 50 and over. The main exception is for the very elderly, where there is a steady increase with age in the likelihood of migration, including moves into residential-care homes.

The table and the map opposite focus specifically on newcomers to the counties and Scottish regions, i.e. residents who had crossed the boundary into these areas during the year before the Census (including from overseas). The table shows that the domi-

nance of young adults in the in-migration streams is not merely a national average but is found for a wide variety of area types. On the other hand, the %-point data reveal considerable variation around the national figures; for instance, London's in-migrants are notably concentrated in the 16–29 age group, Cornwall's share is much below average and Staffordshire's is close to the national pattern across all four age groups.

It is these deviations which are plotted on the map opposite in order to show at a glance how the age structure of newcomers varies across the country. The 16–29 age group has a very distinctive geography, being particularly important amongst migrants to the big-city areas including those of Bristol, Cardiff, and Edinburgh as well as most of the metropolitan counties and especially London. Remoter rural areas, by contrast, tend to be big net losers of young adults.

Rural areas and south coast counties, by contrast, score strongly amongst the 45+ group. Areas with above-average inflows of 30–44 year-olds and children tend to be 'suburban' in nature, like Cheshire, or with buoyant economies at the time of the Census, like Grampian, but are primarily to be found in the 1980s rapid-growth counties of the Greater South East such as Wiltshire and Northamptonshire.

Proportion of 1990–1991 in-migrants, by age: actual share (%) and deviation from national weighted mean (% point)

Area of 1991 residence	Age group				All ages
	1–15	16–29	30–44	45+	
Great Britain:					
%	16.6	45.9	23.6	13.9	100.0
Greater London:					
%	11.9	58.2	21.3	8.6	100.0
% point	−4.7	12.3	−2.3	−5.4	0.0
Greater Manchester:					
%	16.0	51.3	21.6	11.1	100.0
% point	−0.6	5.4	−2.0	−2.8	0.0
Staffordshire:					
%	17.0	44.8	23.6	14.6	100.0
% point	0.4	−1.1	0.0	0.6	0.0
Cheshire:					
%	18.6	41.0	26.1	14.4	100.0
% point	2.0	−4.9	2.5	0.5	0.0
Cornwall:					
%	19.5	34.4	23.4	22.8	100.0
% point	2.9	−11.5	−0.2	8.9	0.0

Note: Numbers calculated to two decimal places and rounded, so totals may not sum exactly.

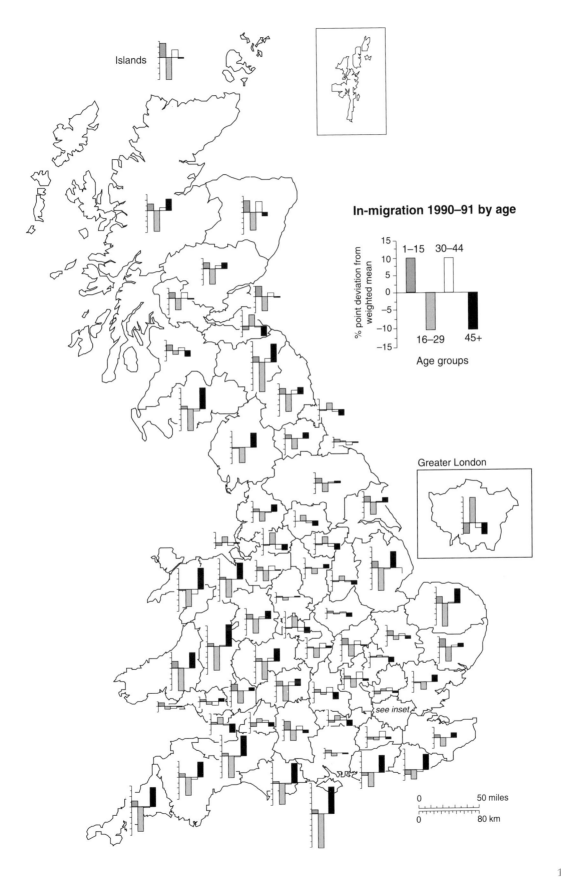

Islands

In-migration 1990–91 by age

1–15   30–44
16–29   45+

% point deviation from
weighted mean

Age groups

Greater London

see inset

0   50 miles

0   80 km

Age structure

The conventional way of portraying the age composition of a population is through what is still known as the 'age pyramid'. In Britain of the 1990s, however, such a triangular shape is clear only in the higher ages of 65 years old and over, where death takes its main toll. At lower ages, the general shape is rectangular, reflecting the existence of birth rates close to replacement level since the 1920s.

Nevertheless, some of the age groups below 50 years old are bigger than others, as shown by the different length of the bars in the diagram. At this national level, these result almost entirely from variations in the birth rate and can be identified by working out the period of birth of each age group. For instance, the longest bar is for those aged 25–29 in 1991 which contains those born in the years 1962–6 at the peak of the 'baby boom', this being followed by a 'baby bust' period in the latter half of the 1970s, seen here in the relatively few 10–14-year-olds.

The dominant theme of the county-level maps is the below-average representation of the younger half of the population (under-45s) in more rural parts of the country. This results principally from decades of out-migration by school-leavers, who gravitate to the larger cities and most economically dynamic areas (map (b)) and tend to settle in the more 'suburban' areas there to raise their own families (map (c)). Also important for many of these more rural and peripheral areas is the tendency for those aged 45 and over to move away from the more crowded and expensive areas, though some of the more urban areas with above-average levels in map (d) result from the ageing of the local work-force.

These patterns are reflected in the district-type graph. Those of older working age (between 45 and pensionable age) form above-average shares of the populations of the industrial areas and other metropolitan districts, as well as the two least urbanized types. The 16–24 year-olds are relatively most important in Inner London, the principal cities of the metropolitan areas and the non-metropolitan cities. London contains the largest proportions of the main working-age group (25–44 year-olds). At the two extremes of the age range, rather predictably, lie the new towns with the largest share of children and the resort, port, and retirement category with their distinctively high level of people of pensionable age.

Age distribution, Great Britain 1991

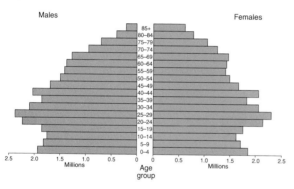

Geographical variations

Differences in age composition around Britain, however, have much more to do with migration than with variations in birth rates. The county maps very much reflect the effects of the patterns of migration examined on the previous pages, though it must be remembered that it is not only recent movements but also earlier ones (when patterns may have been rather different) that have made their imprint.

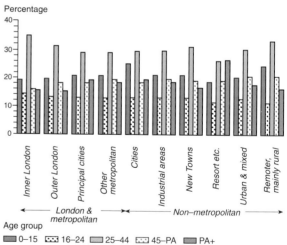

(a)

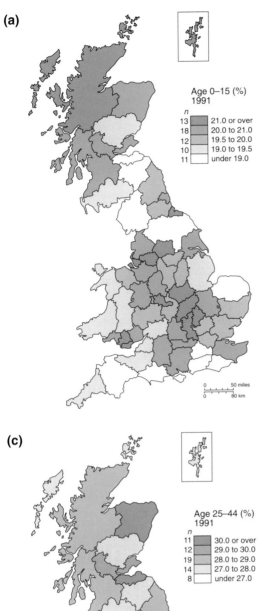

Age 0–15 (%)
1991

n
13   21.0 or over
18   20.0 to 21.0
12   19.5 to 20.0
10   19.0 to 19.5
11   under 19.0

0   50 miles
0   80 km

(b)

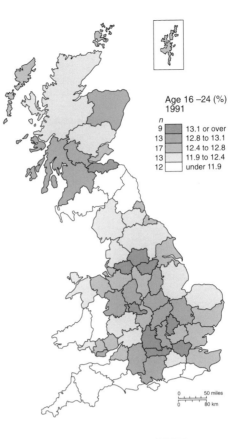

Age 16 –24 (%)
1991

n
9   13.1 or over
13   12.8 to 13.1
17   12.4 to 12.8
13   11.9 to 12.4
12   under 11.9

0   50 miles
0   80 km

(c)

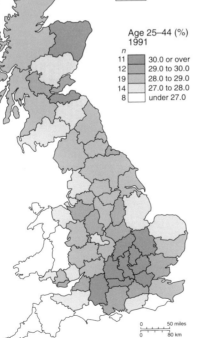

Age 25–44 (%)
1991

n
11   30.0 or over
12   29.0 to 30.0
19   28.0 to 29.0
14   27.0 to 28.0
8   under 27.0

0   50 miles
0   80 km

(d)

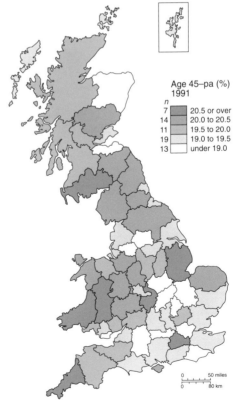

Age 45–pa (%)
1991

n
7   20.5 or over
14   20.0 to 20.5
11   19.5 to 20.0
19   19.0 to 19.5
13   under 19.0

0   50 miles
0   80 km

The elderly

The distribution of people of pensionable age (65 for men and 60 for women at present) is of interest not only in its own right but because of the policy and resource issues which this group raises. Per capita expenditure on health care and social welfare is much higher than for any other age group, and a great deal of support is needed at the local level, especially for the 'old elderly' (normally seen as those of 75 and over). The level of concern is heightened both by the rapid growth of the elderly population nationally and by its very uneven distribution within Britain.

Growth of the elderly population

In 1991 the elderly comprised 18.4% of the national population, up from 16.4% in 1971 and almost three times the proportion at the turn of the century. Over the twenty years to 1991, the actual number of elderly people is estimated to have grown by 16.6%, i.e. one extra person for every six in 1971. The figures for the 75+ group are even more striking: their numbers up from 2.6 to 4.0 million, an increase of 53%— in other words, an extra person in 1991 for every two in 1971, and their share of the total population up from 4.7 to 7.0%.

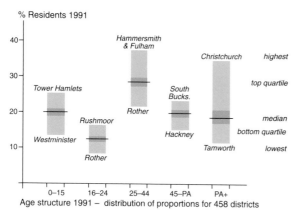

% Residents 1991

Age structure 1991 – distribution of proportions for 458 districts

Geographical variations

The spatial distribution is also more uneven than for any other broad age group. This is seen very well in the district-level analysis shown in the graph, where both the full range and the interquartile range are wider than for the four other groups despite the median level being lower than all but the narrowly defined 16–24 group. In relative terms, the range is even wider for the 75+ group on its own: 15.7% of the population of Rother (East Sussex) to 3.5% of Cumbernauld and Kilsyth (centred on a new town in Strathclyde).

The geographical pattern is also very distinctive. The evidence of the map, together with the listing of the top and bottom ten local authority districts and the district-type graph in *Age structure*, means that a commentary is hardly needed. Coastal resorts dominate, particularly along the south coast, but inland spa towns like Buxton and Harrogate also feature, as do a considerable number of rural districts away from the coast.

Meanwhile, settlements developed under the New Towns Act and the expanded towns programme dominate the bottom ten districts, along with districts with a strong presence of Armed Forces personnel. In general, the areas of the country with fewest elderly in their population are those which recorded the best job prospects for younger people during the previous decade, notably the arc of districts stretching around the edge of south-east England from Hampshire to the Cambridge area but including some more isolated examples such as the main players in the offshore oil industry in northern Scotland.

People of pensionable age: top and bottom ten districts, 1991

Top ten districts	%	Bottom ten districts	%
Christchurch, Dorset	34.6	Tamworth, Staffs	11.6
Rother, East Sussex	34.2	Milton Keynes, Bucks	11.8
Eastbourne, East Sussex	31.9	Cumbernauld and Kilsyth	11.8
East Devon	31.5	Wokingham, Berks	12.0
Arun, West Sussex	31.2	Hart, Hampshire	12.6
Tendring, Essex	30.5	Redditch, Heref. and Worcs.	12.9
West Somerset	30.0	Bracknell, Berkshire	12.9
Worthing, West Sussex	30.0	Surrey Heath	12.9
South Wight	29.8	West Lothian	13.1
Colwyn, Clwyd	27.9	Rushmoor, Hampshire	13.2

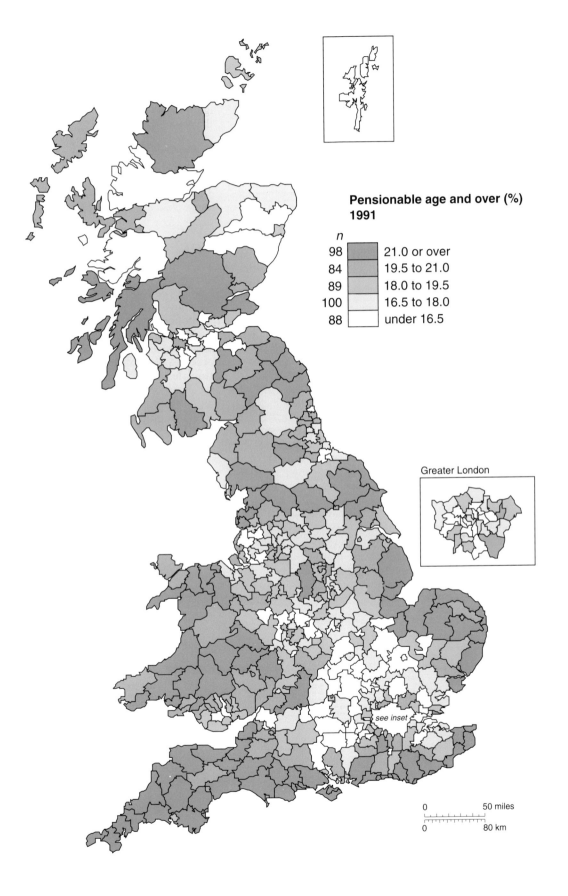

Pensionable age and over (%) 1991

n		
98		21.0 or over
84		19.5 to 21.0
89		18.0 to 19.5
100		16.5 to 18.0
88		under 16.5

Greater London

see inset

0   50 miles

0   80 km

An ageing population

Population ageing is very different from individual people getting older, because the population as a whole is constantly being replenished by new births and by migration exchanges with other areas. In theory, a population can become younger, if the level of births increases or migration involves a net gain of younger people or removes older people. As hinted in *The elderly*, however, this is not the current story because the numbers of children are falling and the numbers of elderly are rising.

The county-level maps concentrate on the two extremes of the age distribution and demonstrate the widespread nature of the ageing process over the 1981–91 period. The keys for maps (a) and (b) show the general distinction between decline in proportions of children and growth in the proportions of people of pensionable age. All areas saw their share of children fall, though by less than the national figure of 2.1% in London and all the metropolitan counties except South Yorkshire as well as in some of the south coast retirement counties which already had low proportions of young people. Nearly all areas saw their proportion of pensionable-age people rise, the exceptions being London, East Sussex, Borders, Grampian, and the Scottish Islands.

The percentage change in numbers is the more significant measure for many policy concerns. Maps (c) and (d) focus on the ages of compulsory schooling and the 'old elderly'. Between 1981 and 1991 the number of 5–15 year-olds fell by 17% nationally, causing great problems for those involved in providing education services, but the scale of change varied enormously: from a fall of almost 25% in Strathclyde region to one of only 6.6% in Cambridgeshire. The numbers aged 75+ rose in all areas: by a massive 38%

Age structure, UK, 1971–2011

Age group	1971		1991		2011	
	000s	%	000s	%	000s	%
Totals	55,928	100	57,801	100	61,110	100
0–4	4,551	8.1	3,873	6.7	3,544	5.8
5–15	9,705	17.4	7,861	13.6	8,311	13.6
16–44	20,839	37.3	24,565	42.5	22,977	37.6
45–pa	11,710	20.9	10,867	18.8	14,178	23.2
pa–74	6,479	11.6	6,589	11.4	7,333	12.0
75+	2,644	4.7	4,046	7.0	4,767	7.8
0–16	14,256	25.5	11,734	20.3	11,855	19.4
16–pa	32,549	58.2	35,432	61.3	37,155	60.8
pa+	9,123	16.3	10,635	18.4	12,100	19.8

pa = pensionable age.

in Hereford and Worcester and by less than 10% in London and the Scottish Islands.

These patterns are set in their longer-term national context in the table and graph. The proportion of under-16s fell from a quarter to a fifth between 1971 and 1991, and is projected to undergo further shrinkage by 2011, though the numbers of compulsory schooling age will rise somewhat. Those of pensionable age seem destined to outnumber children by 2001. The number aged 75+ grew by a massive 53% in 1971–91 and will continue to rise, albeit at a slower rate.

In between, the working-age groups are undergoing a huge change in response to the ageing of the 1960s baby boom mentioned in the section on age structure. This swelled the 16–44 age group in 1971–91, but over the twenty years to 2011 this group starts to shrink and the number of people in the upper working-age group will grow by some 30%.

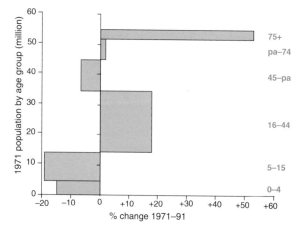

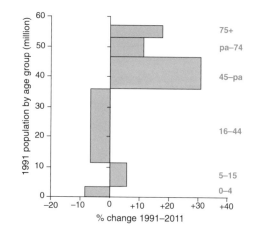

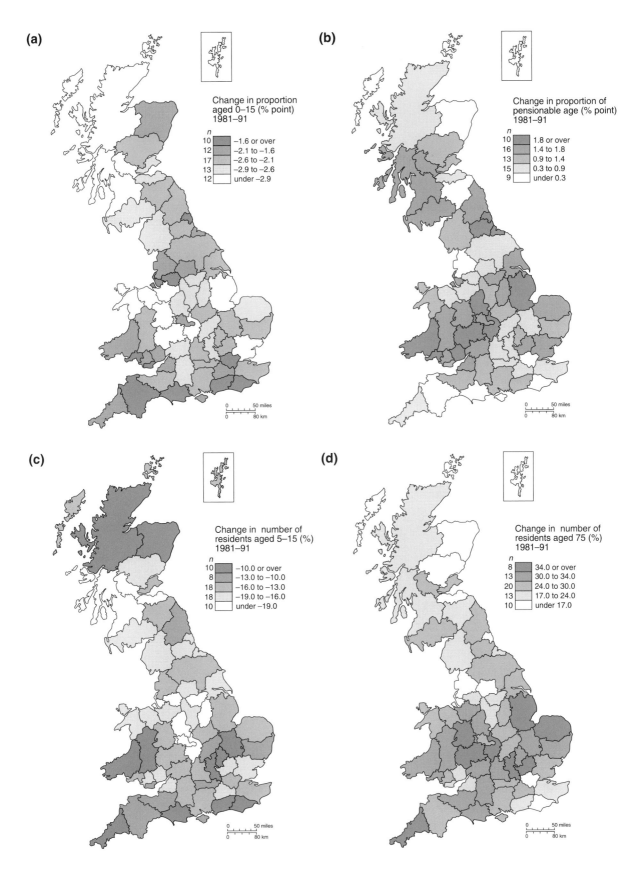

(a)

Change in proportion
aged 0–15 (% point)
1981–91

n
10 −1.6 or over
12 −2.1 to −1.6
17 −2.6 to −2.1
13 −2.9 to −2.6
12 under −2.9

0 ___ 50 miles
0 ___ 80 km

(b)

Change in proportion of
pensionable age (% point)
1981–91

n
10 1.8 or over
16 1.4 to 1.8
13 0.9 to 1.4
15 0.3 to 0.9
9 under 0.3

0 ___ 50 miles
0 ___ 80 km

(c)

Change in number of
residents aged 5–15 (%)
1981–91

n
10 −10.0 or over
8 −13.0 to −10.0
18 −16.0 to −13.0
18 −19.0 to −16.0
10 under −19.0

0 ___ 50 miles
0 ___ 80 km

(d)

Change in number of
residents aged 75 (%)
1981–91

n
8 34.0 or over
13 30.0 to 34.0
20 24.0 to 30.0
13 17.0 to 24.0
10 under 17.0

0 ___ 50 miles
0 ___ 80 km

19

Multicultural Britain

Three nations

Nowadays the term 'multicultural Britain' conjures images of people who have arrived relatively recently from outside the British Isles, but it is important to remember that the longer-established white population of Britain is descended from a variety of distinctive groups, with different languages, cultures, and physical characteristics. The Cornish language is one example of a tradition which has faded away almost completely, whereas Welsh remains relatively strong, and the Gaelic legacy in Scotland lies between these two. The increasing sway of the English language, as well as population movement, continues to threaten these older cultures.

Welsh and Gaelic speakers

Ability to speak a language is the most common measure of the strength of its culture. The graph shows that the Welsh language has survived in Wales much more strongly than Gaelic has survived in Scotland. Both have seen at least a halving of their population shares since 1921, though the rate of decline has diminished since the 1960s, no doubt partly because of education policies and a general upwelling of ethnic consciousness.

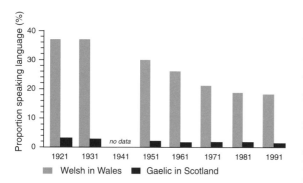

Maps (c) and (d) show that the main areas of Welsh- and Gaelic-speaking tend to be the places most remote from the borders of England. Gaelic has its firmest hold in the Western Isles, where 68% of those aged 3 years and over claim to be able to speak it—not far short of the 75% claiming to speak Welsh in Dwyfor district, Gwynedd. But, whereas in only one other Scottish district is the level above 40% and for half of Scotland the proportion is below 1%, in Wales the 'heartland' is much more extensive and it is only in Gwent that the proportion of Welsh-speakers falls below 5%.

Areas with the highest and lowest proportions of 1991 population born in England, Scotland, and Wales

Birthplace and country of residence in 1991	Proportion of 1991 population (%)	
	Highest	Lowest
England-born		
England	96.4 Durham	74.9 London
Scotland	16.0 Borders	4.3 Strathclyde
Wales	36.6 Clwyd	8.4 Mid Glamorgan
Scotland-born		
England	3.8 Northants	1.0 Merseyside
Scotland	92.2 Strathclyde	80.7 Borders
Wales	1.1 Clwyd	0.5 Mid Glamorgan
Wales-born		
England	5.0 Shropshire	0.3 Tyne and Wear
Scotland	0.5 Islands	0.2 Strathclyde
Wales	89.2 Mid Glamorgan	59.6 Clwyd

Birthplace and lifetime migration

Though the census provides no information on these languages outside their 'home' countries, birthplace data gives some indication of the population mixing which has contributed to the decline in the proportions able to speak these Celtic languages. Maps (a) and (b) show that this 'lifetime migration' reflects the same influences as the one-year migration seen in earlier pages. The areas outside Scotland with most Scotland-born in their populations are either the nearby counties of northern England or the rapidly growing counties of central southern England, while similarly the Wales-born are most common in the West Midlands and the prosperous Bristol–Oxford zone. In all, 20% of the Wales-born recorded by the 1991 Census and 15% of the Scotland-born were living outside their 'home country' at that time.

Substantial movements have also occurred in the opposite directions. In 1991 there were 540,000 England-born people living in Wales, where they made up 19% of the population. For Scotland, the figures were 354,000 England-born making up 7%. The table shows, for each of the three countries, the areas which were most and least English, Scottish, and Welsh in terms of birthplace. On this criterion, Clwyd is the most English part of Britain outside England (with Alyn and Deeside district being 50% England-born). Least 'foreign' penetration in Wales has occurred in Mid Glamorgan (92% Wales-born). In Scotland it is least in Strathclyde, while County Durham is the most 'English' part of Britain. Clearly the traditional mining and industrial areas have not proved very attractive for such long-distance migrants.

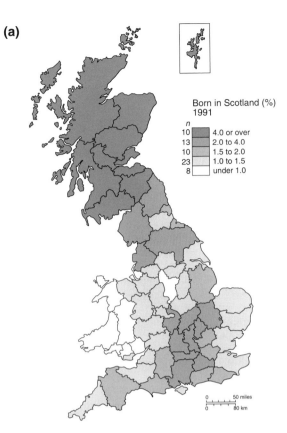

(a)

Born in Scotland (%)
1991

n	
10	4.0 or over
13	2.0 to 4.0
10	1.5 to 2.0
23	1.0 to 1.5
8	under 1.0

0 ___ 50 miles
0 ___ 80 km

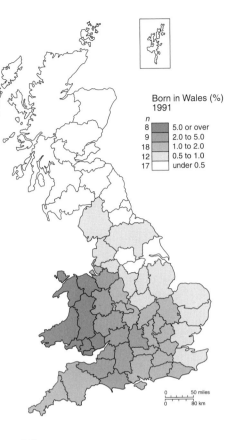

(b)

Born in Wales (%)
1991

n	
8	5.0 or over
9	2.0 to 5.0
18	1.0 to 2.0
12	0.5 to 1.0
17	under 0.5

0 ___ 50 miles
0 ___ 80 km

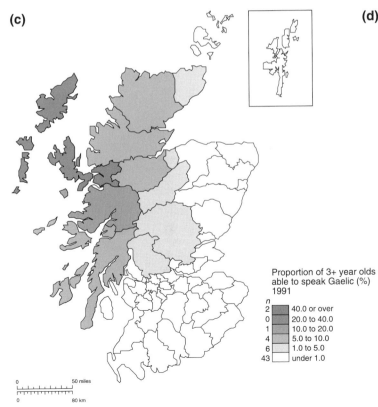

(c)

Proportion of 3+ year olds
able to speak Gaelic (%)
1991

n	
2	40.0 or over
0	20.0 to 40.0
1	10.0 to 20.0
4	5.0 to 10.0
6	1.0 to 5.0
43	under 1.0

0 ___ 50 miles
0 ___ 80 km

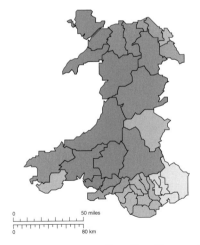

(d)

Proportion of 3+ year olds
able to speak Welsh (%)
1991

n	
8	40.0 or over
7	20.0 to 40.0
5	10.0 to 20.0
12	5.0 to 10.0
5	1.0 to 5.0
0	under 1.0

0 ___ 50 miles
0 ___ 80 km

Born overseas

Out of the 54.89 million residents found by the 1991 Census, just over 4 million, or 7.3%, stated that they had been born outside Great Britain. One in five of these were from Ireland: 245,000 from Northern Ireland and 592,000 from the Irish Republic. One in six, 668,000 in all, gave a birthplace somewhere else in Europe. Immigrants from the New Commonwealth, totalling some 1,688,400, accounted for 42% of all who were born outside Britain and made up almost 3.1% of all residents in 1991. This was nearly ten times the number born in the Old Commonwealth (Canada, Australia, and New Zealand).

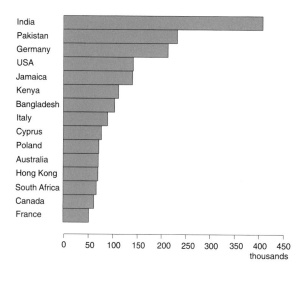

The bar graph shows the fifteen largest sources of people coming to Great Britain, other than from Ireland. New Commonwealth countries are prominent. There is also a sizeable presence of Americans, Italians, and Hong Kong Chinese. The strong showing of Germany and Poland reflects in part survivors of the 1930s flight from the Nazi threat, but some of these figures need careful interpretation, notably because of past and current deployment of people in the armed forces. Thus, a sizeable proportion of the 'immigrants' from Germany and Cyprus comprised children born to British Army families once stationed there, while some of the US-born are American military personnel serving in Britain.

The geographical distribution of the overseas-born is very uneven, as the regional table and subregional maps show. The northern region of England is the most 'British' area in terms of birthplace, with only 2.4% of its 1991 residents hailing from outside Great Britain and with County Durham and Northumberland (along with Mid Glamorgan) being the only places lying in the bottom shading category of all four maps opposite. At the other extreme, London's proportion of overseas-born is almost ten times larger, at 22.4%. Indeed, because of the London factor, the South East is the only region with fewer Britain-born than the national average, and if London is considered separately, even the rest of the South East rises above the average (see the bottom row in the table).

The pattern also varies somewhat between the source areas. While London, and the south-eastern corner of Britain in general, feature prominently on all the maps, the Irish are also relatively numerous in the West Midlands, North West, and Strathclyde, the New-Commonwealth-born in the Midlands, North West, and West Yorkshire, and those from the rest of the world (including the small number from the Old Commonwealth) in Lothian and northern Scotland. The geography of the 'rest of the world' group reflects a significant presence of workers in oil (Grampian) and finance (London and Edinburgh), together with overseas students (London, Oxford, and Cambridge) and American service personnel (Oxfordshire and Suffolk).

Residents of regions, 1991, by place of birth (%)

Region	Place of birth					
	Great Britain	Ireland	Rest of Europe	New CW	Old CW	Rest of World
North	97.6	0.5	0.5	0.8	0.1	0.4
Wales	97.0	0.7	0.7	0.8	0.2	0.5
Scotland	96.5	1.0	0.7	0.9	0.3	0.7
Yorkshire and Humberside	95.4	0.8	0.8	2.2	0.2	0.6
South West	95.4	1.0	1.2	1.3	0.3	0.8
North West	95.1	1.6	0.7	1.9	0.2	0.6
East Midlands	94.4	1.1	1.0	2.7	0.2	0.6
East Anglia	93.9	0.9	1.3	1.4	0.3	2.2
West Midlands	92.9	1.8	0.8	3.9	0.2	0.5
Great Britain	92.7	1.5	1.2	3.1	0.3	1.2
South East	87.0	2.4	2.1	5.7	0.6	2.3
Greater London	77.6	3.8	2.9	11.0	0.8	3.9
Rest of South East	93.0	1.5	1.5	2.4	0.4	1.2

Notes: Regions ranked according to proportion born in Great Britain; CW = Commonwealth.

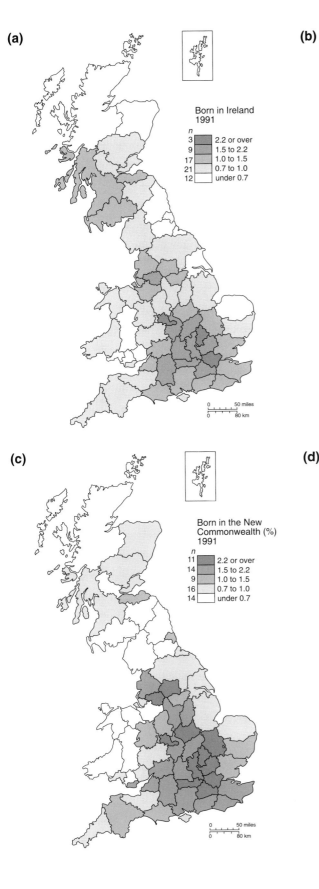

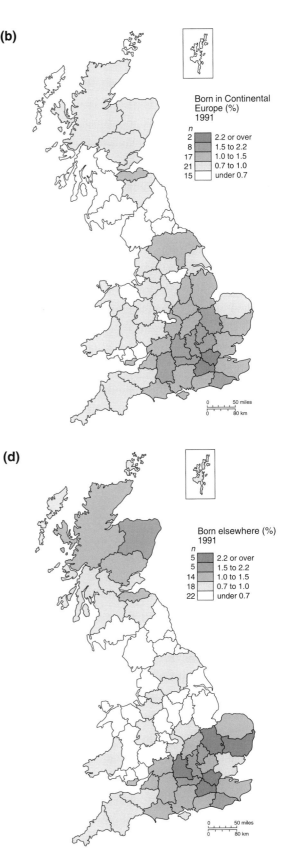

25

Immigrants and non-whites

It is not uncommon for the term 'immigrants' to be equated with the minority ethnic, or non-white, population, yet this is far from the case. The previous page has already shown that the groups of British residents who were born in Ireland, the rest of Europe, and the three Old Commonwealth countries together number almost as many as those who originate from the New Commonwealth. In 1991, for the first time ever, the Census asked about people's ethnic group and so it is now possible to provide precise details of the degree of overlap between these two aspects of local, as well as national, populations.

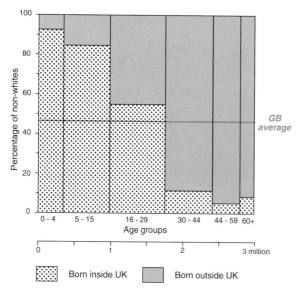

Born inside UK   Born outside UK

The national picture is as follows. The proportion of non-whites is 5.5%, while that of people born outside the UK is 6.9%. But the cross tabulations in the Census show that only 42.5% of British residents born outside the UK were in fact non-white and also that almost half (46.8%) of non-whites living in Britain in 1991 had been born in the UK. The latter group mainly comprises the children of immigrants and are almost all aged under 30 years old, as the graph shows. One result is that non-whites make up a significantly larger proportion of Britain's 0–15 year-olds than of the total population, 9.0% compared to the average of 5.5%.

The geographical distribution of the non-white population is also significantly different from that of all immigrants. Maps (a) and (b) opposite show that non-whites are much more concentrated; whereas only four counties, plus the Scottish Islands, had fewer than 2.0% of their population born outside the UK, non-whites make up under 1.0% of the population in many parts of Britain and 2.0% or over in relatively few. There is a strong urban–rural component to this contrast, as can also be seen from the first two columns of the table.

There is also a clear geography to the proportion of non-whites who are not immigrants. As shown in map (c) opposite, the proportion is particularly high in the western half of England in a zone stretching from Lancashire and West Yorkshire down through the north and west Midlands towards the South West. In terms of district types, the table (third column) shows the highest values to be in the metropolitan districts and industrial areas. This is largely a reflection of the history of non-white immigration, because the collapse of staple northern industries like textiles since the mid-1960s has meant that more recent immigration has thereby been dominated by movement to London and the South East.

As a result, some parts of Britain have remarkably high proportions of non-whites in their 0–15 year-old population: fully a third of London's 0–15 year-olds, and one in six for the principal metropolitan cities (see table). Concentration of non-whites, however, means that this proportion is below average in all but nine counties, as shown in map (d).

Immigrants and non-whites, by type of district

District type	% immigrant	% non-white	% non-white born in UK	% 0-15 non-white
Great Britain	6.9	5.5	46.8	9.0
Greater London				
Inner London	27.9	25.6	45.1	41.2
Outer London	18.0	16.9	41.2	25.0
Metropolitan				
Principal cities	7.5	9.5	53.6	16.8
Other districts	4.5	5.1	53.1	9.2
Non-metropolitan				
Large cities	6.2	6.0	47.8	10.2
Small cities	6.3	4.0	47.3	6.7
Industrial areas	3.4	2.6	50.4	4.6
New towns	4.4	2.7	46.7	4.3
Resort, port, and retirement	4.2	1.1	42.2	1.7
Urban and mixed urban–rural	5.7	2.3	43.4	3.7
Remoter mainly rural	3.2	0.6	43.7	1.1

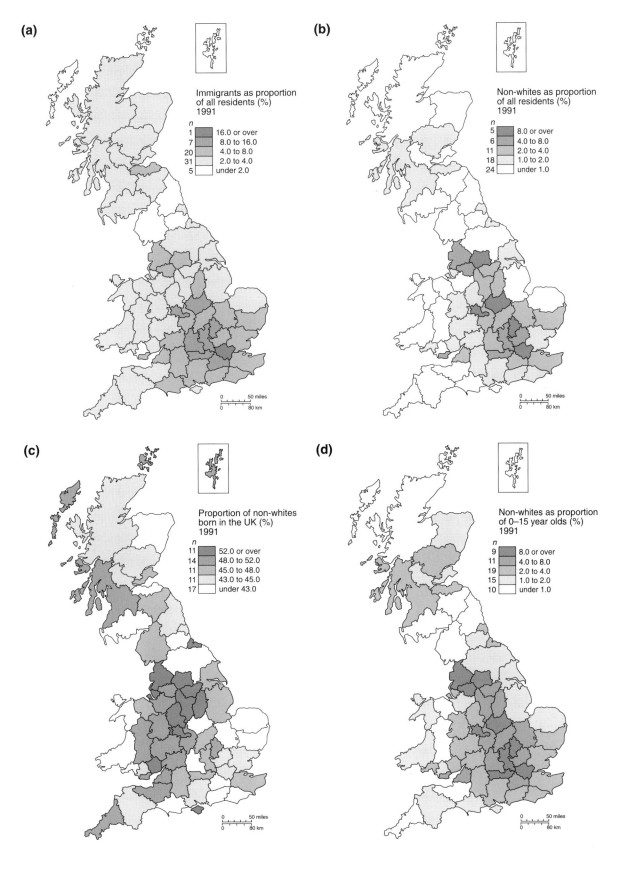

(a)

Immigrants as proportion
of all residents (%)
1991

n	
1	16.0 or over
7	8.0 to 16.0
20	4.0 to 8.0
31	2.0 to 4.0
5	under 2.0

0   50 miles
0   80 km

(b)

Non-whites as proportion
of all residents (%)
1991

n	
5	8.0 or over
6	4.0 to 8.0
11	2.0 to 4.0
18	1.0 to 2.0
24	under 1.0

0   50 miles
0   80 km

(c)

Proportion of non-whites
born in the UK (%)
1991

n	
11	52.0 or over
14	48.0 to 52.0
11	45.0 to 48.0
11	43.0 to 45.0
17	under 43.0

0   50 miles
0   80 km

(d)

Non-whites as proportion
of 0–15 year olds (%)
1991

n	
9	8.0 or over
11	4.0 to 8.0
19	2.0 to 4.0
15	1.0 to 2.0
10	under 1.0

0   50 miles
0   80 km

The growth of the ethnic-minority population

This section develops one of the themes of the previous two pages, namely the increasing proportion of non-whites who are UK-born and the implications which this has for the way in which the size of the non-white population can be gauged. Until the early 1970s it was assumed that the vast majority of non-whites in Britain were immigrants from the former 'Third World' colonies which had become known as the New Commonwealth. Since then, however, the increasing proportion of the UK-born in the non-white population has undermined the value of this measure. This change was one of the key reasons for introducing the question on ethnicity in the 1991 Census. This point is demonstrated here at national, regional, and subregional levels.

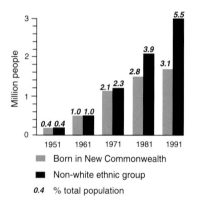

Born in New Commonwealth

Non-white ethnic group

0.4 % total population

National trends

The graph shows that for 1951, 1961, and 1971 the numbers of people in Britain who had been born in what has become the New Commonwealth are very close to the estimated size of the non-white population at each date, even though it is known that not all the non-whites had originated there. By 1981, however, the size of the non-white population had become much larger than the number born in the New Commonwealth, mainly as a result of newcomers becoming parents after arriving in the UK but also due to the death or return migration of earlier immigrants. The gap grew even more quickly between 1981 and 1991. Over the last two decades, the non-white population has grown by over 1.8 mil-

lion, while the number born in the New Commonwealth has risen by less than one-third of this amount.

Geographical patterns

The maps opposite show that, even on the basis of the 'born in the New Commonwealth' definition, there were some significant changes in population composition between 1971 and 1991. Maps (a) and (b) have the same shading intervals and show very clearly the increasing number of areas qualifying in the higher categories, although the areas with under 1.0% have altered rather little. The percentage point changes shown in map (c) are a pale shadow of those shown in map (d) which estimates change in the proportion of non-whites for the twenty-year period (see technical notes for details of the method of calculation). Only four counties are shown as having a rise of 1.6% or more in the proportion of people born in the New Commonwealth, whereas sixteen counties are estimated to have seen the non-white shares of their populations grow by at least 2.0% points.

The table provides the full set of data for both measures at regional level, with regions ranked according to the share of their non-white population in 1991. Notably, on both measures, the degree of regional concentration appears to have increased, with the largest rises occurring in regions with the highest proportions in 1971. There is also an interesting contrast between the top five and bottom five regions in the difference between each of their two measures in 1971.

'Non-whites' in the population, 1971–1991, by region

Region (ranked on % non-white 1991)	Born in New CW			Non-white		
	1971 %	1991 %	1971–91 % point	1971 %	1991 %	1971–91 % point
South East	3.8	5.7	1.88	4.0	9.9	5.86
West Midlands	3.1	3.9	0.78	4.0	8.2	4.23
East Midlands	1.7	2.7	0.98	1.9	4.8	2.85
Yorks. and Humb.	1.6	2.2	0.59	1.8	4.4	2.62
North West	1.2	1.9	0.66	1.3	3.9	2.64
East Anglia	1.0	1.4	0.38	0.6	2.1	1.51
Wales	0.5	0.8	0.34	0.3	1.5	1.12
South West	1.2	1.3	0.13	0.6	1.4	0.71
North	0.5	0.8	0.31	0.3	1.3	0.94
Scotland	0.6	0.9	0.33	0.3	1.3	0.95

CW = Commonwealth.

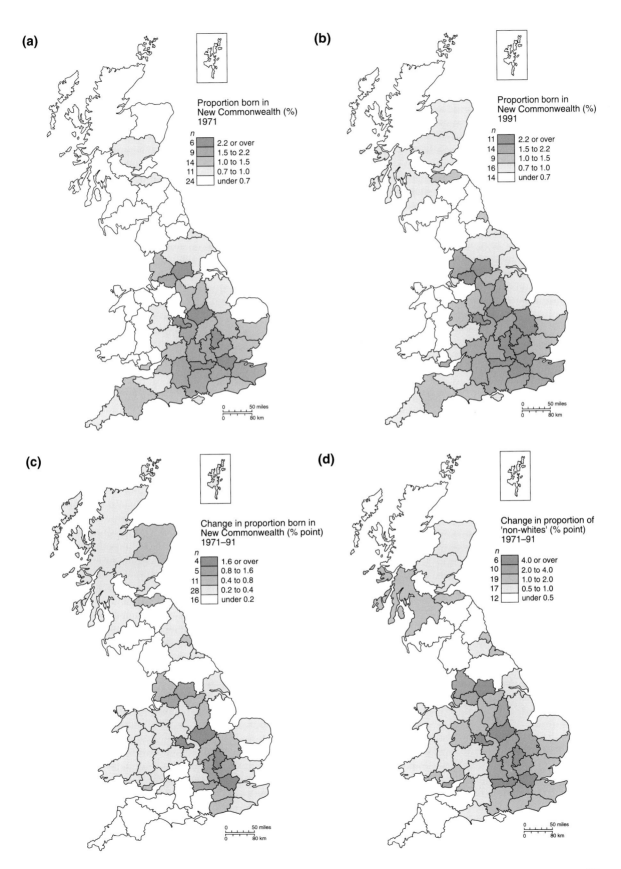

(a)

Proportion born in
New Commonwealth (%)
1971

n
6   2.2 or over
9   1.5 to 2.2
14   1.0 to 1.5
11   0.7 to 1.0
24   under 0.7

0   50 miles
0   80 km

(b)

Proportion born in
New Commonwealth (%)
1991

n
11   2.2 or over
14   1.5 to 2.2
9   1.0 to 1.5
16   0.7 to 1.0
14   under 0.7

0   50 miles
0   80 km

(c)

Change in proportion born in
New Commonwealth (% point)
1971–91

n
4   1.6 or over
5   0.8 to 1.6
11   0.4 to 0.8
28   0.2 to 0.4
16   under 0.2

0   50 miles
0   80 km

(d)

Change in proportion of
'non-whites' (% point)
1971–91

n
6   4.0 or over
10   2.0 to 4.0
19   1.0 to 2.0
17   0.5 to 1.0
12   under 0.5

0   50 miles
0   80 km

29

The ethnic-minority groups

Over 3 million residents of Britain did not identify themselves as 'White' in answer to the 1991 Census question on ethnicity. This 'non-white' population covers a great variety of racial and ethnic groups, but the history of immigration to the UK ensures that certain groups are very much more prominent than others. There are also significant variations between groups in their characteristics and geographical distribution.

in the UK partly reflects their higher turnover, while the high proportions for the Black Other and Other Other groups reflects the increasing number of people who are of mixed descent or who identify with Britain more strongly than with country of ancestry. These factors contribute to the variations between groups in the proportion of under-16 year-olds (see final column of the table).

Regional distribution

As shown in the graph, the South East contains over half Britain's non-whites, though accounting for less than one-third of the country's total population. The West Midlands is the only other region to record a greater share of non-whites than of the total population, while the top five regions (these plus the North West, Yorkshire and Humberside, and the East Midlands) contain all but 8.3% of Britain's non-white population.

The South East contains over half of the members of all but one of the broad categories shown in the graph. The exception—the Pakistani group, for which the South East accounts for just under 30%—is particularly prominent in Yorkshire and Humberside, and also forms a well-above-average share of the non-white populations of both the North West and Scotland. Indians make up over half the non-white population of the East Midlands, while the contribution of the Black category to the non-white population is almost as high in East Anglia and the South West as it is in the South East. These variations are reflected in the maps opposite and are described in more detail in *Black and white Britain*.

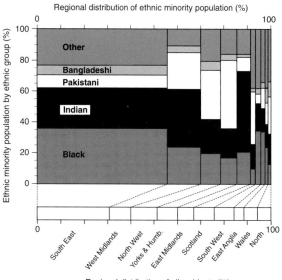

The table shows that Indians form the single largest group at over a quarter of the total ethnic-minority population, with West Indians and Pakistanis coming next with roughly one in six each of the total. The Black African, Black Other, Bangladeshi, and Chinese groups each contribute 5–7%. Altogether, those of South Asian extraction account for almost half the total, and the three Black groups a further 30%.

The proportion of each group made up of people born in the UK, also shown in the table, closely reflects the phasing of immigration over time. West Indians dominated immigration to the UK in the 1950s, with the result that well over half the Black population is UK-born. The Pakistanis and Indians were the main groups to enter in the 1960s and 1970s, while the 1980s was the main period for the arrival of Bangladeshis. The low proportion of Chinese born

The non-white population of Britain, 1991, by ethnic group

Ethnic group	Persons (000s)	% GB's non-whites	% born in UK	% aged 0–15
all non-white	3,015.1	100.0	46.8	33.0
Black	870.7	29.5	55.7	29.4
Caribbean	500.0	16.6	53.7	21.9
African	212.4	7.0	36.4	29.3
Other	178.4	5.9	84.4	50.6
South Asian	1,479.6	49.1	44.1	35.7
Indian	840.3	27.9	41.9	29.5
Pakistani	476.6	15.8	50.5	42.6
Bangladeshi	162.8	5.4	36.6	47.2
Chinese and Others	644.7	21.4	40.6	32.0
Chinese	156.9	5.2	28.5	23.4
Other Asian	197.5	6.6	21.9	24.4
Other	290.2	9.6	59.8	41.7

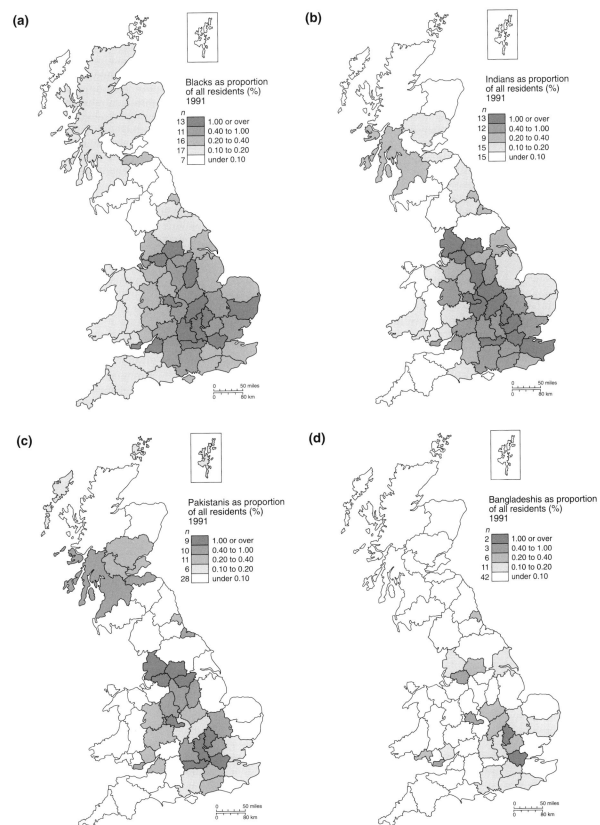

(a)

Blacks as proportion
of all residents (%)
1991

n
13 | 1.00 or over
11 | 0.40 to 1.00
16 | 0.20 to 0.40
17 | 0.10 to 0.20
7 | under 0.10

0 ___ 50 miles
0 ___ 80 km

(b)

Indians as proportion
of all residents (%)
1991

n
13 | 1.00 or over
12 | 0.40 to 1.00
9 | 0.20 to 0.40
15 | 0.10 to 0.20
15 | under 0.10

0 ___ 50 miles
0 ___ 80 km

(c)

Pakistanis as proportion
of all residents (%)
1991

n
9 | 1.00 or over
10 | 0.40 to 1.00
11 | 0.20 to 0.40
6 | 0.10 to 0.20
28 | under 0.10

0 ___ 50 miles
0 ___ 80 km

(d)

Bangladeshis as proportion
of all residents (%)
1991

n
2 | 1.00 or over
3 | 0.40 to 1.00
6 | 0.20 to 0.40
11 | 0.10 to 0.20
42 | under 0.10

0 ___ 50 miles
0 ___ 80 km

31

Black and white Britain

Distribution by district

The district-level map opposite shows, to an even greater extent than the county maps on the previous page, the high degree of concentration of the ethnic-minority population. Though all 459 districts of Great Britain contained at least one non-white resident at the 1991 Census, those districts where non-whites made up under 1.0% of the population tend to be very extensive.

At the same time, there is no district where the ethnic-minority population is in the majority. As the graph shows, Brent came close to this in 1991, with almost 45% of its population accounted for by non-whites, followed by Newham with 42%, and another five London boroughs with levels of at least 29%. The highest proportions outside London are those of Leicester and Slough (Berkshire).

Variations between minority groups

The graph also reveals that the spatial patterns vary between the ethnic groups to an even greater extent than at regional and subregional levels shown on the previous two pages. In most cases the non-white population of the districts shown are dominated by one particular group: Bangladeshis in Tower Hamlets, Blacks in Hackney, Indians in Ealing, and so on. Brent and Newham are the clear exceptions with roughly similar proportions of Blacks and Indians in both.

The table provides an alternative way of looking at these distinctive geographies, showing the top five districts in terms of the proportion of their populations made up by each of the four ethnic-minority-groups. Tower Hamlets is clearly distinctive because of its large Bangladeshi presence, while Leicester is in this sense the Indian 'capital' of Britain. For Pakistanis, Bradford tops the list, but is rivalled by Pendle (Lancashire) and Slough (Berkshire), while the top five for Blacks are all London boroughs.

London boroughs feature to some extent in all four lists, reflecting the importance of the national capital in the distribution of the ethnic minorities and accounting very largely for the dominance of the South East in the graph of regional distribution (see *The ethnic-minority groups*). Greater London accounts for approaching half (44.6%) of all Britain's non-white residents. This proportion varies between the main ethnic groups, being particularly high for Blacks (60.1% of the national total) and Bangladeshis (52.7%), somewhat lower for Indians (41.3%), and very much lower for Pakistanis (18.4%).

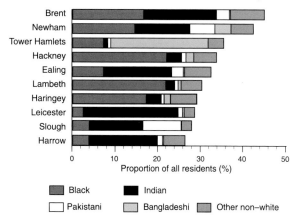

Proportion of all residents (%)

Legend: Black | Indian | Pakistani | Bangladeshi | Other non–white

The top five districts for each of four ethnic groups, ranked in terms of proportion of residents, 1991 (%)

Black		Indian	
22.0	Hackney	22.3	Leicester
21.8	Lambeth	17.2	Brent
17.8	Southwark	16.1	Ealing
17.1	Haringey	16.1	Harrow
16.5	Brent	14.3	Hounslow
Pakistani		**Bangladeshi**	
9.9	Bradford	22.9	Tower Hamlets
9.4	Pendle	3.8	Newham
9.1	Slough	3.5	Camden
6.9	Birmingham	2.7	Luton
6.3	Waltham Forest	2.4	Oldham

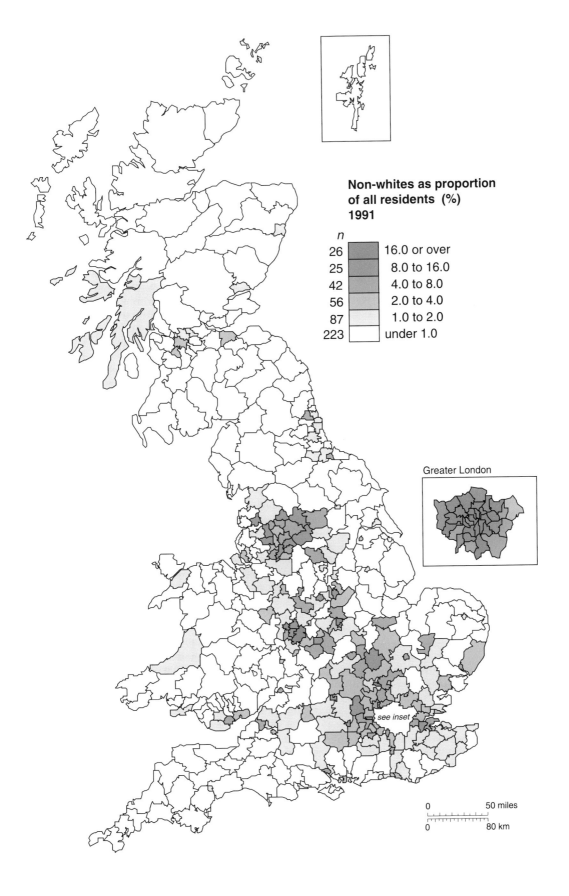

**Non-whites as proportion
of all residents (%)
1991**

n	
26	16.0 or over
25	8.0 to 16.0
42	4.0 to 8.0
56	2.0 to 4.0
87	1.0 to 2.0
223	under 1.0

Greater London

see inset

0		50 miles
0		80 km

Ethnicity and the labour-market

People play a variety of different roles in the household, the wider community and also in society at large. The aspect which is most thoroughly measured is position in the labour-market, notably whether people consider themselves as available for formal paid employment as opposed to being 'economically inactive'. The latter category includes people who have retired from work, children aged under 16 and older students who are not formally employed, those who are not available for work now or in the future because they are 'permanently sick', and a whole range of people for whom duties as carers in one form or another (for frail elderly, sick, children, or the household in general) deter them from seeking formal jobs.

Because children aged under 16 are not considered eligible for formal employment, 'economic activity rates' are normally calculated by reference to the population aged 16 and over. Even on this basis, there are considerable variations in labour-force participation between people and areas, not least between ethnic groups. These result notably from differences in age composition (mainly because those of retirement age are included), in numbers taking early retirement (by choice or through redundancy packages) and in the proportion of women not seeking work outside the home.

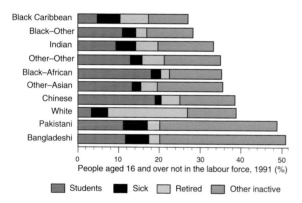

Black Caribbean
Black–Other
Indian
Other–Other
Black–African
Other–Asian
Chinese
White
Pakistani
Bangladeshi

0 10 20 30 40 50
People aged 16 and over not in the labour force, 1991 (%)

Students ▨ Sick ■ Retired ▨ Other inactive ▨

The bar graph shows, for the ten ethnic groups distinguished in the 1991 Census, the proportion of people aged 16 and over that is not economically active. The majority ethnic group of Whites, with its rate of 39%, provides a reference point for comparison

with the various minority groups. Inactivity rates are significantly lower than this for Black Caribbeans, at barely a quarter, but are much higher for Pakistanis and Bangladeshis at around a half of all aged 16 and over.

The direct reasons for these differences are evident from the breakdown in the bar graph and from the gender and age-based analyses in the table. In particular, the White population contains more retired people than the groups dominated by recent immigrants—a contrast which is only partially offset by the larger proportions of students for most of the minority groups. The levels of inactivity which are not attributable to students, sickness and retirement are particularly high for Bangladeshis and Pakistanis, who both have very low levels of labour-force participation amongst their working-age women arising from Islamic cultural tradition. At the other extreme, the 'other inactive' category is especially low for Black Caribbeans, for whom working-age participation rates are very high for both women and men.

Geographical variations in economic activity rates are sizeable, as shown in the maps for men aged 16 and over. For Whites and Blacks, the highest rates occur in central southern England as a result of a traditionally tight labour-market and relatively youthful age structure. For South Asians and Others, the highest rates are found in some of the more remote, mainly rural counties, often areas with relatively small numbers of these groups and where only those who are strongly placed in the labour-market have been able to move in.

Labour-force participation rates for men and women of working age, by ethnic group, Great Britain, 1991 (%)

Ethnic group	Men aged 16–64	Women aged 16–59
All groups	86.6	67.6
White	87.0	68.3
Non-white	79.6	56.6
Black	81.9	69.2
Caribbean	86.4	73.3
African	70.4	61.4
Other	83.7	64.8
South Asian	79.6	47.6
Indian	82.3	60.4
Pakistani	75.7	28.3
Bangladeshi	74.3	22.2
Chinese and Others	76.7	57.0
Chinese	72.4	56.7
Other Asian	78.0	56.2
Other	78.5	58.2

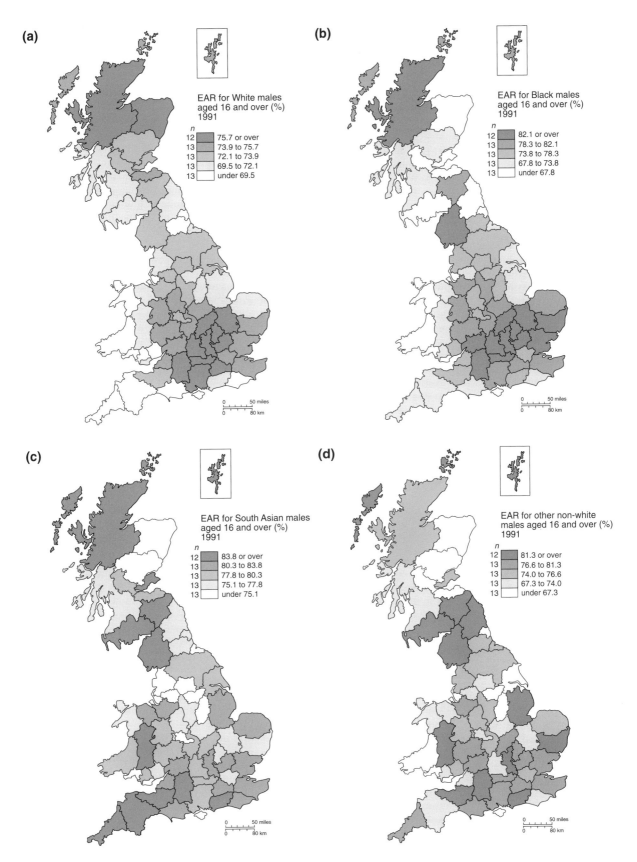

(a)

EAR for White males
aged 16 and over (%)
1991

n
12	75.7 or over
13	73.9 to 75.7
13	72.1 to 73.9
13	69.5 to 72.1
13	under 69.5

0   50 miles
0   80 km

(b)

EAR for Black males
aged 16 and over (%)
1991

n
12	82.1 or over
13	78.3 to 82.1
13	73.8 to 78.3
13	67.8 to 73.8
13	under 67.8

0   50 miles
0   80 km

(c)

EAR for South Asian males
aged 16 and over (%)
1991

n
12	83.8 or over
13	80.3 to 83.8
13	77.8 to 80.3
13	75.1 to 77.8
13	under 75.1

0   50 miles
0   80 km

(d)

EAR for other non-white
males aged 16 and over (%)
1991

n
12	81.3 or over
13	76.6 to 81.3
13	74.0 to 76.6
13	67.3 to 74.0
13	under 67.3

0   50 miles
0   80 km

Ethnicity and opportunity

Unemployment is a problem which is far from equally shared across Britain's population. This is not simply a question of the uneven distribution of job opportunities (as charted on later pages). There is also the issue of who gets the jobs which *are* available. Britain is unique among European Union countries in having lower unemployment among women than men. However, it is unfortunately true that there is nothing unusual in the level of unemployment suffered by ethnic-minority groups being substantially higher than that faced by the White population. The map measures the differential unemployment problem suffered by non-white groups in each of a specially defined set of 'places' (which have been defined as local labour-market areas—see the note in the Appendix).

The map shows, in degrees of blue shading, those areas where ethnic-minority groups make up more than 3% of the labour-force (see also *Black and white Britain*). The overall picture is of concentration in the larger cities and/or central England. Because most immigration took place over the 1960s and 1970s, most non-white in-migrants went to those areas extending from London to Birmingham which were growing then. Thus the larger cities with relatively few ethnic minorities are Liverpool, Newcastle, and Glasgow—the centres of regions which were fuelling the 'North–South drift' over that period. The other element of the picture is that textile towns in Lancashire, Yorkshire, and the East Midlands also attracted ethnic minority in-migrants, even though they were not attracting White migrants from the rest of Britain.

The map also shows where the unemployment problem for non-whites is substantially higher than that for Whites. The calculation involved here takes the local unemployment rate for Whites (the substantial majority of the labour-force in all areas) and works out how many non-Whites 'should' be unemployed if they suffered the same level of joblessness. The differential in unemployment levels is then revealed by subtracting this 'expected' number of non-white unemployed people from the actual number reported by the Census.

A small number of areas on the map are hatched black and white: these are the areas where the differential is *negative*—fewer non-white people are unemployed than are to be 'expected' according to the analysis. All these areas have very low numbers of non-white residents, in many cases because they have been relatively unattractive to most migrants due to their relative remoteness and/or dependence on declining industries such as coal-mining (e.g. the south Wales valleys). These factors came together to mean that the few in-migrants in these areas from ethnic minorities tended to have been recruited for secure jobs (e.g. as doctors) and so they are less likely to become unemployed than the local White residents.

The areas shaded blue on the map all have substantial ethnic-minority populations, and in all these areas the minority groups had *higher* rates of unemployment than their white neighbours. The map plots a '+' for each 1,000 non-white unemployed people who would have had a job if that area's minority population had had the same unemployment rate as the White members of the local labour-force. Some of the more prosperous central areas, such as Northampton and Milton Keynes, do not have a large differential unemployment problem. However, the general picture is of depressingly widespread evidence of, on the face of it, racial discrimination. It is possible to see hints of variation within this pattern: for example the inset map suggests that east London has substantially higher differential non-white unemployment than does west London, which houses similar numbers of non-white residents. In this respect, the analysis conforms with the widespread evidence for greater racial tension in the East End than in other parts of London.

The graph plots the change over the last decade in the unemployment rates of Whites and non-whites nationally. The scale of the differential between the groups is shown by the distance by which the curve lies above the lower diagonal on the graph. As unemployment fell during the 1980s it seems that the differential between ethnic groups may have fallen slightly too, with the 1988–90 values nearer to the diagonal than those for 1984–6 had been. However, the return to rising unemployment fuelled the evidence of apparent discrimination still further and 1993 saw the non-white rate at more than double the White unemployment rate for the first time for at least a decade. Moreover, the picture is equally bleak for both men and women when they are analysed separately.

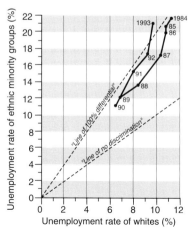

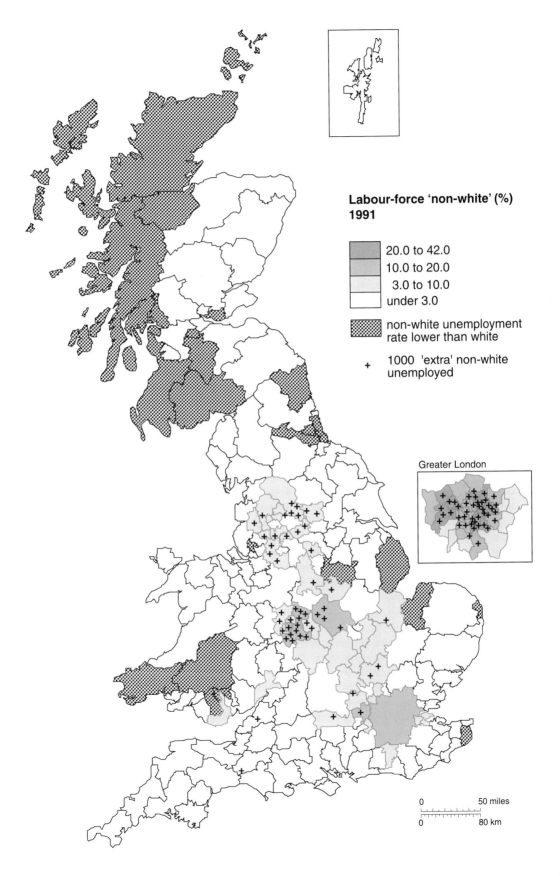

Labour-force 'non-white' (%) 1991

- 20.0 to 42.0
- 10.0 to 20.0
- 3.0 to 10.0
- under 3.0

non-white unemployment rate lower than white

+ 1000 'extra' non-white unemployed

Greater London

0   50 miles
0   80 km

Ethnicity and unemployment

The extent of joblessness varies considerably between ethnic groups. This is clear from the maps opposite, notably in terms of the number of areas with unemployment rates in the top categories. Thus, while no area had a rate of 20% or more for White males, twenty-four areas did for Black males, ten areas did for South Asian males, and three areas did for the Chinese and Others category. The same descending order of ethnic minority rates is found for the highest-unemployment county for each group: for Black males, it is 36.3% in Merseyside; for South Asians, 30.5% in South Yorkshire; and for Chinese and Others, 22.3% in West Midlands.

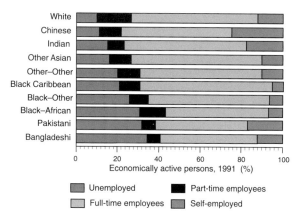

Economically active persons, 1991 (%)

Unemployed   Part-time employees

Full-time employees   Self-employed

Unemployment rates for men and women, by ethnic group, Great Britain, 1991 (%)

Ethnic group	Men	Women
All groups	12.6	7.9
White	12.0	7.4
Non-white	22.6	18.4
Black	28.2	19.5
Caribbean	26.6	15.9
African	33.2	29.0
Other	29.5	22.1
South Asian	21.1	19.3
Indian	15.1	14.7
Pakistani	31.1	34.5
Bangladeshi	32.7	42.4
Chinese and Others	17.9	14.6
Chinese	11.9	10.0
Other Asian	17.0	15.5
Other Other	22.3	17.5

The table gives a breakdown for the nine ethnic-minority groups, and for women as well as men. Clearly, even within the three broad minority groupings, there are considerable variations. For instance, the rate for Chinese men is barely half that for the Other Other category. Even more strikingly, the rates for Pakistani and Bangladeshi men are over twice that for Indian men, and the rate for Bangladeshi women is almost three times that of Indian women. Not only, as seen previously, do remarkably few Bangladeshi women want to work, but among those that do a substantial number are unable to find a job.

The bar graph shows the employment position of the whole labour-force, men and women combined, with the ten ethnic groups ranked on the basis of

overall unemployment rate. First, this reinforces the fact that the rate of unemployment for Whites is only about a third of those for Bangladeshis, Pakistanis and Black Africans. It also shows that the Chinese level is not much above that for Whites, and those for Indians and Other Asians are also comparatively low.

Also evident from the bar graph are significant differences between groups in the pattern of employment amongst those with work. Self-employment is very much more important amongst the Chinese than any other single group, with the level for Indians and Pakistanis being about two-thirds of this, and that for Bangladeshis also being above average. Less than half the Pakistanis and Bangladeshis in the labour-force are full-time employees, and the only groups which exceed the white rate for this category are the Black Caribbeans and Other Asians.

Part-time employment is less important for all nine ethnic-minority groups than it is for Whites. Given that part-time work in Britain is predominantly female work, this is partly due to the below-average labour-force participation of women of most ethnic-minority groups (see the table in *Ethnicity and the labour-market*), but not entirely because of this. The Census also shows that, amongst those women who are in the labour-force, fewer non-whites are engaged in part-time work than Whites (17.7%, as opposed to 34.4%) and more are in full-time employment (57%, compared to 52% of economically active White women).

(a)

Unemployment rate for
White males (%)
1991

n	
0	20.0 or over
6	15.0 to 20.0
15	11.0 to 15.0
25	8.0 to 11.0
18	under 8.0

0   50 miles
0   80 km

(b)

Unemployment rate
for Black males (%)
1991

n	
24	20.0 or over
22	15.0 to 20.0
12	11.0 to 15.0
2	8.0 to 11.0
4	under 8.0

0   50 miles
0   80 km

(c)

Unemployment rate for
South Asian males (%)
1991

n	
10	20.0 or over
16	15.0 to 20.0
11	11.0 to 15.0
13	8.0 to 11.0
14	under 8.0

0   50 miles
0   80 km

(d)

Unemployment rate for
other non-white males (%)
1991

n	
3	20.0 or over
12	15.0 to 20.0
19	11.0 to 15.0
18	8.0 to 11.0
12	under 8.0

0   50 miles
0   80 km

Employment and Education

Men without work

Unemployment is a central issue for people and governments in virtually every country of the world. The map shows the male unemployment rate in each part of Britain (using the 'places' which were defined in the notes to *Ethnicity and opportunity*). The graph shows the relationship between this level of male joblessness and the unemployment rate for the whole local labour-force. Statistical confusion has always surrounded debates over the apparently straightforward question of how many people are unemployed at any one time; there is a table in the notes on this topic which measures some of the factors contributing to these debates.

The many different positions in which people are to be found in the labour-market are summarized in the table in the notes. The traditional aim of someone seeking work, full-time employment, is the status of 16.1 million British people—not much more than a third of the total potential work-force. Even so, the only other category of the over-15s to constitute such a major share of the total is the retired group (14.1 million).

The economically inactive category includes many other subgroups as well as the elderly retired. There is an increasing number of men who have been encouraged to retire from the labour-market before reaching their pensionable age (a strategy which is often termed 'natural wastage' when it is part of the major job losses from a pit closure, for example). Next to the retired, 'housewives' are the largest inactive group, although their numbers have been steadily declining as more mothers return to work while their children are young. The crucial point to draw from thinking about these two groups is that the dividing line between those who are actively in or out of the labour-market cannot be firmly drawn. This fact, that many people are undecided about whether to seek a job, becomes an intractable problem when trying to calculate an unemployment rate because the basic idea is to divide the numbers unemployed by the total number of people who are active in the labour-market.

The question remaining to be considered is who should be counted as 'unemployed' or, perhaps, fall within a wider 'underemployed' category. The largest group which might be included in the latter, wider, category is part-time workers—although official surveys have found that less than a million part-time workers say that they really wish to gain a full-time post. The problem of identifying who is unemployed is particularly acute for the measurement of unemployment among women, so male unemployment rates are more often used to compare the level of joblessness in different areas.

For all areas of Britain—unlike the position in all the other European Union countries—male unemployment rates are higher than those for women. The graph shows that the differential between the rate for men and that for the two genders combined increases in proportion with the place's level of unemployment. There is a surprisingly slight difference between the South and the rest of Britain, with northern areas having a steeper slope of the graph. The highest rates are restricted to the most industrial areas, where job losses were most acute in the industrial sectors more likely to have employed men.

The influence of industrial decline on local levels of male unemployment is easily seen on the map. The major concentrations of the highest rates are on Merseyside and Clydeside, and in north-east England and South Yorkshire. Elsewhere there are 'black spots' in each industrial region: Manchester itself, Smethwick near Birmingham, the south Wales valleys, plus many inner London boroughs (shown on the inset). The 'white spots' of low unemployment are mainly in the region of sustained growth to the west of London, together with more isolated areas of prosperity due to local growth in sectors such as oil and tourism.

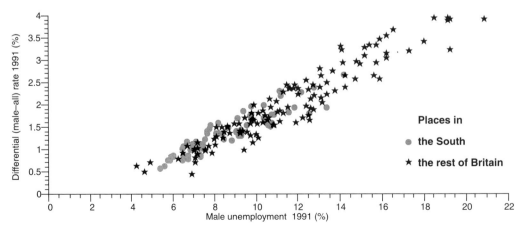

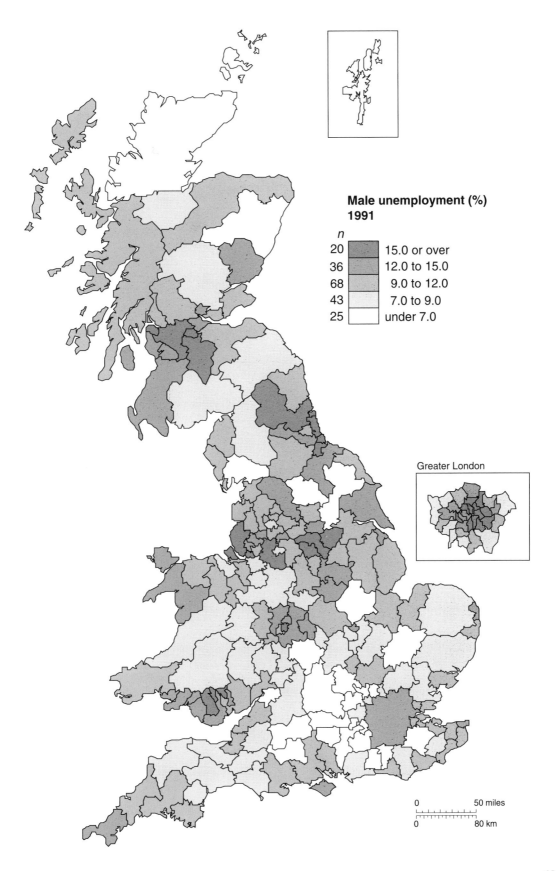

Male unemployment (%)
1991

n		
20		15.0 or over
36		12.0 to 15.0
68		9.0 to 12.0
43		7.0 to 9.0
25		under 7.0

Greater London

0   50 miles
0   80 km

Lacking skills and jobs

The early 1990s were a period when regional variations had temporarily narrowed, due to the recession centred around 1990 in the usually prosperous south of England. After this, the gap between North and South widened again: even so, dividing Britain into the ten 'standard' regions rarely finds a scale of variation in which the highest rate is as much as double the level of that in the least-affected region. In fact, the single most important factor influencing a person's chances of gaining a job is having skills and education. However, the map does show a substantial variation between areas in the level of unemployment for those people who have few skills.

Dividing the labour-force according to their level of education reveals that the unemployment rate of those with no qualifications is over three times that of those with degrees or diplomas. The distinctions become greater once people have gained work experience in the sorts of jobs which are associated with each level of qualification. Data from the Spring 1992 Labour Force Survey shows that the unemployment rate among people who have worked in a professional occupation is under 3%—which is the level often seen as 'full employment' (because there will always be some people who are between jobs). On the other hand, all the mainly industrial manual occupation groups had unemployment rates at least six times higher.

The map presents the 1991 Census data on the local unemployment rates of those who were either unskilled or semi-skilled: all agricultural workers were included, but personal-service workers were excluded. The majority of the people in these groups would be looking for jobs such as drivers or machine operatives. The geographical pattern is a familiar one, with most of the areas with high rates clustered in northern conurbations where there has been long-run industrial decline. The other concentration is in the eastern inner London Boroughs (shown in the inset). Here, the problem is more likely to be a reduction in demand for low-skilled labour among the service industries which are dominant in London—and also in the Isle of Wight and a few other southern areas with higher rates of joblessness.

The cliché of 'getting on your bike' suggests that migration might ease unemployment problems. The diagram dramatizes the superficial evidence in favour of this prescription: not one place in southern England has a very high low-skill unemployment rate, while none of the northern metropolitan areas has a very low rate. Yet no southern area has a low-skill rate below the 3% 'full employment' level, so there cannot be many low-skill jobs being left unfilled. A fair summary seems to be that migration might level out the unemployment rates and so alter *who* is unemployed, but the current shortage of jobs for those with few skills would remain at much the same level.

The need to have skills to compete in the labour-market follows from British firms having to compete with firms in the many countries where skill levels are higher. The summer 1993 LFS shows that even having a degree is no longer a secure and direct route into a job: among the under-25s there was little difference in unemployment rates according to their level of qualification. However, it seems certain that, as they get older, their experiences will be similar to their parents'—so that those who remain without skills will remain the most vulnerable to unemployment.

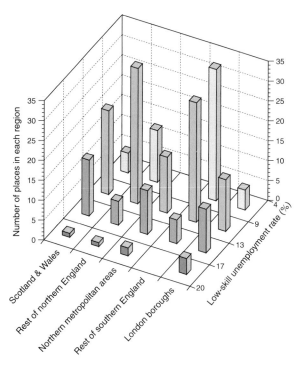

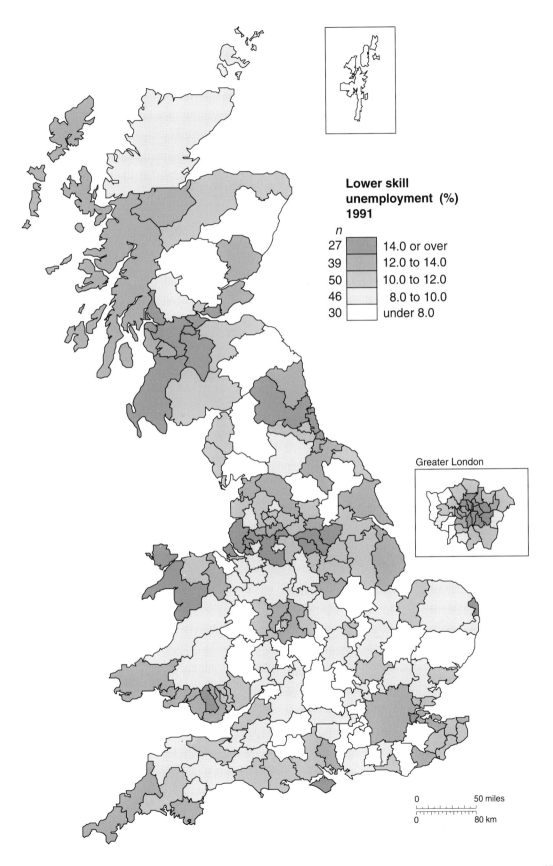

**Lower skill
unemployment (%)
1991**

n		
27		14.0 or over
39		12.0 to 14.0
50		10.0 to 12.0
46		8.0 to 10.0
30		under 8.0

Greater London

0   50 miles

0   80 km

Young people and work

For most people, their late teens and early twenties form the most formative period of their lives as they conclude education and enter the labour-market. How they go through this period has a very strong influence on the way in which they will spend the rest of their working lives. There are clear regional and local differences in people's experiences of this crucial time.

A general picture of people's progression through the ages of 16 to 24 is given in the graph, distinguishing men from women. The most obvious change is the fall in the proportion who are 'inactive', i.e. not part of the labour-force, from the level of just over two-thirds at age 16. This largely reflects the end of the education process (see *Staying on at school*), but for women the proportion stabilizes from age 19 largely as a result of many leaving the labour-force for child birth and care.

The difficulties faced in this transition are seen in the share of each age group in unemployment and working on a Government Scheme. The proportion unemployed increases to age 19, but would be highest at age 17 if Government Schemes were not available. In terms of all who want to work, the level of unemployment (including those on Schemes) is highest at age 16, involving two in five men and one in three women, and in fact falls steadily with increasing age.

The table shows regional patterns averaged across the whole age group, with the regions ranked according to the proportion employed. The proportion of people in employment exhibits a clear North–South progression, though Wales is lower than it usually is

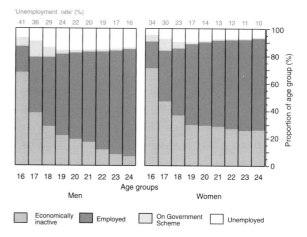

on such rankings and Scotland higher—both these partly being related to their overall activity rates and proportions of students. Government Schemes absorb a smaller proportion of this age group in the South, and are especially important in the North region. It seems that these schemes are put in place where the government expects unemployment to be high.

Map (a) provides the subregional picture of labour-force participation for these young people. This largely reflects the extent of continuing with education, with Welsh counties predominating amongst the lowest values (the lowest being Dyfed at 63%) and with Essex and Grampian (both 75%) at the other extreme.

In maps (b) and (c), the main feature is the strong showing of the metropolitan counties and the former areas of mining and heavy industry. The highest proportion of the whole age group that was unemployed at the time of the 1991 Census is for Merseyside (17%), followed by Tyne and Wear, Strathclyde, Cleveland, and Mid Glamorgan. The highest proportions on Government Schemes were for the four counties of north-east England led by Cleveland (6.8%).

The proportion of 16–24 year-olds who wanted to work but at best could only find a place on a Scheme, shown in map (d), ranged from 33% in Merseyside and 31% in Cleveland to under 12% for Grampian, Surrey, and Berkshire. Also, young adults in remoter rural areas appear to face greater difficulties in getting jobs than their counterparts in the more accessible shire counties, notably those in southern England.

The economic position of 16–24 year-olds, 1991 (%)

Region (ranked on % employed)	Employed	Unemployed	On GS	Active	Unemployment rate	Students
Great Britain	57.1	11.0	3.0	71.1	19.7	24.8
East Anglia	62.0	8.7	2.4	73.0	15.1	23.9
South West	59.3	9.2	2.8	71.3	16.7	26.0
East Midlands	58.9	10.1	3.1	72.0	18.2	23.8
South East	58.9	10.2	1.6	70.7	10.2	26.5
Scotland	57.3	11.9	4.0	73.1	21.7	22.7
West Midlands	56.9	11.4	3.4	71.6	20.6	23.4
Yorkshire and Humberside	55.8	11.5	3.9	71.2	21.7	23.2
North West	53.8	12.8	3.5	69.9	23.2	24.6
North	52.3	13.1	5.9	71.3	26.6	22.5
Wales	51.3	11.8	4.2	67.3	23.8	26.2

Notes: Active = in the labour-force, i.e. employed (including self-employed), unemployed, or on a Government Scheme (GS). Students may be in the labour-force. Unemployment rate is the percentage of the active that are unemployed or on a Government Scheme. Other data are percentages of all persons aged 16–24.

(a) Proportion of 16–24 year olds in labour force (%) 1991

n	
12	73.5 or over
10	72.0 to 73.5
18	70.5 to 72.0
14	69.0 to 70.5
10	under 69.0

0   50 miles
0   80 km

(b) Proportion of 16–24 year olds unemployed (%) 1991

n	
11	12.0 or over
12	10.5 to 12.0
18	9.0 to 10.5
14	8.0 to 9.0
9	under 8.0

0   50 miles
0   80 km

(c) Proportion of 16–24 year olds on Government Scheme (%) 1991

n	
10	5.0 or over
10	4.0 to 5.0
15	3.0 to 4.0
14	2.0 to 3.0
15	under 2.0

0   50 miles
0   80 km

(d) 'Unemployment rate' for 16–24 year olds (%) 1991

n	
12	23.5 or over
13	19.5 to 23.5
13	17.0 to 19.5
11	14.5 to 17.0
15	under 14.5

0   50 miles
0   80 km

47

Staying on at school

The proportion of young people staying in education, after the minimum school-leaving age of 16, has been growing for many years. The map shows the large variation in the share of an area's 16 and 17 year-olds who are full-time at school or college: the highest value (for the area centred on High Wycombe) is well over half as high again as the lowest (Falkirk). The graph reviews the 1981–91 trends which indicate that this strong contrast in areas' staying-on rates is by no means a new development.

It is immediately obvious from the map that most of the very low rates are to be found in the more urban areas of Scotland. Of course, the very different Scottish educational system makes comparisons difficult, although this particular analysis is less affected than are most educational measures (because some contrasts are solely due to the differing exam systems north and south of the Border, for example). The lower rates in Scottish urban and industrial areas are, however, echoed by a similar urban/rural contrast elsewhere, and especially in Wales.

Whilst the map clearly shows that more southern areas had higher proportions of youngsters remaining in education in 1991, the graph reveals that these regional contrasts are not unprecedented. Along with the three regions of northern England, Scotland had very many more low rates than high in 1981, whereas Wales and the two Midland regions included similar numbers of high and low rates, and high rates were predominant in London and southern England.

The graph also shows the 1981–91 change for each of these broad regions' set of places. London boroughs show some widening in the contrasts between them: most boroughs with high 1981 rates also had

rapid 1981–91 increases, whereas few of those with lower rates showed the rapid increases they would have needed to keep pace, let alone to catch up. The rest of the South saw a similar pattern of 1981–91 change to that which occurred in the North and Scotland (namely fairly steady increases in staying-on, whether the place had had a high *or* a low rate in 1981). With a similar level of change in both regions, the broad North–South contrast which existed in 1981 can thus be seen to have been largely unaffected by the substantial national trend towards more young people staying in education.

It is Wales and the Midlands where the trend to higher rates has been weakest. Half of the places in these regions which had had high rates in 1981 have experienced 1981–91 increases of under 6% (the lowest bands shown in the figure). If this pattern is continuing through the 1990s then it might be said that this is a 'North–South divide' whose boundary is shifting southwards—so that the Midlands is becoming more of an extension of the North than of the South.

The areas on the map with low staying-on rates—including many in east London, the Black Country, some Lancashire cotton towns and the Scottish and north-east coalfields—mostly have chronic unemployment problems. In such places the explanation for low staying-on rates cannot be that young people can easily get jobs by leaving school as soon as possible. The more likely answer is that these areas' young people see how many of their predecessors—even those who did gain good educational qualifications—have become unemployed. It is not so surprising then if young people in these areas see less incentive to stay on in education.

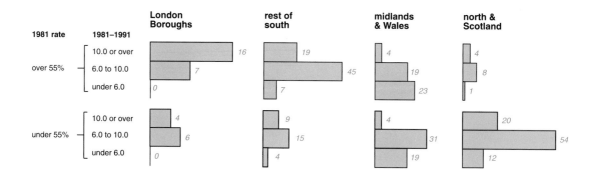

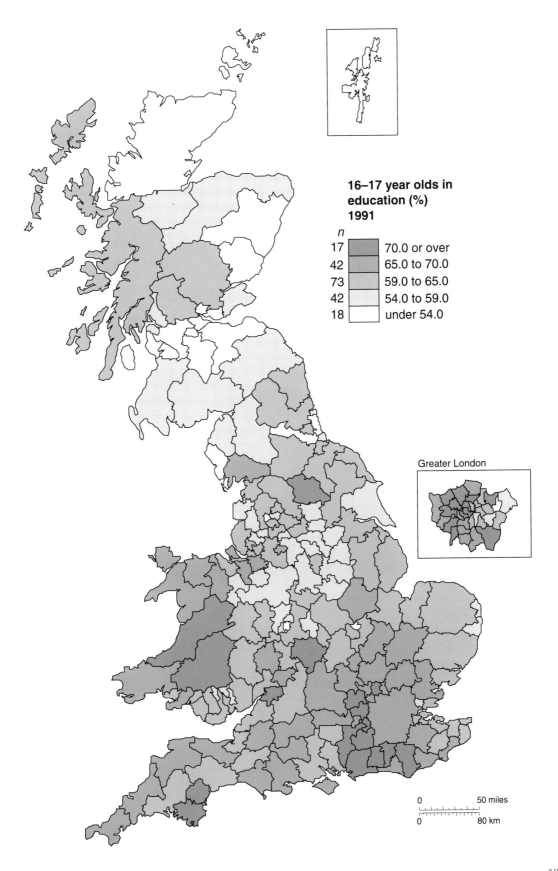

16–17 year olds in education (%) 1991

n	
17	70.0 or over
42	65.0 to 70.0
73	59.0 to 65.0
42	54.0 to 59.0
18	under 54.0

Greater London

0   50 miles

0   80 km

Exam results and qualifications

Over the years there has been a great improvement in the educational achievements of the population as a whole. For every fifteen children who were in their final year of compulsory education in Britain in 1991 only one left school without a nationally recognized qualification. Twenty years ago three times as many children were leaving school with no qualifications, and twenty years before that, in 1951, at least ten in every fifteen children left school by the time they were 14 years old with no nationally recognized qualification.

Geographical variations in exam results

However, this improvement has not been evenly spread across the country. The map shows how great are the differences between school pupil exam results even when these differences are averaged out across whole counties. A child growing up in Surrey is almost two-and-a-half times more likely to leave school with A levels than is a child in Tyne and Wear. (Note that the proportions in Scotland appear even higher than for Surrey, but this is in part due to the fact that the statistics treat the Scottish Highers as the equivalent of A levels.) At the other end of the scale, the contrasts are even more marked, with 20% of Mid Glamorgan's 1991 school-leavers having no graded results compared with under 2% for Bedfordshire, Shropshire, and Somerset.

Even at the broad regional level there are considerable disparities, as more detailed statistics show. Boys leaving school in Wales are four times more likely to leave with no qualifications as compared with boys leaving school in the South West region. At the local level the differences between different areas and schools are very stark, as has been highlighted by the publication of school league tables.

Thus, although there has been a great improvement in educational standards over the last forty years, that improvement has resulted in a map of exam results which shows that where a child grows up in Britain today matters far more than it used to. In the past most children would have left school with no qualifications, regardless of where they lived.

Importance of qualifications

These geographical differences are vital because of the growing importance of qualifications in ensuring employment or access to higher education when children leave school. For instance, in 1988 only 6% of school-leavers in Scotland left school to be unemployed. Just four years later that rate had doubled (note: school-leaver destinations are systematically surveyed only in Scotland). In *Lacking skills and jobs*, the importance of skills and education were shown for people's chances of gaining employment.

The graph on this page shows just how important exam results can be for determining the kind of work people find. Most professional workers have a degree while the majority of semi-skilled or unskilled workers in Britain have no qualifications. People who are employers and managers or skilled workers are unlikely to hold anything less than five GCSE results at grades A to C. Less than a quarter of junior non-manual workers (junior secretaries for instance) have no qualification.

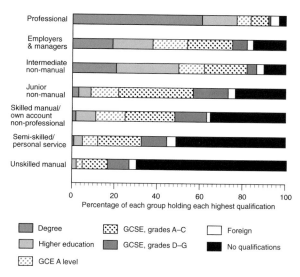

These are the figures for the population as a whole. For the young, who are experiencing the highest rates of unemployment in Britain, the qualifications needed to find work are generally much higher. The rising level of qualifications among school-leavers has encouraged employers to raise the 'entry standards' for the limited numbers of jobs for which young people are competing.

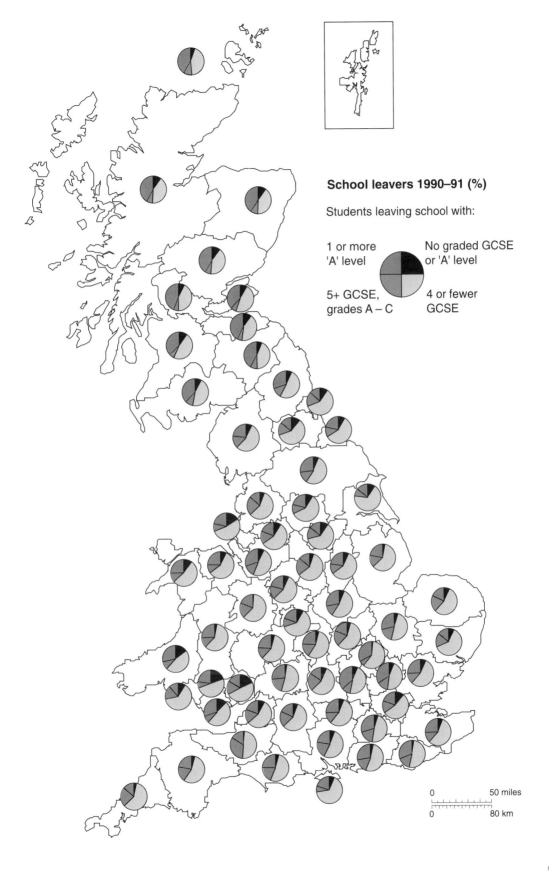

School leavers 1990–91 (%)

Students leaving school with:

1 or more
'A' level

No graded GCSE
or 'A' level

5+ GCSE,
grades A – C

4 or fewer
GCSE

| 0 | | | | | 50 miles |
| 0 | | | | | 80 km |

Going to school

Many important policy issues are raised by child care and school. Amongst these are the extent to which parents, particularly mothers, can be released from child-care responsibilities in order to stay in the labour-force and pursue careers. Once at school, there is the question of class size and the amount of attention given to individual students. The signs are that these vary considerably across the country, often in quite regular patterns.

Day care and the under-5s

As more and more mothers of young children have wanted to keep working, the number of day-care places for the under-5s has grown considerably. For every two places available in 1981, there were three places in 1992. As shown in the graph, the biggest absolute increase was with registered child-minders, but the greatest percentage growth was for places in registered day-nurseries.

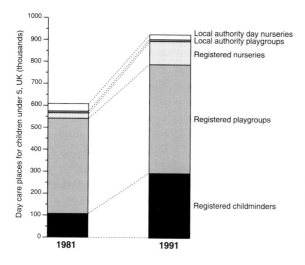

Map (a) shows great variation round the country in part of this child-care provision. In 1992 the number of day-nursery places (local authority and registered) ranged from 55 per 1,000 children aged under 5 in East Sussex to under 10 in Northumberland and Derbyshire and nil for the Isle of Wight. The best served regions were the North West and the West Midlands (47 and 40 per 1,000 respectively), with the poorest—excluding Scotland where the data refers only to local authority provision—being Wales and East Anglia (both 25 per 1,000).

The number of under-5s that have started school has also increased substantially since the early 1980s, and indeed has trebled since the mid-1960s, as shown in the table. This growth has occurred principally through rising part-time attendance at primary schools.

The number of under-5s in schools, expressed in map (b) as a proportion of 3 and 4 year-olds, varies geographically almost as much as nursery provision. The highest figure in 1992 was for Cleveland (91%), followed by West Glamorgan, Clwyd, and Tyne and Wear (all at least 75%), while at the other extreme the figure for Wiltshire was 19% and for Hampshire 20%. The regional patterning is quite strong, ranging from Wales, the North West and the North (all over 60%) to East Anglia and the South West (35–6%).

Pupil : teacher ratios

At school, national standards ensure a fair degree of consistency in pupil : teacher ratios, although maps (c) and (d) both reveal a clear contrast between the situation in England and Wales and the separate arrangements in Scotland. At primary level the most adverse level in Scotland in 1992 was for Central (20.4 pupils per teacher), a figure that is bettered elsewhere in the country only by Dyfed (19.7) and compares very favourably with Greater Manchester's ratio of 27.8, the highest in England.

Even more impressively, at secondary level, Scotland's highest ratio in 1991 (Fife at 13.2) is well below that of the lowest county south of the Border (Gwynedd's 14.3) and so is in stark contrast to the many areas in England and Wales with at least 16.5 pupils per teacher.

Numbers of children aged under 5 in public-sector schools (000s)

	1970/71	1980/81	1990/91	1992/93
Nursery schools:				
Full-time	20	22	16	15
Part-time	29	67	68	70
Primary schools:				
Full-time	263	281	357	376
Part-time	38	167	303	329
Non-maintained:				
Full-time	19	19	28	29
Part-time	14	12	20	21
Special:				
All	2	4	4	4
Totals	**384**	**573**	**799**	**848**

(a)

Day nursery places
(per 1000 under 5s)
1992

n	
13	42.0 or over
13	28.5 to 42.0
13	24.0 to 28.5
13	13.5 to 24.0
12	under 13.5

0   50 miles
0   80 km

(b)

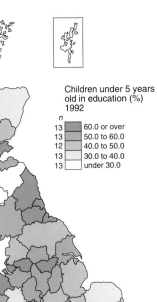

Children under 5 years
old in education (%)
1992

n	
13	60.0 or over
13	50.0 to 60.0
12	40.0 to 50.0
13	30.0 to 40.0
13	under 30.0

0   50 miles
0   80 km

(c)

Primary school
pupil/teacher ratio
1992

n	
12	23.0 or over
13	22.5 to 23.0
13	22.0 to 22.5
13	21.0 to 22.0
13	under 21.0

0   50 miles
0   80 km

(d)

Secondary school
pupil/teacher ratio
1992

n	
13	16.5 or over
12	15.9 to 16.5
13	15.6 to 15.9
13	15.0 to 15.6
13	under 15.0

0   50 miles
0   80 km

New and old universities

The map shows the distribution of those centres of higher education which held the title 'University' by the mid-1990s. The symbols are shaded according to the era from which they date (see note in Appendix 1) while the size of each symbol indicates the size of the institution. In the diagram, the UK is divided into seven regions of roughly the same size population; the symbols then show the growth in numbers of universities in each region over the last two centuries.

In this analysis, collegiate universities such as Oxford and London are each counted as a single large institution, whereas each of the main centres of the University of Wales, for example, is shown separately. The reason is that the rule applied here was that each 'university' should have its own royal charter and, unlike London University colleges, each Welsh institution does indeed have a separate charter. One effect of this approach is that some universities which are mapped as single symbols are in fact spread across two or more centres which may be quite some distance apart.

The scale of the symbols on the map reveals that nearly all the largest universities had been established in either medieval or Victorian times. The size measure used here is the number of academic staff, which includes researchers as well as lecturers, and as such is the relevant measure for anyone considering the potentially beneficial economic effect on a town or city of housing a university. This measure puts the simple count of universities (used in the figure) in perspective: London University on its own (i.e. *not* including the other eleven universities in Greater London) has over 10,000 academic staff—almost as many as the sum of all the eighteen universities across the whole of Scotland *and* Wales!

The diagram shows the explosive growth in the number of universities in recent years. The most recent period has mainly been one of re-labelling, in that almost all of the forty latest university charters were bestowed on former polytechnics. Yet it is true to say that most of these centres—together with most of the 'modern' universities shown on the map—were either non-existent or very modest institutions before the major expansion which started in the 1960s.

Taking together these two categories of recently created universities, the map makes it clear that providing local access has been a major effect of extending the distribution. Indeed the current pattern could be seen as taking this dispersal to excess because every county and Scottish region now either houses at least one university, or is adjacent to at least one area which does. Plans are underway to extend the

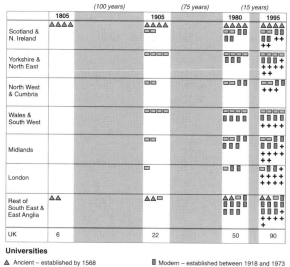

Universities

△ Ancient – established by 1568

▣ Redbrick – established between 1826 and 1905

▤ Modern – established between 1918 and 1973

+ Latest – established since 1990

network still further with, in particular, a University of the Highlands based in Inverness. Another way in which local access can be brought to an area which was without a university is by a new 'remote' campus being opened by an existing university. For example, De Montfort University (formerly Leicester Polytechnic) has looked beyond its home area—where there are competing universities—to adjacent Northamptonshire and Lincolnshire, where they could open a new 'academic branch plant' which would be the first campus in either of those counties.

The diagram shows clear evidence of the trend towards a universal coverage of the country with universities. Even allowing for all other factors, it is remarkable that until less than 200 years ago Scotland had twice as many universities as England. The 'redbrick' era brought universities to the industrial conurbations (note: at first northern England had just the single 'Victoria University' with colleges spread from Liverpool to Leeds—Manchester University still in fact retains this title). The 'modern' growth period of the 1960s and 1970s particularly favoured the smaller cities which are most numerous in southern England. The diagram shows that there was still a wide variation in the number of universities per region until 1980, but the last column indicates that the regional counts have strongly converged (apart from the North West, where there are many large towns between Liverpool and Manchester which have no local university).

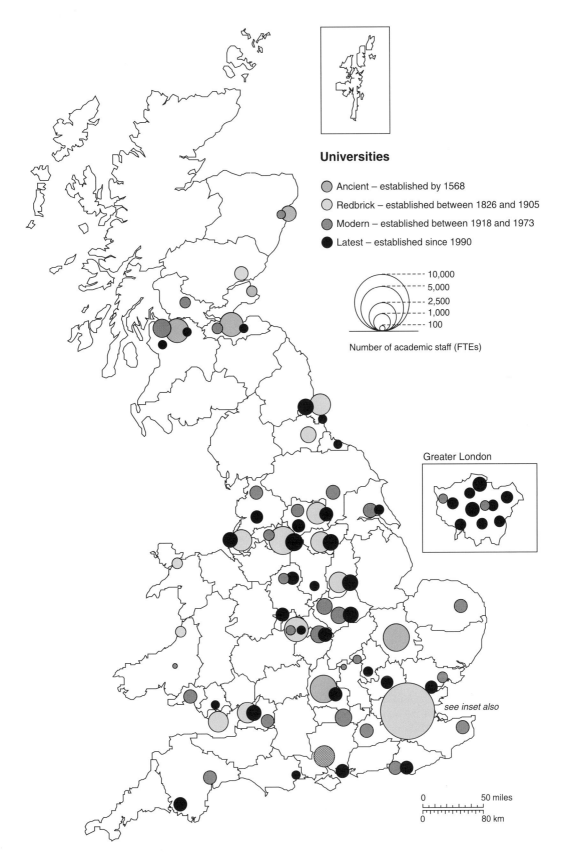

Universities

- Ancient – established by 1568
- Redbrick – established between 1826 and 1905
- Modern – established between 1918 and 1973
- Latest – established since 1990

10,000
5,000
2,500
1,000
100

Number of academic staff (FTEs)

Greater London

see inset also

0   50 miles

0   80 km

Matching ability to responsibility

There is little doubt that if Britain is to thrive economically then an increasing proportion of its economy must be based on those activities which pay high incomes to a highly qualified work-force. In fact, the graph shows that some areas have quite high unemployment rates among the better qualified members of their work-force. Even so, current government policies acknowledge the need for a widespread and rapid increase in skill levels in order to compete with other countries where qualification levels are not only higher but are continuing to rise rapidly. At present, there is considerable variation between parts of Britain in the availability of more highly qualified people. The map uses a measure of 'overqualification' which expresses, for each area, the number of working residents who have a degree (or equivalent) *as a percentage* of the number who work in the types of jobs which typically recruit those with degrees, namely managers, professionals, and semi-professionals.

The places which appear white on the map can thus be said to have an overqualified work-force, and are mainly in south-west England or the Lake District, or much of Wales and Scotland away from the old industrial areas. These are places where there is strong evidence of a relative surplus of well-qualified people in the local work-force. Many of these areas have seen strong net in-migration to their attractive towns and countryside.

In the places with the darkest shading on the map, employers seem likely to have a problem in finding enough well-qualified people for their higher level jobs. Areas such as Oldham, Walsall, and parts of east London are suffering from high unemployment overall, but at the same time they face a shortage of people with degrees and similar qualifications. Some of the places which have seen rapid growth in recent decades, such as Peterborough and Basingstoke, are also areas where a less well-qualified person may be able to get a better paid job than he or she would in areas where underqualification is less acute. In these areas, growth in employment opportunities for well-qualified people has not been matched by the distribution of the well-qualified work-force (nor, perhaps, by the level of education qualifications obtained by young people locally). Yet the single most important factor is likely to be migration among the age groups who are finishing further and higher education. The patterns on the map will substantially reflect the drift of many better qualified younger people—the most mobile group in society—from their original home areas to those places which attract them.

If migrants are accepting jobs for which they are overqualified, then much of the attraction of areas such as the Lake District must not be related to job opportunities but to factors such as life-style and environment. The graph shows the pattern of unemployment rates among well-qualified people, in each of four broad regions (with London boroughs also being shown, by way of contrast). The two highest rates are west Cornwall (Truro and Penzance) and Brighton—areas where the flow of in-migrants has clearly outstripped the growth of high-level jobs.

An intriguing contrast can be made with the similar graph of unemployment rates for those with few skills (*Lacking skills and jobs*); southern England provides several of the places with the highest unemployment rates for the better qualified, but none of its areas are among those with very high unemployment rates for those with few skills. It is still important to remember that within any single place the low-skilled always have a higher unemployment rate than their neighbours with good qualifications. Even so, the patterns of migration—of the better qualified in particular—seems to have the effect of levelling-off the contrast between the unemployment rates of the different skill groups *both* in the high unemployment areas (such as the older industrial regions) which migrants are tending to leave, *and* in the more rural areas which attract them.

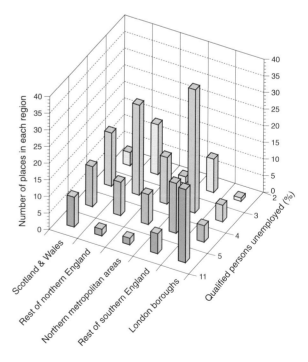

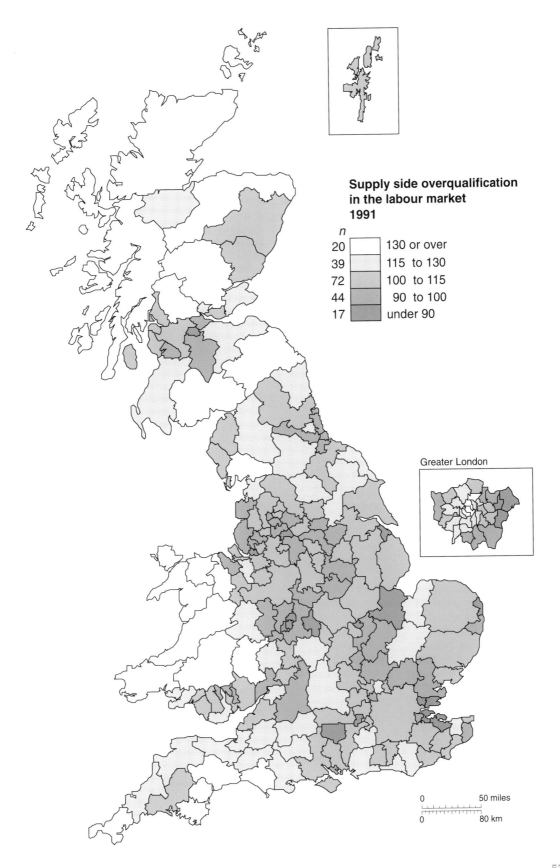

Supply side overqualification in the labour market 1991

n		
20		130 or over
39		115 to 130
72		100 to 115
44		90 to 100
17		under 90

Greater London

0   50 miles

0   80 km

Projecting future employment patterns

Looking at the various employment sectors, and considering expert views of their likely growth or decline over the coming years, allows projections to be made for future patterns of employment. Predictions of this kind are usually made on a national basis, but it is possible to estimate them on a county basis. This may be achieved by examining the employment profile of each county and then assuming that within a county each sector will have the same rate of growth or decline as has been predicted for the nation as a whole.

The national forecast of employment change by industry for 1991–2001 is shown in the table. Clearly it is expected that agriculture, mining, and most manufacturing industries will have experienced substantial contractions in jobs by 2001, most by at least 10% and mining etc. by over a third. By contrast, considerable growth is expected in parts of the service sector. Other things being equal, areas that are more dependent on production sectors than average can expect to perform more poorly than average in terms of overall job growth, and vice versa.

Map (a) shows the total change in jobs that each county (and Scottish region) will experience over the decade up to the year 2001. Obviously counties having a larger proportion of jobs in those sectors predicted to expand in the next few years, notably in miscellaneous service industries, are expected to see an overall expansion in work available. Many of these areas will be in the southern and south-eastern parts of England, although other areas such as north Wales and the south-west England will also experience expansion.

Over the last decade, the public sector has shrunk notably. Many of the categories in the table, such as mining, utilities, and transport and communication, would have contributed to the public sector, but recent trends in privatization have created a situation where although these categories still contribute a small amount, the public sector is mostly dominated by health and education and public administration. Assuming that these core categories will continue to be the only notable contributors to the public sector in 2001, a projection of public-sector employment is given in map (b). This shows a very different geographical pattern from the first map, particularly for Greater London—with its high projected rate of overall employment growth and its very low public-sector profile in 2001—and northern England where the reverse is the case.

The sector predicted to grow the fastest is miscellaneous services. These include many private-sector personal services, such as hairdressing and health clubs, and also commercial services such as office cleaning. It is interesting to note that this sector is expected to expand by almost 31% by the year 2001, a rate of expansion that is ten percentage points larger than the next fastest growing sector, health and education.

Map (c) shows the proportion of the work-force employed in this sector in 1991. It is clear that in Greater London and the South East, there is a relatively strong dependence on this particular type of employment. There are also other areas of the country having proportions close to that of the South East.

In map (d), a projection of the percentage of the work-force employed in miscellaneous services is made for the year 2001. As the map is drawn using the same class-shading intervals as map (c), the extent to which this sector is expected to grow becomes apparent. Although there are still high percentages in the South East, it is clear that there are higher levels in many other parts of the country. Impressively, while there were only six counties in the top category in 1991, the number is projected to rise to thirty-seven in the figures for 2001 illustrated in map (d).

Projected change in employment by industry, Great Britain, 1991–2001 (%)

Industry	Projected change	Industry	Projected change
Agriculture	−15	Construction	+5
Mining etc.	−35	Distribution etc.	+6
Utilities	−26	Transport and communication	−5
Metal, minerals, etc.	−17	Banking, insurance, and business services	+13
Engineering	−18	Miscellaneous services	+31
Chemicals	−6	Health and education	+21
Motor vehicles	−3	Public administration	+5
Food, drink, and tobacco	−25		
Textiles and clothing	−23		
Other manufacturing	−10		

(a)

Projected change in
total employment (%)
1991–2001

n		
13		3.0 or over
18		1.0 to 3.0
29		−1.0 to 1.0
3		−3.0 to −1.0
1		under −3.0

0   50 miles
0   80 km

(b)

Projected employment in
the public sector (%)
2001

n		
18		17.0 or over
21		15.0 to 17.0
18		13.0 to 15.0
6		11.0 to 13.0
1		under 11.0

0   50 miles
0   80 km

(c)

Employment in
miscellaneous services (%)
1991

n		
8		11.0 or over
13		9.0 to 11.0
17		7.0 to 9.0
19		5.0 to 7.0
7		under 5.0

0   50 miles
0   80 km

(d)

Projected employment in
miscellaneous services (%)
2001

n		
37		11.0 or over
21		9.0 to 11.0
6		7.0 to 9.0
0		5.0 to 7.0
0		under 5.0

0   50 miles
0   80 km

Contrasting employment sectors

Throughout history, an area's economic prospects have tended to hinge on the fortunes of its 'staple' industry. It is only necessary to refer to the diagram in *New enterprise* to see how dramatically the overall trend in any one sector of industry can alter within quite a short period. Two of the maps opposite are based on forecasts for the year 2001 of employment levels in contrasting industrial sectors. It is notable that these forecasts were made at the start of the 1990s, projecting forward trends from the late 1980s such as the strong increase in employment in banking and finances: in fact, that sector—which is not featured here—has since then experienced job loss at a faster rate than almost any other sector. The employment prospects in some individual industries clearly call for careful review.

Job forecasts are available for seventeen sectors of the economy, ranging from the predicted job loss of over one in three jobs in mining to an expected growth in jobs of over 30% in miscellaneous services (see *Projecting future employment patterns*). The latter sector is very largely made up of smaller private businesses, and as such makes a notable contrast with the health and education sector which was forecast to see the next fastest growth in job levels. It is worth noting here that *growth* in job numbers can in some cases be mainly due to full-time jobs being replaced by part-time posts, so that firms' wages bills may be *lower* as a result. Even so, an area will clearly face a more prosperous future if a high proportion of its jobs are in growth sectors rather than those which are confidently expected to lose jobs rapidly.

Services

In map (a), the balance between the number of jobs in the public services of health and education and the miscellaneous services sector is shown. Given the very different ownership and other characteristics of these two sectors, considering the balance between them (expressed as a ratio) reveals the dependence of those areas with high values on the level of government spending on health and education in the near future. London and the South East have more of their jobs in miscellaneous services, whereas many other parts of the country rely more on public services and so the projected job growth there is dependent on government policy.

Production

Map (b) shows the current proportion of the workforce employed in the production sector. This sector is the one in which jobs are expected to be lost heavily, as they have been since the 1960s. The map shows a low concentration in London and the South East, with much higher levels in the Midlands and northern England, together with parts of Scotland and Wales. Taken together with the service-sector forecasts described above, this could be a scenario for a further strengthening of the 'North–South divide' over the coming decade.

However, map (b) is not the entire story, since it refers to all jobs in the production sector, not simply those in the *most* threatened industries. When each area's mix of individual industries is considered, predicted percentage falls in jobs in the production sector may be computed. These are illustrated in map (c), and they make it clear which northern areas are particularly likely to lose jobs. A rather more surprising feature of the map is the large predicted drop in the Grampian area. This should be regarded with some suspicion, since the figure arrived at here classes the oil industry as mining and therefore presumes a level of decline which should only be associated with the coal-mining industry. If nothing else, this is a salutary lesson that one should always check the assumptions made in economic predictions, and their underlying models. The law of 'garbage in garbage out' applies very strongly here!

If some industry sectors are in decline, then it is essential that others expand in order to maintain employment bases within regions. Clearly, from the table in *Projecting future employment patterns*, the miscellaneous services sector has been tipped to have the greatest expansion. It is therefore useful to compare the ratio of jobs in this part of the service sector to those in the production sector on a county basis (map (d)). As one would expect, this ratio is high in London, but is also surprisingly high in certain other areas of the country. Tyne and Wear has a particularly strong ratio amongst counties in northern England, reflecting the fact that its previous production jobs were in sectors such as mining which are projected to continue their long-term decline so that the forecast adds up to a 'post-industrial' area in 2001.

(a)

Ratio of public to
miscellaneous services
1991

n	
12	2.0 or over
13	1.8 to 2.0
13	1.7 to 1.8
13	1.5 to 1.7
13	under 1.5

0 50 miles
0 80 km

(b)

Employment in the
production sector (%)
1991

n	
13	30.0 or over
15	25.0 to 30.0
18	20.0 to 25.0
15	15.0 to 20.0
3	under 15..0

0 50 miles
0 80 km

(c)

Projected fall in
employment in
production sector (%)
1991–2001

n	
2	19.0 or over
5	17.0 to 19.0
9	15.0 to 17.0
41	13.0 to 15.0
7	under 13.0

0 50 miles
0 80 km

(d)

Ratio of miscellaneous
services to production
sector, 2001

n	
13	0.55 or over
18	0.45 to 0.55
9	0.35 to 0.45
11	0.25 to 0.35
13	under 0.25

0 50 miles
0 80 km

Life Chances

New enterprise

Until very recently, a key feature of any atlas such as this would have been maps of industries and their work-forces. In 1971 for example, dramatic contrasts could be made between the 52% of workers in the East Midlands and the 33% in East Anglia who worked in the mining and manufacturing industries. By 1991 the figures were 32% and 23% respectively. Thus it is no longer realistic to map the remaining vestiges of individual traditional industries and so to characterize whole swathes of Britain as mining, steel-making, shipbuilding, or textile districts. The graph reveals the sheer scale of job loss in five key traditional industries.

It is worth remembering that the first year shown here was barely twenty-five years ago—and the mining industry, for example, was already then less than half the size it had once been. The graph shows that this decline has accelerated (even though the available data combines the prosperous oil industry with coal-mining). The other industries shown have each had their crisis periods too, and all have lost over half of their 1971 work-force. Yet the influence of these past industries continues to be observable in many of the economic and social patterns which are mapped in this atlas, and not least in the map here of the growth of new small firms, on which many rely to provide jobs as replacements for those lost in the old industries.

The skills and experience of an area's work-force were largely shaped by those industries which were its main local employers. Many industries operated mainly through large 'branch plants' which were located away from the firms' head offices. When such plants close down, the work-force in those areas have little experience of management—and research shows that most successful small firms are set up by people with past management experience. For this map, then, each area's managers and professionals are taken to be its 'seed bed' of potential new-firm founders. The number of people in these groups, in each place, is thus divided into the number of local new firms (i.e. registering for VAT purposes for the first time in 1991) to produce the 'new firms per 10,000' value which is mapped.

Producing this 'standardized' new-firm formation rate can be seen as a rather sweeping attempt to discount the statistical effect of places' past industrial structure. The map shows that it has indeed succeeded in removing the stark North–South regional contrast which is present in the non-standardized rates. However, the map also shows that *within* most

regions there is still a mix of both high and low values after the standardization. This remaining pattern at the local level can be seen to be influenced by the areas' past industrial histories. In Wales, Scotland, and northern England, for example, it is clear that the higher values are largely restricted to the rural areas—into which heavy industry scarcely penetrated. In the South East, too, the lower rates are to be found in areas where there was a significant level of manufacturing industry, notably along the Thames estuary and in some new towns (e.g. Hatfield, Bracknell, and Crawley).

The detailed pattern within London (see inset) may seem to run counter to the argument developed here about the influence of past industrialization. Most of London's industry was in the inner areas, yet it is the inner boroughs which are prominent among those with high rates of new-firm formation. Part of the explanation lies in the fact that some of these inner areas include many solicitors and other business-service firms, whose offices are often used as business addresses of firms which are likely to be located in outlying places. An *indirect* effect of industrialization on new-firm formation rates in inner London—and also in many textile towns—is the strong presence in these areas of ethnic-minority population. These in-migrants are largely from the South Asian countries, and they have a strong tendency to be new-firm founders (see the bar graph in *Ethnicity and unemployment* for self-employment levels among different ethnic groups).

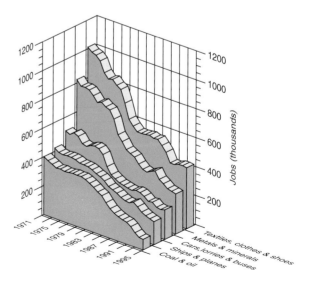

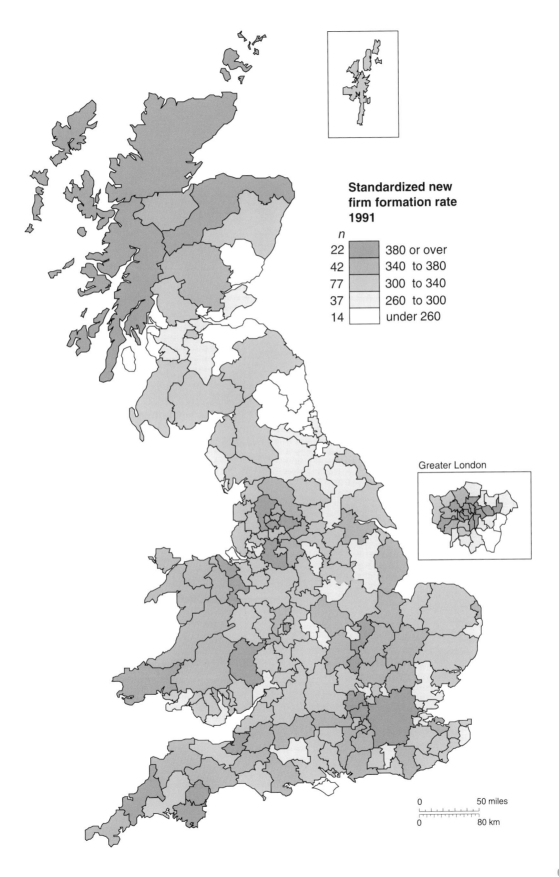

Standardized new firm formation rate 1991

n		
22		380 or over
42		340 to 380
77		300 to 340
37		260 to 300
14		under 260

Greater London

0   50 miles

0   80 km

Wealth

There is very little information on the wealth of people in Britain broken down by geographical area. The Inland Revenue publishes the vast majority of its statistics at the level of the United Kingdom. However, a variety of unofficial statistics can be used to gauge the extent of wealth in Britain. The most obvious example is information from building societies on wealth held in the form of bricks and mortar: housing equity (see *House prices and negative equity*). But most wealth is not held in the form of property, but as savings, investments, or pension plans. An indication of the extent to which people in different areas hold assets in more liquid form can be gauged from looking at the distribution of share-ownership in Britain and the value of those shares at one point in time. Here a sample of shareholders has been taken from each district in Britain to estimate the mean value of assets held by shareholders in that district.

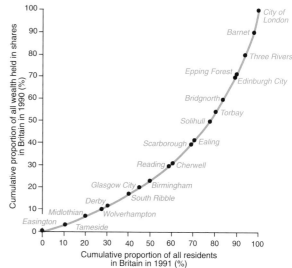

Geography of wealth held in shares

The map uses 'coins' with areas proportional to the average value of shares held in each district. The richest district in Britain by this measure was Kensington and Chelsea, where the average shareholder had assets in this form worth £20,900 in 1990. The poorest district was Blyth Valley (Northumberland), where the average value of shares held by these investors was only £1,600. These figures refer only to shareholders.

When the wealth held in shares in each district is divided among all the population living there, the divide between rich and poor areas is much wider than the above figures would suggest. Averaged out, each resident in Kensington and Chelsea had £43 held in the form of shares for every £1 held by the residents of Blyth Valley. However, by this measure these two areas no longer form the most extreme cases in Britain.

Concentration of share wealth

The graph shows how only a quarter of the population of Britain lived in districts which contained people holding over half of the share wealth of the country. The poorest quarter of the population lived in districts whose residents held less than 9% of the country's share wealth, while the poorest 10% of the population (by district) held less than a fortieth of the share wealth. These people live in forty-six districts of which Easington is the most poor and Tameside the least poor. The graph shows the districts that bound each decile of the population, ending with Epping Forest and the City of London, which bound the fifty-two districts whose residents are the richest 10%, holding almost 30% of share wealth.

Below the Gini Curve of wealth inequality are listed the names of the eleven districts which bound the population that holds ten equal portions of the nation's wealth in progressively greater concentrations. At the extreme, less than one person in every fifty in Britain lives in districts found on this scale to be lying between the London Borough of Barnet and the City of London, yet these people hold one-tenth of the share value of this country.

It is important to remember that only a minority of people in each district hold shares and that within districts there is great variation in the wealth held by people living in different neighbourhoods. Nevertheless, wealth held in this relatively common form is highly concentrated between different parts of the country. It would not be surprising, were the information available, to find that wealth held in all forms was even more concentrated than this.

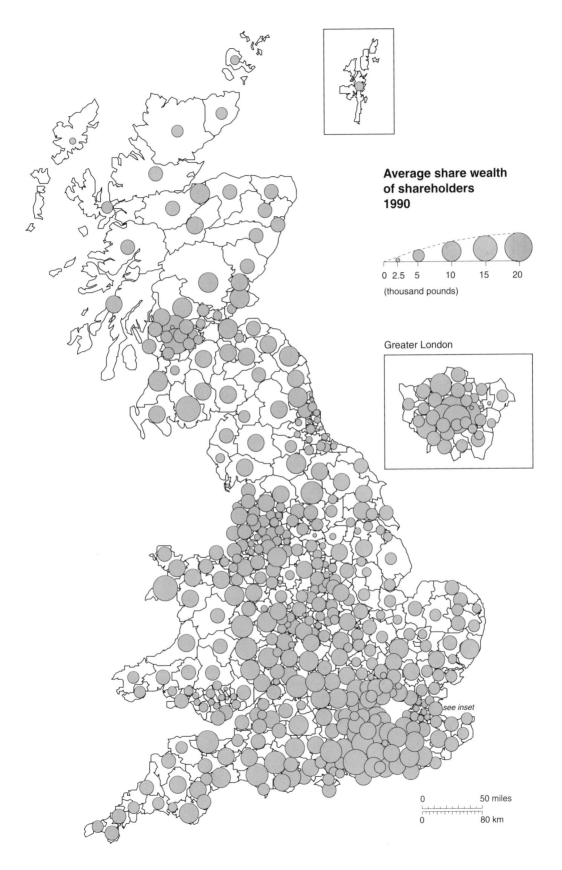

**Average share wealth
of shareholders
1990**

0 2.5 5 10 15 20

(thousand pounds)

Greater London

see inset

0   50 miles

0   80 km

Social class

Social class is closely related to wealth, in that it is defined on the basis of occupation—which is also the main influence on income levels. It is traditional to recognize six separate social groupings, even though—rather confusingly—the Social Classes are numbered I to V (and their precise definitions have changed over time). These are identified in the graph.

The national picture

The graph shows how numerous each of the six groupings was in 1991 in terms of men, women, and heads of household. Note that men are over three times as likely to be in professional occupations as are women, and that the proportion in Social Classes IV and V is somewhat higher for women than for men. The biggest difference between the sexes, however, is within the very large Social Class III, which is subdivided into non-manual and manual. Here women are highly concentrated into the former, with men being much more heavily represented in the latter. The predominance of males as household heads is reflected in the fact that more of the latter were classified as IIIM than IIIN.

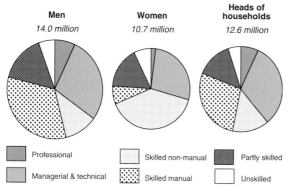

Men
14.0 million

Women
10.7 million

Heads of households
12.6 million

Professional

Managerial & technical

Skilled non-manual

Skilled manual

Partly skilled

Unskilled

Variations across Britain

Map (a) and the district-level table confirm the geographical patterns found for *Wealth*. At county level, Surrey leads the way, with 54% of households headed

by a person in Social Class I or II, followed by Berkshire, Buckinghamshire, and Hertfordshire, all with at least 48%. At district level, the City of London comes top with 75%, followed by two London boroughs, two 'exclusive' Clydeside suburbs and a number of London's high-status dormitory towns.

At the other end of the district rankings come the two former steelworks towns of Scunthorpe and Corby, with under one in five of household heads in professional or managerial occupations. The lowest counties are Mid Glamorgan (30%), Tyne and Wear, South Yorkshire, Cleveland, and Humberside, reflecting the legacy of mining and industry for occupational profiles.

The position in relation to partly skilled and unskilled occupations, shown in map (d), is very largely a mirror image of map (a), though in this case it is rural areas rather than older industrial areas that score highest—Scottish Islands, Borders, and Dumfries and Galloway have at least 25% of households headed by someone in Classes IV or V.

The industrial/mining counties of Staffordshire, Mid Glamorgan, and South Yorkshire head the rankings on the skilled manual occupations shown in map (c). Meanwhile, the highest proportions of skilled non-manual occupations, shown in map (b), are found for the three national capital areas of Greater London, South Glamorgan, and Lothian, no doubt related to the large numbers of support in the administrative and service sectors.

Percentage of households headed by person in Social Classes I and II, 1991: highest and lowest districts

Highest	%	Lowest	%
City of London	74.6	Scunthorpe	19.4
Kensington and Chelsea	64.8	Corby	19.5
Richmond upon Thames	64.6	Barking	19.6
Bearsden and Milngavie	63.9	Easington	20.9
Eastwood	63.4	Sandwell	21.2
Wokingham	61.4	Stoke	21.8
Elmbridge	61.2	Knowsley	22.5
Chiltern	60.4	Port Talbot	22.9
St Albans	60.3	Rhondda	23.0
South Buckinghamshire	58.5	Blaenau Gwent	23.5

(a)

Proportion in
Social Classes I & II (%)
1991

n	
10	43.0 or over
15	39.0 to 43.0
12	36.0 to 39.0
13	34.0 to 36.0
14	under 34.0

0   50 miles
0   80 km

(b)

Proportion in
Social Class III N (%)
1991

n	
9	15.0 or over
14	13.5 to 15.0
16	12.5 to 13.5
11	12.0 to 12.5
14	under 12.0

0   50 miles
0   80 km

(c)

Proportion in
Social Class III M (%)
1991

n	
14	31.5 or over
11	29.5 to 31.5
16	27.5 to 29.5
10	25.5 to 27.5
13	under 25.5

0   50 miles
0   80 km

(d)

Proportion in
Social Classes IV & V (%)
1991

n	
8	23.5 or over
19	21.0 to 23.5
15	19.0 to 21.0
11	17.5 to 19.0
11	under 17.5

0   50 miles
0   80 km

69

Waged and unwaged

There is a long-standing belief among the collectors of Britain's official statistics that British people will not tolerate being asked about their income. This belief continues to prevent the inclusion of an income question in the Census—despite the evident success of many commercial surveys in asking people about their income level. Unlike in countries such as the USA, then, measures of poverty have to be estimated from other data. When comparing areas, an important part of the picture is the proportion of all people in each place who are not earners.

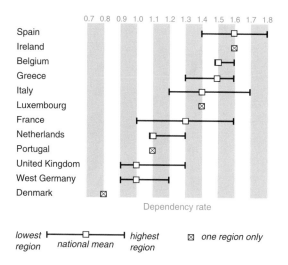

Dependency rate

lowest region ⊢——□——⊣ highest region
national mean
⊠ one region only

A simple approach to dependency identifies all non-earners as dependants, whether they are children, housewives, unemployed, or retired people. Thus a pensioner couple would be counted as two dependent people, as would two unemployed people living alone, or two children in a family. Yet the levels at which pensions and benefits are set is just one sign that the 'earnings requirement' for each of these dependants is not the same (e.g. the pension for a couple is far less than the sum of the pensions for two single pensioners living alone). One approach used in Europe makes a start on allowing for these factors by calculating 'adult equivalent' earnings requirements. It is not suggested that 'two can live as cheaply as one' but the second (and any subsequent) adult in a household is counted as needing only 0.7 of the earnings of the first member. Children are assumed to live with at least one adult, so the presence of a child is taken to imply an additional earnings need equivalent to 0.5 of the adult level.

The calculation underlying the map relies upon first measuring the 'adult equivalent' requirement of

each area's population. This will present higher values where there are large numbers of single person households, and lower values for areas with large families, than would a simple measure based on a head count. The map shows the relationship between this measure and the count of dependants—whether children, pensioners, unemployed, or otherwise not active. A very clear picture emerges, with low values in an arc to the west and north of London where the high numbers of children are more than offset by the low number of retired people (see *Age structure*). These areas also have many single employed people and DINKY (Double Income No Kids Yet) households, who will make the biggest contribution to lowering this form of dependency rate.

In a rough and ready way, the map can be said to be contrasting areas making the biggest net payments into the welfare state (namely the lightest shaded areas) with those which are probably receiving more. The former areas have a high proportion of earners, all of whom will pay National Insurance contributions and other direct taxes. The latter areas include a mix of pensioners, children (whose parents receive Child Benefit), and the unemployed (most of whom are paid benefits). The inset map of London illustrates the contrast, with south-west London including many earners who will help to pay for the higher proportion of non-earners in eastern areas nearer to Docklands.

Of course, the fuller picture is much more complex: for example, many earners also have children so they too receive substantial Welfare State payments. It is also important that the range of dependency values, between highest and lowest, is not very great. Yet the map does still draw attention to some important patterns. In particular, the areas with higher values are not restricted to regions like north-east England with problems such as long-term unemployment; high values are also characteristic of retirement areas along the south coast from Margate to Torquay and west Cornwall.

Concerns about Welfare State expenditure—especially with the increasing numbers of older people—are common to many other Western countries. The figure presents 1990 European Union data, which is calculated in a slightly different way from that used for the map. Britain can be seen to be similar to the other mainly Protestant countries in having a relatively high proportion of its people who are earners. The value for Northern Ireland is 1.3 and if this was ignored—to consider only the values of regions in Great Britain—then the range (from 0.9 to 1.1) would be less than for any other large European country.

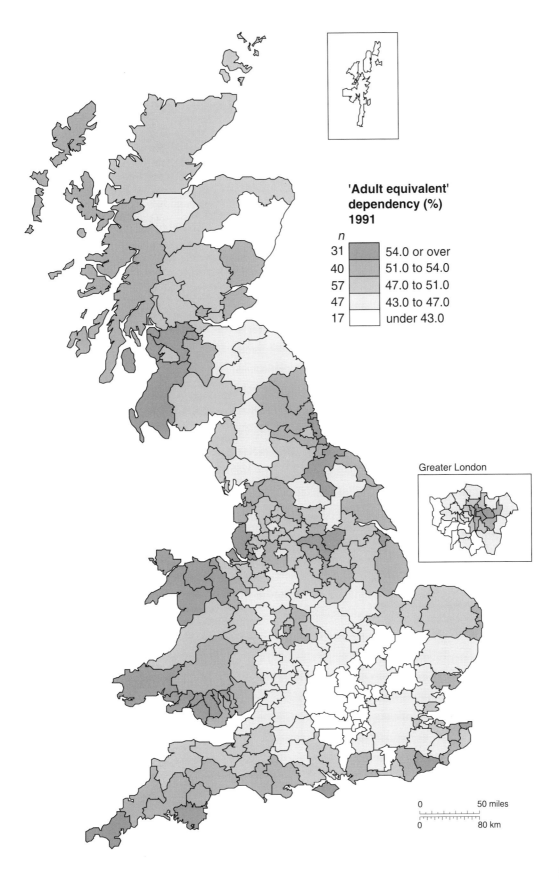

'Adult equivalent'
dependency (%)
1991

n		
31		54.0 or over
40		51.0 to 54.0
57		47.0 to 51.0
47		43.0 to 47.0
17		under 43.0

Greater London

0   50 miles

0   80 km

Growing up in poverty

There is widespread concern at the increasing problem of child poverty in 1990s Britain. A growing proportion of all children are living in households which, without Benefit payments, would fall below the 'poverty line' set by the government. In most of these households, no one has been able to get a job; the diagram classifies children according to whether or not they live in such a 'no earner' household, and then examines how far this is related to other aspects of their standard of living. The map takes a slightly broader view of child poverty by also including children in households with a lone parent who has just a part-time job (because these are also likely to be households with low incomes).

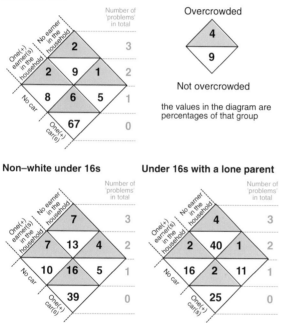

All under 16s

Number of 'problems' in total

Overcrowded

Not overcrowded

the values in the diagram are percentages of that group

Non–white under 16s

Under 16s with a lone parent

Number of 'problems' in total

Although the Census in Britain does not ask a question about income, there is little doubt that child poverty is likely to be most widespread in those areas with the darkest shading on the map. It is these areas—Clydeside, Merseyside, south Wales, and north-east England—where unemployment has been a long-term concern, and child poverty is one consequence. It is notable that those areas in which severe job loss has been a more recent development, such as South Yorkshire and the West Midlands, have a slightly lower proportion of their children in low income households.

The one place in the West Midlands which the map shows to have over one in four of its children in low-income households is West Bromwich—this is an inner urban area and so can be compared with the Inner London areas where high rates of child poverty are also to be seen (in the inset). Many residents of these areas have low educational levels, and also many are from ethnic minorities. These are categories of people who are more at risk of being unemployed *wherever* they live, and it should be remembered that many other cities will have similar neighbourhoods of concentrated disadvantage.

To explore this question of 'risk factors' further, the diagram focuses on the extent to which one problem can lead to another until a family can be said to be multiply deprived (see the note in Appendix 1).

One group of children who can be seen to be particularly at risk of poverty-related problems are those who live with lone parents. Although the category of lone parents includes people in a very wide range of circumstances, the overall picture is of a strong contrast between these families and those with two parents: for example, in 1992 (*Social Trends* 24, 37) 63% of children with lone parents lived in housing rented from a local authority or a housing association, compared to only 18% of children living with a couple. The lower part of the diagram confirms that being with a lone parent—or being from an ethnic minority group—increases the risk of experiencing the three forms of material deprivation measured in this analysis.

The two groups differ noticeably, with ethnicity associated with the highest proportion (7%) of children suffering *all* three problems, yet also including a higher proportion (39%) than those with lone parents having *none* of these three. The most distinctive feature of the diagrams is probably the fact that 40% of all children with lone parents are in a household with no earner and no car—but are *not* suffering overcrowding (see notes).

This gloomy picture for children in certain lone-parent households is confirmed by the fact that the seven places where having a lone parent is least common (all located in the Home Counties to the west of London) are also among those areas which the map shows to have very few low-earner households. Further, the two measures show similar areas with the highest values: Glasgow, Manchester, and Liverpool have approaching 20% of children in lone-parent families, and all three cities are also in the heaviest shaded category on the map of children living in low-earner households.

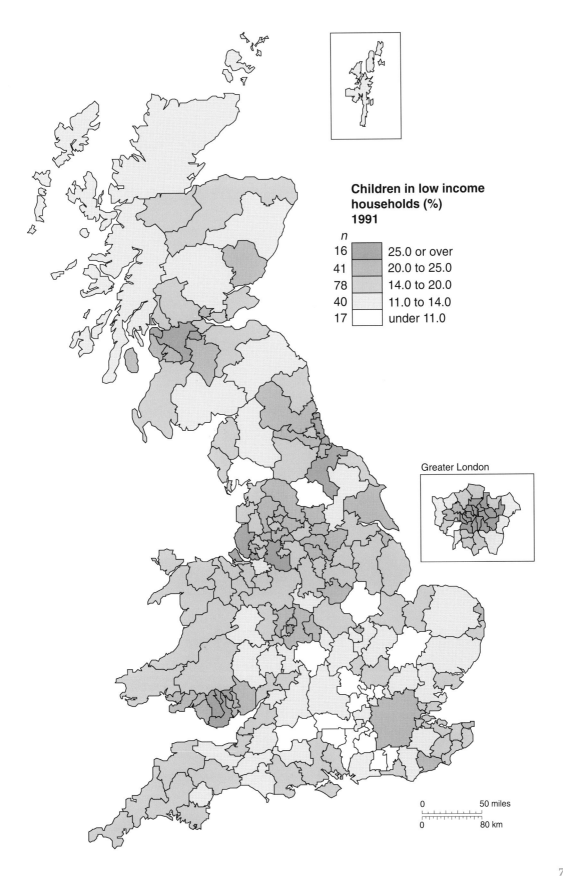

Children in low income
households (%)
1991

n		
16		25.0 or over
41		20.0 to 25.0
78		14.0 to 20.0
40		11.0 to 14.0
17		under 11.0

Greater London

0   50 miles

0   80 km

Born outside marriage

Related to the increase in the number of children in poverty, in many people's minds at least, is the growth in the number of births occurring to unmarried mothers. Certainly, the past two decades have seen a huge change in sexual behaviour and living arrangements, part of what some have called 'the demographic revolution' or 'the second demographic transition'. But, broadly viewed in that way, this development is very pervasive and certainly not restricted to particular groups of people or parts of the country.

The general trend is shown in the graph. Less than one in twenty births occurred outside marriage in the mid-1950s, but a figure of one in three looks likely during the 1990s. The rise has been very consistent from year to year over most of these four decades—pretty gradual till the 1970s, particularly strong in the 1980s, and then decelerating somewhat since 1991.

One element of popular stereotyping is confirmed by panel (a) of the table, concerning the much higher probability of mothers aged under 20 giving birth out of wedlock than for older women. As long ago as 1971 fully a quarter of births to these young mothers were 'illegitimate', as they were termed then, and by 1992 this proportion had risen to five out of every six. Nevertheless, the proportion of all births to unmarried mothers accounted for by women under 20 years old has almost halved since the 1970s, standing at only 18.6% in 1992. This has resulted from the big increases in births outside marriage to all the other age groups of women as well, with the proportion increasing sixfold for 20–24-year-olds and fivefold for 25–29-year-olds.

Also shown by the table (panel (b)) is that the biggest contributor to the increase in births outside marriage has not been to 'single mothers' (except in the legal sense) but to the category where the mother is living with her child's father as a 'cohabiting' couple. Births registered by parents living at the same address now account for over half of all births outside marriage and were responsible for virtually all the increase since 1986, whereas the share of all births registered by the mother only has changed very little.

The map shows how widespread this phenomenon is across the country. Even so, in 1992 the proportion of children born out of wedlock was twice as high in some areas as in others, ranging from 42% to just under 20%. The patterns are quite clear, with urban and industrial areas coming highest (Merseyside, Cleveland, Tyne and Wear, Greater Manchester, Mid Glamorgan, and Humberside, in that order) and suburban and rural areas lowest (Surrey, followed by Scottish Islands, Borders, Oxfordshire, Berkshire, and Buckinghamshire). As with most widespread trends, however, the fastest increases are often in the areas which had low values initially. Thus the percentage at least trebled over the decade in areas as diverse as Mid Glamorgan and West Sussex, and the smallest proportionate rise was in Greater London.

Births outside marriage, by age of mother and type of registration

(a)

Age of mother at birth	% all births to age group				
	1971	1976	1981	1986	1992
Under 20	26.1	34.2	46.7	69.0	83.7
20–24	7.7	9.1	14.8	28.2	47.2
25–29	4.7	4.4	6.6	12.1	22.8
30–34	5.7	5.2	6.2	10.1	17.3
35 and over	7.4	8.9	8.7	12.9	19.8
All ages	8.4	9.2	12.8	21.4	31.2

(b)

Type of registration	% all births				
Joint by mother and father	3.8	4.7	7.4	14.2	23.7
Same address	n.a.	n.a.	n.a.	10.0	17.3
Different address	n.a.	n.a.	n.a.	4.2	6.4
Mother only	4.6	4.5	5.4	7.2	7.5

(c)

	% births outside marriage				
Births outside marriage to mothers aged under 20	32.9	36.8	32.6	28.0	18.6

n.a. = not available.

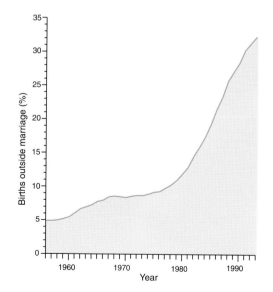

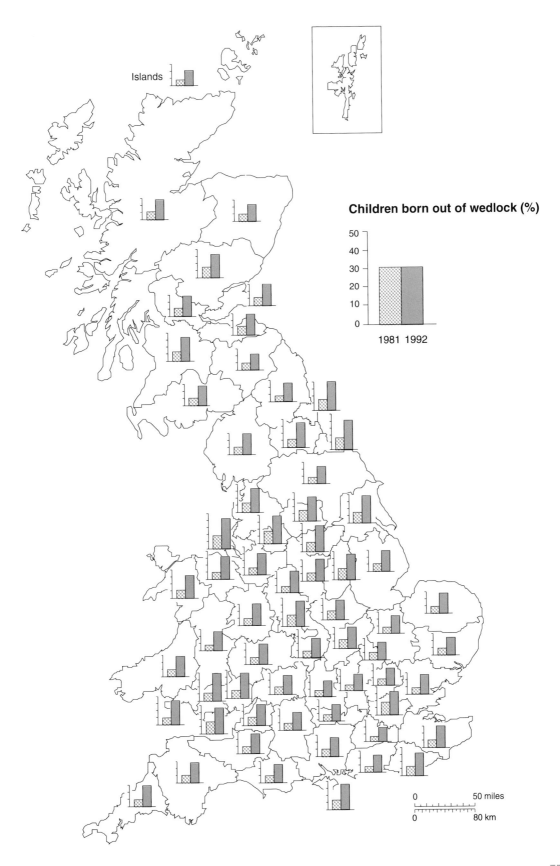

Islands

Children born out of wedlock (%)

1981 1992

0   50 miles
0   80 km

75

Who lives with whom

To judge by the clichés of TV advertising, most households in Britain comprise a mother, a father, and a couple of children—but nowadays reality is much more complicated. With long-established trends for the elderly to live independently of their children and for young adults to move away from home for further education and jobs, and also with increased rates of divorce and separation, a variety of other household types have grown more common. These trends, along with lower fertility than thirty years ago, have led to a marked reduction in average household size.

National trends in household type and size

The graph presents the national picture as of 1981 and 1991. It can be seen that couples with dependent children accounted for only one-quarter of all households in Britain in 1991. Lone parents with dependent children made up another 6%, so that dependent children were present in less than one-third of all households. Fully a quarter of households comprised individuals living alone, the majority of them being aged 60 or over—this latter group accounting for one in six of all households. The main changes since 1981 have been the reduction in the proportion of couples with dependent children and the increase in 16–59-year-olds living alone.

The table shows how these changes have impacted on size of households. Consistently over the past two decades the proportion of households containing only one or two persons has risen, while the proportion which are larger households has fallen. As a result, average household size has fallen steadily, so that by 1991 it was 15% lower than in 1971 and 8% lower than in 1981. This has important implications for housing needs, as many more houses—and preferably smaller houses and flats—are needed, irrespective of any increase in total numbers of people.

Geographical variations

The maps show that there is a clear geography to these household patterns. The main concentration of high-average household size in 1991 was central southern England, where strong economic growth over the previous few years had attracted young families. For instance, Buckinghamshire, Bedfordshire, and Berkshire average at least 2.58 persons per household. Below-average size is generally associated with more remote rural areas which have gained retirement migrants, the extreme case being East Sussex at 2.24.

The main conurbations and some other urban and industrial counties have rather distinctive profiles. In the first place, as map (d) shows, they have more than their fair share of lone-parent households: Merseyside heads the list with 5.8%, followed by Cleveland, Strathclyde, Tyne and Wear, Greater Manchester, and London. They also tend to have above-average proportions of both very small and very large households, as shown in maps (b) and (c) respectively. Various factors lie behind this, including their attractiveness for both young adults and minority ethnic groups.

Household size, Great Britain

Number of persons	Percentage of households of each size						
	1971	1981	1983	1985	1987	1989	1991
1	17	22	23	24	25	25	26
2	31	31	32	33	32	34	34
3	19	17	17	17	17	17	17
4	18	18	18	17	17	16	16
5	8	7	7	6	6	6	6
6 or more	6	4	3	2	2		22
Average household size	2.91	2.70	2.64	2.56	2.55	2.51	2.48

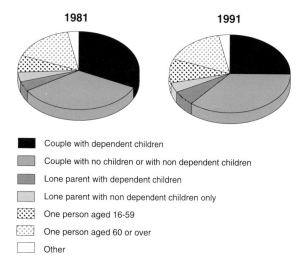

1981   **1991**

- ■ Couple with dependent children
- ▨ Couple with no children or with non dependent children
- ▨ Lone parent with dependent children
- ▨ Lone parent with non dependent children only
- ▨ One person aged 16-59
- ▨ One person aged 60 or over
- □ Other

(a)

Average household size
(persons per household)
1991

n
12 2.54 or over
13 2.50 to 2.54
12 2.47 to 2.50
14 2.44 to 2.47
13 under 2.44

0   50 miles
0   80 km

(b)

One-person households
as proportion of all
households (%) 1991

n
11 28.0 or over
13 26.5 to 28.0
13 25.5 to 26.5
16 24.0 to 25.5
11 under 24.0

0   50 miles
0   80 km

(c)

Households with 6+
persons as proportion of
all households (%) 1991

n
11 2.5 or over
12 2.1 to 2.5
20 1.8 to 2.1
13 1.6 to 1.8
8   under 1.6

0   50 miles
0   80 km

(d)

'Lone parent' households
as a proportion of all
households (%) 1991

n
12 4.2 or over
12 3.4 to 4.2
11 3.0 to 3.4
17 2.7 to 3.0
12 under 2.7

0   50 miles
0   80 km

Limiting long-term illness

In 1991, for the first time, the Census included a question on 'limiting long-term illness'. This is broader than the traditional question on 'permanent sickness' and is designed to discover how many and what type of people are affected by medical problems which seriously restricted the things that they could do. In all, one in eight people in Britain indicated that they were affected in this way, but the detailed results showed a wide range across the country and some clear geographical patterns.

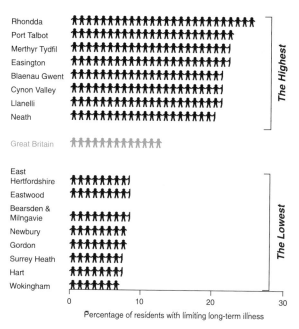

The scale of the range at district level is shown in the graph. Wokingham, in Berkshire, reported the smallest percentage of ill people, followed by Hart in Hampshire and Surrey Heath, all with under 7.5%. At the other extreme, for three districts in south Wales and Easington in County Durham, the level was at least three times higher than this.

The map helps to show that two types of areas have particularly high incidence of illness. One comprises traditional industrial and mining areas, such as in south Wales, north-east England, Clydeside, north-east and south Lancashire, and the Yorkshire-Derbyshire-Nottinghamshire coalfield. The other consists of districts which are popular with retirement migrants, like the south and east coast resorts,

north Wales, and the Lancashire coast. Meanwhile, the lowest proportions are found across a wide zone of inland southern England, as well as northern Scotland.

Variations between district types

These patterns are reflected in the analysis by district types presented in the table. Highest, on average, come the seven Principal metropolitan cities (Birmingham, Glasgow, Leeds, Liverpool, Manchester, Newcastle upon Tyne, and Sheffield). This group is followed by the Resort, port, and retirement category, the Other metropolitan districts, and the Industrial areas. Well below average are the Urban and mixed urban–rural districts and Outer London boroughs, followed by the New Towns and Remoter mainly rural areas.

The table also shows that the age factor does play a part in these patterns. If the proportions of people suffering from limiting long-term illness are examined for the four separate age groups, it can be seen that the Resort, port, and retirement category has much lower rates of illness than its all-ages figure would suggest. Conversely, the age-specific rates for the New Towns are higher than its overall average suggests.

Limiting long-term illness, 1991, by district type and age

District type (ranked by all ages rate)	Percentage of age group ill				
	All ages	0–29	30–pa	pa-74	75+
Principal metropolitan cities	15.6	3.7	15.6	35.7	55.8
Resort, port, and retirement	15.1	3.0	10.8	27.9	51.2
Other metropolitan districts	14.8	3.3	13.9	35.5	56.9
Industrial areas	14.3	3.2	13.2	35.3	56.6
Large non-metropolitan cities	14.1	3.3	12.8	32.6	54.3
Small non-metropolitan cities	13.2	3.2	11.6	30.4	52.7
Inner London	12.7	3.4	12.6	32.3	52.5
Remoter mainly rural	12.4	2.6	9.3	26.8	50.0
Districts with New Towns	12.4	3.0	11.5	32.8	54.6
Outer London	11.1	2.6	9.0	27.6	50.5
Urban and mixed urban–rural	10.3	2.4	7.5	25.8	50.7
Great Britain	13.1	3.0	11.2	30.9	53.1

pa = pensionable age (65 for men, 60 for women).

On the other hand, apart from these two district types with their extremes of elderly and youthful age profiles respectively, the patterns of age-specific illness are broadly similar to the ranking for all ages. This suggests that other factors besides age contribute to the variations observed. This aspect is taken further over the page.

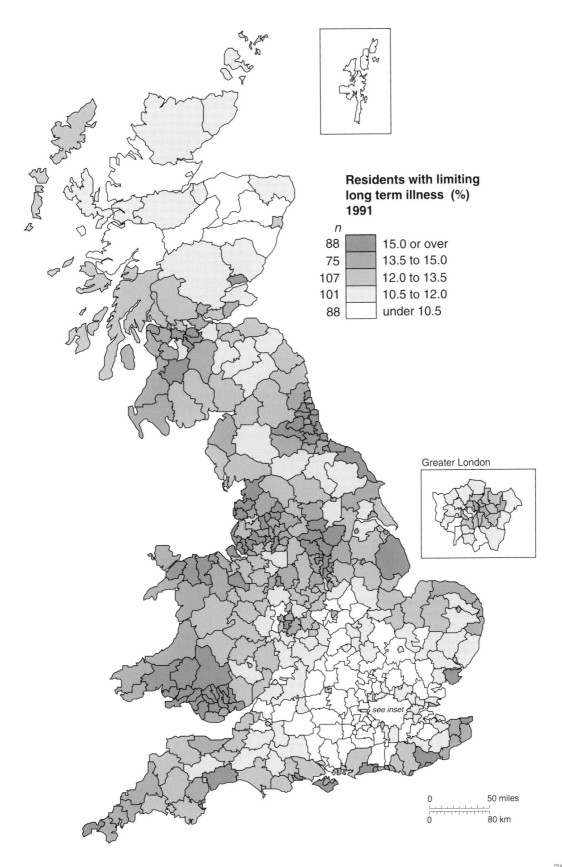

**Residents with limiting
long term illness (%)
1991**

n	
88	15.0 or over
75	13.5 to 15.0
107	12.0 to 13.5
101	10.5 to 12.0
88	under 10.5

Greater London

see inset

0   50 miles

0   80 km

Who the ill are

The geographical incidence of limiting long-term illness shown on the previous two pages is only partly the result of variations between places in the importance of the elderly in their populations. Clear geographical patterns remain after allowing for age—patterns which are pretty consistent across all age groups and which must therefore be related to some potent factors.

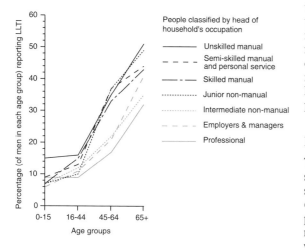

This high degree of consistency is readily demonstrated. Each of the four age-specific maps presents basically the same pattern of well-above-average rates of illness in south Wales, west-central Scotland, and the industrial Midlands and north of England, with the lowest rates in central southern England. As shown in the table, Mid Glamorgan records the highest incidence of illness for all four age groups, with neighbouring West Glamorgan coming second in every case. There is rather greater variation at the other end of the scale, but Surrey features in the top three of all four age groups and in all cases the top three are representatives of either south-east England or remote rural Scotland.

The same is also true at district level. According to the 1991 Census, Rhondda (Mid Glamorgan) looks to be the most unhealthy place in Britain for three of the four age groups, the only exception being for those who manage to reach the age of 75. Merthyr Tydfil (Mid Glamorgan) appears in the list of five worst districts for all four age groups, Port Talbot (West Glamorgan) and Easington (Durham) three

times, Rhymney Valley and Cynon Valley (both Mid Glamorgan) and Blaenau Gwent two out of four times. In the four lists of five most healthy districts, Eastwood and Bearsden and Milngavie (both in Strathclyde) and the Scilly Isles each appear three times, and Elmbridge (Surrey) twice.

Such consistency must clearly be related to aspects of the localities involved, in terms of underlying social and environmental factors and/or the conditions to which people are—or have been—exposed in their work. In particular, a close link has been identified between coal-mining and illness, not so much because of accidents as through the lung disorders brought on by exposure to coal dust. More recently, the rapid rundown of the mining industry has brought joblessness and its own range of health problems.

Differences between occupations

The general relationship with occupation is demonstrated in the graph, using data on 'limiting long-standing illness' regularly provided by the annual *General Household Survey*. A considerably higher proportion of manual workers suffer from such illness than do non-manual, and notably professional, workers. The contrast is particularly glaring in the older working ages, and presents a major challenge to a country that has operated the National Health Service for nearly half a century, aiming for greater equality in life chances.

Limiting long-term illness by age, 1991: extreme areas (% of population)

Age group	Highest	%	Lowest	%
All ages	Mid Glamorgan	20.5	Berkshire	8.9
	West Glamorgan	19.4	Buckinghamshire	9.1
	Durham	17.4	Hertfordshire	9.8
0–29	Mid Glamorgan	4.5	Scottish Islands	2.0
	West Glamorgan	4.1	Surrey	2.2
	Merseyside	3.8	Hertfordshire	2.3
30–pa	Mid Glamorgan	22.2	Buckinghamshire	6.6
	West Glamorgan	19.1	Surrey	6.7
	Gwent	17.1	Berkshire	6.9
pa–74	Mid Glamorgan	47.6	Surrey	22.6
	West Glamorgan	41.9	Borders	23.5
	Gwent	40.4	West Sussex	24.2
75 +	Mid Glamorgan	63.1	Borders	47.0
	West Glamorgan	60.4	Surrey	48.8
	West Yorkshire	59.9	Highland	48.8

pa = pensionable age (65 for men, 60 for women).

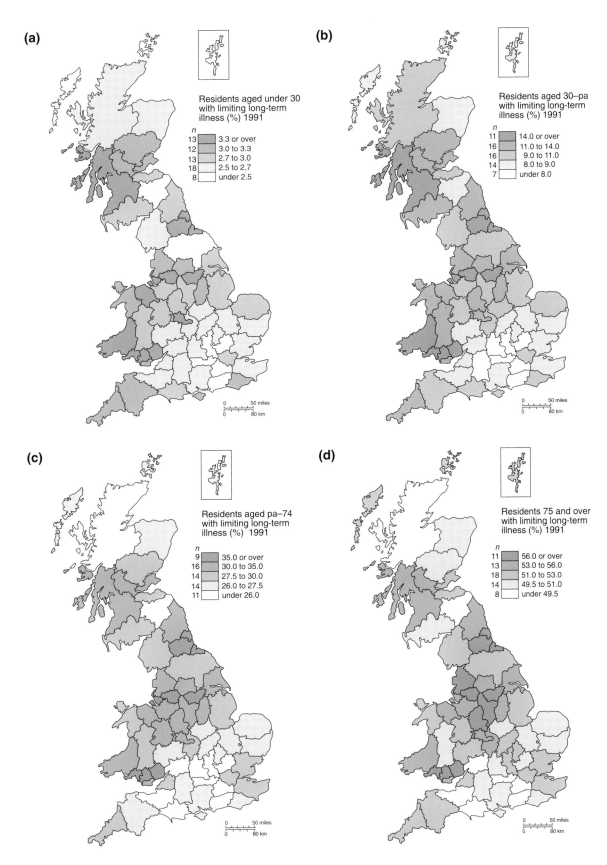

(a)

Residents aged under 30
with limiting long-term
illness (%) 1991

n
13   3.3 or over
12   3.0 to 3.3
13   2.7 to 3.0
18   2.5 to 2.7
8   under 2.5

0   50 miles
0   80 km

(b)

Residents aged 30–pa
with limiting long-term
illness (%) 1991

n
11   14.0 or over
16   11.0 to 14.0
16   9.0 to 11.0
14   8.0 to 9.0
7   under 8.0

0   50 miles
0   80 km

(c)

Residents aged pa–74
with limiting long-term
illness (%) 1991

n
9   35.0 or over
16   30.0 to 35.0
14   27.5 to 30.0
14   26.0 to 27.5
11   under 26.0

0   50 miles
0   80 km

(d)

Residents 75 and over
with limiting long-term
illness (%) 1991

n
11   56.0 or over
13   53.0 to 56.0
18   51.0 to 53.0
14   49.5 to 51.0
8   under 49.5

0   50 miles
0   80 km

Death chances

There are many ways in which good and poor health can be measured and mapped. The previous two topics on *Limiting long-term illness* and *Who the ill are* have discussed what the census can tell us about the variation in health across areas by looking at the numbers of people who claim to be ill. There are, however, significant problems in assessing its extent: one person's mild headache can be another's severe migraine.

Measuring mortality

Problems of measuring ill health accurately have led many authorities, including the World Health Organization, to suggest that there is still great merit in looking at variations in mortality rather than morbidity—looking at the extent to which people die rather than at what they complain about when they are alive. This may sound quite severe, given that very few people die young in Britain nowadays. Nevertheless, mortality rates have been shown to reflect aspects of a great many other more complex measures of health, and mortality rates are also quite simple to calculate.

If simple mortality rates were calculated for an area, then they would merely reflect the age structure of that area. We would expect places with more elderly people to see a greater proportion of their population dying each year than places containing more young people. To overcome this problem and to be able to investigate the differences between people's chances of dying in different places, irrespective of their age, the standardized mortality ratio (SMR) is commonly calculated. This is the ratio of actual deaths occurring in a particular place to the number of deaths that would be expected if each age-sex group in that place had experienced the national average mortality rates for that age-sex group. If the actual deaths are higher than expected, then the SMR is above 100, whereas a ratio of under 100 signifies lower death chances, or conversely better life chances, than average (see the note in Appendix 1).

Geography of death chances

The map shows these ratios for local authority districts. Note how the light blue and unshaded districts are almost always to be found in the rural south of England. This is where people are most likely to live to an old age. The areas where people are particularly likely to die prematurely are almost all to be found in the cities of the north of England and Scotland. The one exception to this pattern is the high ratio for Corby (Northamptonshire), but this may well be due to the high in-migration rate of people who lived most of their lives in Scotland (see *Three nations*). Differential rates of migration can affect these mortality ratios, but the ratios do, in turn, reflect the wide variety of the influences which place of residence appears to have on people's chances of survival.

The pattern of mortality ratios shown opposite reflects many of the other distributions displayed elsewhere in this volume, such as the availability of work, the proportion of children in low-income households and the scale of share ownership. This provides further evidence of the continued importance of differences in people's life chances in Britain today. Where you are born and what you do has a very strong effect on how long you are likely to live.

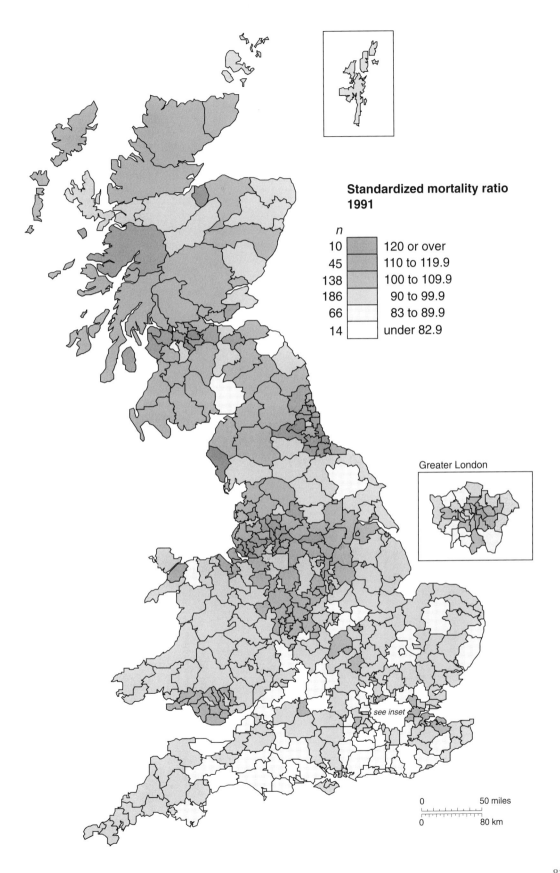

Standardized mortality ratio
1991

n		
10		120 or over
45		110 to 119.9
138		100 to 109.9
186		90 to 99.9
66		83 to 89.9
14		under 82.9

Greater London

see inset

0   50 miles

0   80 km

Offenders and crimes

Over the past decade, crime has often been in the news. Much has been written about young offenders, and about certain cities having 'no-go' areas, where levels of crime are so great that most people are afraid to enter them. Some important geographical questions are raised here, such as: 'Are cities more susceptible to crime than rural areas?', 'Do different cities fall prey to different types of crime?', and 'Who are the offenders?'

Where the crimes occur

When considering crime statistics, one way of breaking them down is in terms of victims and offenders (although some offenders may themselves be victims). In maps (a) to (d), information about the number of crimes in 1991 is given per head of population for police-force areas in England and Wales. In map (a) the total number of crimes is shown. From this it may be seen that most of the metropolitan areas have a relatively high rate of reported crime per head, with non-metropolitan areas in the south of England having much lower rates. Note also the extremely low presence of reported crime in rural Wales.

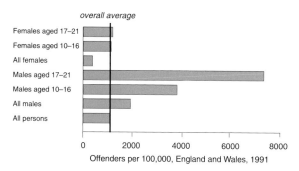

Offenders per 100,000, England and Wales, 1991

Map (b) for violence against the person shows a somewhat different story, with Nottinghamshire and the London Metropolitan area having very high rates. Note, however, that in absolute terms there are relatively few reported crimes of this type.

Contrast this with household burglaries, which are one of the commonest forms of crime. In map (c) it may be seen that the population living in the region served by the Northumbria Police Force experience the highest rates of burglary. In general, the other areas suffering from the highest rates of burglary are also in northern England.

Map (d) shows the incidence of criminal damage per head of population. Typically, reported cases of vandalism are classed as criminal damage. From map (d), it can be seen that this is mostly an urban phenomenon, with rural areas having very low rates, although there are some exceptions to this.

Who the offenders are

The geography of crime should be considered in terms of offenders as well as offences. Who are the offenders? The graph shows offence rates for different subgroups of the population. The category with the most prevalent rate, by a long way, is that for males aged 17–21, with males aged 10–16 next. Policemen may not be getting younger every day, but burglars probably are!

Looking at a breakdown of these offender rates by police-force area for the most prevalent group, we see from the table that Merseyside has the highest rate of male offenders in the 17–21 age group, and Bedfordshire the least.

Finally, it should be noted that all of these figures are based on reported crime rates; in many instances crimes are not reported and will not therefore appear on official statistics such as these.

Police-force areas with highest and lowest rates of 17–21 year-old offenders

Highest	per 100,000	Lowest	per 100,000
Merseyside	11,151	Bedfordshire	5,193
Gwent	9,703	Thames Valley	5,301
Nottinghamshire	9,602	Surrey	5,511
Lancashire	9,587	Avon and Somerset	5,695
Cleveland	9,571	North Yorkshire	5,788

(a)

Total crimes

16
12
8
6
4

Number of crimes
(per million people)

0   50 miles
0   80 km

(b)

Violence against person

8
5
4
3
2

Number of crimes
(per million people)

0   50 miles
0   80 km

(c)

Burglaries

4
3
2
1.5
1

Number of crimes
(per million people)

0   50 miles
0   80 km

(d)

Criminal damage

20
15
10
7.5
5

Number of crimes
(per million people)

0   50 miles
0   80 km

Housing

Overcrowding and underoccupancy

Matching housing supply to the population of an area—most often measured by the number of persons per room in a dwelling—has been a major issue since the nineteenth century, but the nature of that interest has changed over time. Until quite recently, most attention was given to the problem of overcrowding, originally defined as a situation in which there were more than 1.5 persons per room. Partly because average dwelling sizes have increased and mainly because households have become smaller (see *Who lives with whom*), this issue has become less important. Even with the overcrowding standard now lowered to 'more than 1 person per room', only 2.2% of Britain's households are affected—though there are a few places with significantly higher levels than this. A much more widespread situation is that of 'underoccupancy', which for present purposes will be defined as there being at least twice as many rooms as there are residents.

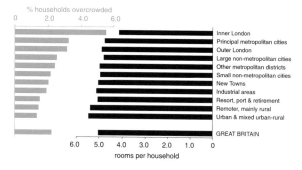

Overcrowding and dwelling size

Overcrowding is essentially an urban phenomenon. At district level, two parts of Britain stand out: London and Clydeside, as shown in the table. The level of overcrowding in Tower Hamlets is five times the national proportion, with those for Newham, Hackney, Monklands, and Brent being over three times the British average. In terms of the eleven district types (see the diagram), Inner London clearly comes out with the highest level, followed by the Principal metropolitan cities. Outer London, the Large non-metropolitan cities and the Other metropolitan districts also have above-average levels, while it is the three least urban categories that have the lowest overcrowding levels.

To some extent, these patterns of overcrowding can be related to the nature of the housing stock in an area, measured in terms purely of their number of rooms. It can be seen from the diagram that the aver-

age number of rooms across all households in Inner London in 1991 was significantly lower than for other district types, at only 4.1, whereas for the Remoter mainly rural and Urban and mixed urban–rural categories it was around 5.4. The figure for Glasgow was 3.8, and for Strathclyde region as a whole was 4.3. It was below average for several of the English metropolitan counties and most Scottish regions, as shown in map (a) opposite. The highest average dwelling sizes were concentrated in the more rural counties of southern Britain, with Wales averaging 5.4 rooms and East Anglia and the South West with around 5.3. These areas have seen a great deal of new building in the past four decades and have traditionally not faced the high cost pressures on space characteristic of London and the Home Counties.

Underoccupancy

The other three maps opposite focus on underoccupancy and demonstrate a clear correlation with the patterns of dwelling size. The counties with the highest levels of underoccupancy on the three measures are all found in Wales: 70% of households in Powys live at a density of under 0.5 persons per room, 58% of Mid Glamorgan's one-person households live in dwellings with five or more rooms, and one-person households living in dwellings of at least five rooms comprise over 15% of all Gwynedd's households. Strathclyde lies at the other extreme, with figures of 54%, 17%, and 5% for these three measures respectively. These patterns reflect a combination of factors including the size of the housing, the proportion of small households (especially elderly couples and surviving spouses), and the extent to which market forces and other factors stimulate the matching process.

Districts with the highest levels of overcrowding, and average dwelling size, 1991

District	% Households overcrowded	Average rooms per household
Tower Hamlets (Inner London)	11.1	3.93
Newham (Inner London)	7.6	4.47
Hackney (Inner London)	7.5	4.06
Monklands (Strathclyde)	7.1	4.29
Brent (Outer London)	6.7	4.54
Glasgow (Strathclyde)	6.1	3.83
Motherwell (Strathclyde)	6.0	4.23
City of Westminster (Inner London)	5.7	3.73
Inverclyde (Strathclyde)	5.6	4.25
Slough (Berkshire)	5.5	4.61

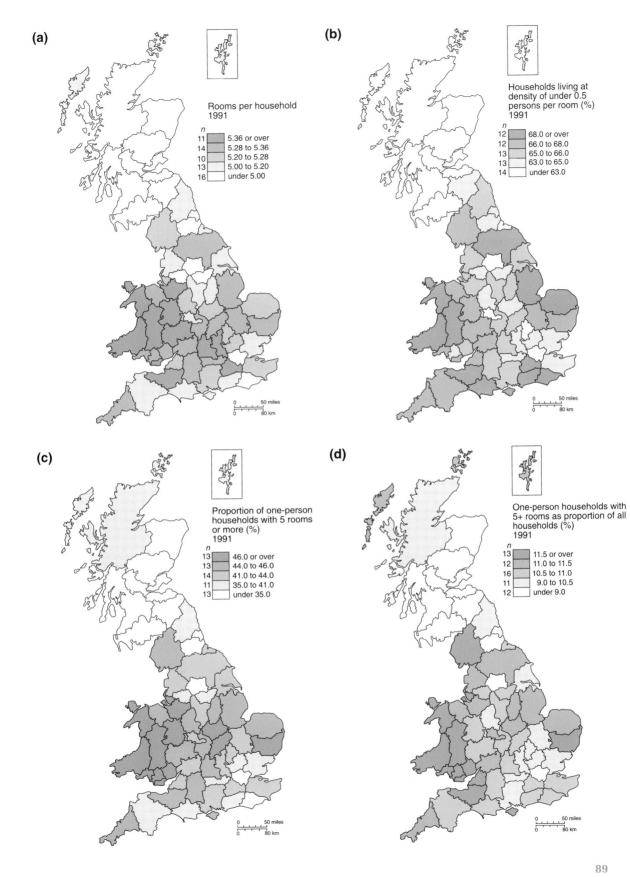

(a)

Rooms per household
1991

n	
11	5.36 or over
14	5.28 to 5.36
10	5.20 to 5.28
13	5.00 to 5.20
16	under 5.00

0   50 miles
0   80 km

(b)

Households living at
density of under 0.5
persons per room (%)
1991

n	
12	68.0 or over
12	66.0 to 68.0
13	65.0 to 66.0
13	63.0 to 65.0
14	under 63.0

0   50 miles
0   80 km

(c)

Proportion of one-person
households with 5 rooms
or more (%)
1991

n	
13	46.0 or over
13	44.0 to 46.0
14	41.0 to 44.0
11	35.0 to 41.0
13	under 35.0

0   50 miles
0   80 km

(d)

One-person households with
5+ rooms as proportion of all
households (%)
1991

n	
13	11.5 or over
12	11.0 to 11.5
16	10.5 to 11.0
11	9.0 to 10.5
12	under 9.0

0   50 miles
0   80 km

Amenities and gadgets

The criteria which have traditionally been the main measure of household amenities are no longer a significant problem in numerical terms. Even as recently as 1971 one in six households did not have exclusive use of the three basic amenities of hot-water supply, fixed bath/shower, and inside WC, but by 1991 the proportion was down to only 1.2%. Because of this major improvement, attention has now turned to other amenities, with a question on the availability of central heating being introduced in the 1991 Census and with data on durable household goods being collected by the General Household Survey.

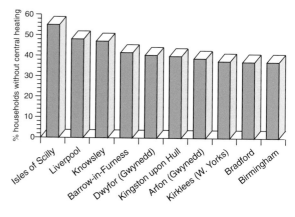

Access to basic amenities

Map (a) opposite suggests that there is remarkably little variation across the country in the proportion of households that do not have access to, or have to share with another household, at least one of the three basic amenities. Dyfed represents the most extreme case with 2.5% of households not having exclusive use of all these amenities, followed by London (2.4%), the Scottish Islands (2.3%) and Mid Glamorgan and Powys (both 2.2%). In regional terms, Wales was the most poorly served in 1991, with a level of 1.7%, and Scotland the best served, with only 0.6% of households without exclusive access.

This situation represents a huge improvement on the situation twenty years earlier for most of the areas that were particularly disadvantaged at that time. As can be inferred from map (b), in 1971 at least one in five households did not have exclusive access in central and south Wales, London, parts of midland and northern England, and the Scottish Islands. Over the two decades, the biggest fall in the percentage of households in this category occurred for Mid Glamorgan (32% in 1971). Nevertheless, at district level there remain distinct pockets with relatively high proportions of households without exclusive use, notably in Inner London (e.g. Newham 4.7%, Kensington and Chelsea 4.4%) and south Wales (e.g. Rhondda 4.4%).

Central heating and other features

Nowadays, four out of every five households have some form of central heating, but this too varies considerably between districts, as shown in the graph. At county level Merseyside was the worst-off (37% of households), followed by Gwynedd (34%) and West Yorkshire (33%). At the other extreme, north-east England and the outer South East stand out as the best equipped, as shown in map (c).

Only a very small proportion of dwellings consist of non-permanent structures, a category that includes trailer homes and caravans that perform the function of usual residences. As map (d) shows, these are very rare in the major conurbations and most common in more rural counties, and particularly in their most rural districts where they can form a significant proportion of all occupied household spaces; for instance, 4.3% in Skye and Lochalsh (Highlands), 3.1% in Restormel (Cornwall), and 3.1% in Radnor (Powys).

The table provides a regional summary for central heating and a range of household goods. It confirms the position of the North as the best served region in terms of central heating, and also for washing machines, but the North comes out bottom on dish washers and telephones. Scotland and Yorkshire and Humberside have the fewest households with deep freezers and home computers, and Wales is bottom for compact-disc players. The South East and South West generally come out top for these latter durable goods.

Percentage of households with selected facilities, by region, 1991–1992

Region	Central heating	Washing machine	Dish-washer	Telephone	Deep-freezer	Home computer	Compact-disc player
North	87	91	8	82	81	22	26
Yorks. and Humb.	75	88	10	86	79	19	25
East Midlands	86	89	14	87	85	22	30
East Anglia	85	87	14	90	84	23	31
South East	85	85	20	92	87	24	35
South West	80	86	20	92	87	22	30
West Midlands	77	87	11	87	84	20	28
North West	76	87	12	86	83	22	28
Wales	82	88	12	84	85	22	24
Scotland	78	90	12	84	79	19	26
Great Britain	81	87	15	88	84	22	30

(a)

Households without exclusive use of amenities (%) 1991

n	
11	1.5 or over
11	1.2 to 1.5
15	1.0 to 1.2
14	0.8 to 1.0
13	under 0.8

0   50 miles
0   80 km

(b)

Reduction in proportion of households without exclusive use of amenities (% point) 1971–91

n	
13	19.0 or over
14	16.0 to 19.0
12	13.5 to 16.0
13	11.0 to 13.5
12	under 11.0

0   50 miles
0   80 km

(c)

Households without central heating (%) 1991

n	
12	24.0 or over
13	19.0 to 24.0
17	15.0 to 19.0
10	12.0 to 15.0
12	under 12.0

0   50 miles
0   80 km

(d)

Households in non-permanent accommodation (%) 1991

n	
14	0.85 or over
11	0.65 to 0.85
12	0.45 to 0.65
9	0.25 to 0.45
18	under 0.25

0   50 miles
0   80 km

Vacant and vacation housing

At any one time there is a proportion of the housing stock that is not anyone's usual residence. The main situations in which this occurs fall into two categories, as shown in the diagram. The larger is vacant housing, detected by Census enumerators largely through the absence of furniture and through information from neighbours. The other main category comprises accommodation which is occupied (though not necessarily on Census night) but is not the usual residence of a household. The majority of this category can be termed vacation housing.

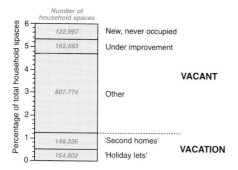

Vacant housing

Vacant housing includes new dwellings which have not yet been occupied for the first time and older housing which is being rehabilitated, but the majority comprises housing which is empty because of lack of immediate local demand. There is always the need for some available housing to allow turnover to occur smoothly, but the amount can vary over space and time. Vacant housing is usually more common in areas of more sporadic demand (as in more rural areas) and at times when it is difficult to sell housing for the price expected (as in the property-market recession at the time of the 1991 Census).

The geography of vacant housing is shown in maps (a) and (b). The areas with the largest proportion of their housing stock vacant because of undergoing improvement are found in more peripheral rural regions and certain urban and metropolitan localities. Mid Glamorgan, Gwynedd, Borders, and the Scottish Islands come out highest with around 1.1% of their housing stock in this category, but at district

level the proportion is highest in inner city locations, led by Salford (2.1%), Kensington and Chelsea (2.0%) and City of Westminster (1.9%).

Vacant housing that is not under improvement has a similar distribution, except for a larger occurrence in south-west and eastern England. It is most common in the Scottish Islands (6.8%), followed by Gwynedd, London, and East Sussex (around 5.5%), and is lowest in 'suburban' contexts near to but outside major conurbations, such as Hertfordshire (2.8%), Surrey, and Central Region (Scotland).

New but never-yet occupied housing is one element of this and has a distinctive distribution that can be related to the level of building activity and the speed of selling. As the table shows, this type of vacant housing is principally a phenomenon of rural areas that were experiencing strong in-migration until the housing-market collapse at the end of the 1980s, but the leading district is Tower Hamlets where the 1980s Docklands property boom had turned to bust by 1991.

Vacation housing

Vacation housing falls into two main categories, as shown in the diagram. Second homes, which are owned by individual households and serve as their secondary residences, can include weekday *pieds-à-terre* in cities, but form a much more significant share of the housing stock in traditional rural and seaside holiday areas, as shown in map (c). Holiday accommodation, shown in map (d), largely comprises dwellings that are rented out by private companies, farmers, and so on, and are even more highly concentrated in these holiday areas. Turn the page to obtain more details of the most popular vacation housing areas—and also of where holiday-makers choose not to go!

Percentage of household spaces that are new and not yet occupied

Top counties	%	Top districts	%
Lincolnshire	1.17	Tower Hamlets	1.83
Cornwall	1.01	Mid Suffolk	1.69
Powys	0.98	South Pembrokeshire	1.62
Isle of Wight	0.95	East Lindsey	1.55
Dorset	0.90	South Holland	1.52

(a)

Vacant: not under
improvement (%)
1991

n	
12	4.6 or over
15	4.1 to 4.6
13	3.7 to 4.1
14	3.4 to 3.7
10	under 3.4

0   50 miles
0   80 km

(b)

Vacant: under
improvement (%)
1991

n	
11	0.90 or over
10	0.75 to 0.90
19	0.60 to 0.75
16	0.50 to 0.60
8	under 0.50

0   50 miles
0   80 km

(c)

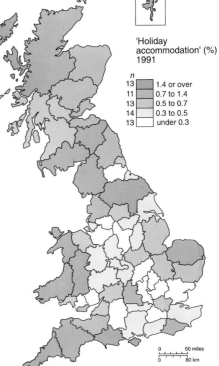

'Second homes' (%)
1991

n	
11	1.6 or over
13	0.8 to 1.6
16	0.4 to 0.8
16	0.2 to 0.4
8	under 0.2

0   50 miles
0   80 km

(d)

'Holiday
accommodation' (%)
1991

n	
13	1.4 or over
11	0.7 to 1.4
13	0.5 to 0.7
14	0.3 to 0.5
13	under 0.3

0   50 miles
0   80 km

Second homes and holiday lets

The district-level map picks out much more clearly than the maps on the previous page the parts of Britain that are so popular with holiday-makers that many people are prepared to buy or rent accommodation there when it is not their main place of residence.

Coastal and rural areas

By and large, these holiday areas are coastal, but there are also some inland areas which are noted for the attractiveness of their rural scenery and where status as National Parks or Areas of Outstanding Natural Beauty allows the strict enforcement of controls on new building. Clearly identifiable are the Cotswolds, the Gower peninsula, the Peak District, the North York Moors, the Yorkshire Dales, the Lake District, and the Northumberland National Park, as well as the upland areas of Wales, the Scottish Borders, and the Highlands. Also favoured are cities renowned for their architectural splendours such as Bath, Oxford, Cambridge, and York.

Central London and other cities

The main departure from this pattern is provided by central London, which contains a clear concentration of housing which is not used by anyone as their main residence. The 'Square Mile' of the City of London provides the most extreme case, with 12.6% of its household spaces considered to be second homes and 4.6% as housing which was classified by the Census enumerator either as 'holiday accommodation' or containing people who were not owner-occupiers and for whom this was not their main residence. This accommodation can include flats owned by companies for temporary use by staff and visitors, as well as housing used during the working week by people who have their main residence elsewhere in the country, or presumably elsewhere in the world (but it is meant to exclude housing occupied solely by students, for which there is a separate category in the Census).

Kensington and Chelsea and the City of Westminster also feature in the top quintile on the map, and it is also noticeable that the levels in most large cities are higher than in their surrounding areas. These include not only the national centres of government (Edinburgh and Cardiff), but also the prin-

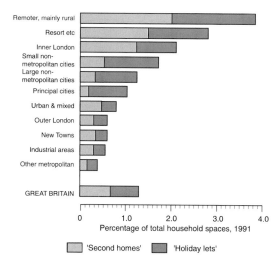

Percentage of total household spaces, 1991

'Second homes' 'Holiday lets'

cipal regional financial centres like Birmingham, Manchester, Leeds, and Glasgow.

The graph and table reinforce this picture. Not surprisingly, the district types with the greatest concentration of this form of housing are the Remoter mainly rural and Resort, port, and retirement categories. In the Scilly Isles, almost a third of the housing falls into one of these categories, and the proportion is at least one in ten in several Scottish and Welsh districts. Inner London is also high in the ranking of district types.

At the other extreme are the Other metropolitan districts, Industrial districts, and New Towns, with only around 0.5% of their housing being used in this way. Scunthorpe and Ashfield make it into the bottom six districts on this criterion, along with several parts of Clydeside and Merseyside.

Districts with the largest and smallest percentages of housing in the form of second homes and holiday lets, 1991

Largest	%	Smallest	%
Scilly Isles	31.6	Knowsley	0.13
Badenoch and Strathspey	22.6	Motherwell	0.15
Dwyfor	18.9	Clydebank	0.15
City of London	17.2	St Helens	0.16
Meirionnydd	16.3	Ashfield	0.17
Skye and Lochalsh	15.9	Scunthorpe	0.17
Sutherland	12.8	Walsall	0.17
Lochaber	11.3	Rotherham	0.17
Argyll	11.1	Monklands	0.18
North Norfolk	10.6	Corby	0.18

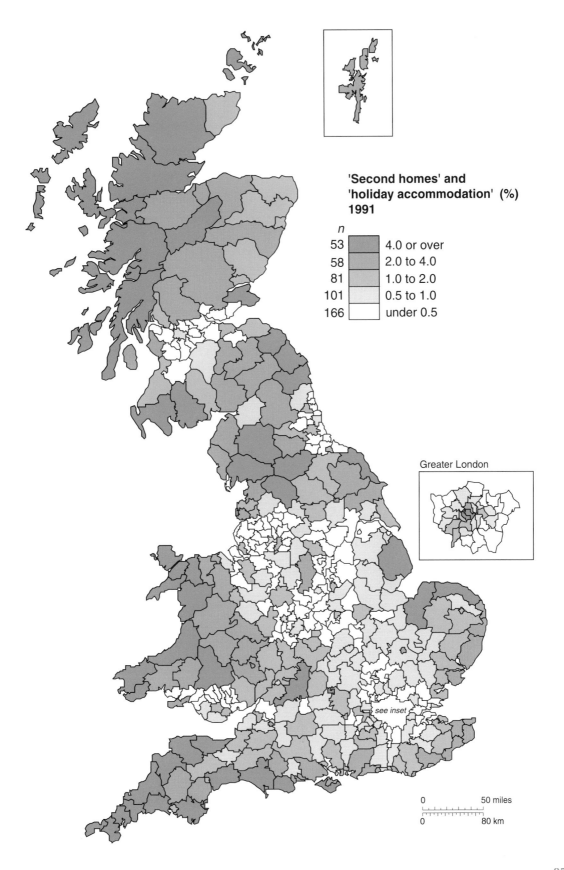

'Second homes' and
'holiday accommodation' (%)
1991

n		
53		4.0 or over
58		2.0 to 4.0
81		1.0 to 2.0
101		0.5 to 1.0
166		under 0.5

Greater London

see inset

0   50 miles

0   80 km

Semi-detached Britain?

Britain is renowned for the popularity of semi-detached housing, but this dwelling type is perhaps not as common as might be thought and is associated with some periods of construction more than others and, partly because of this, with some localities more than others.

Dwelling type by date of construction

The table reveals that semi-detached houses comprised just over a quarter of England's dwellings in 1991, and also shows the estimated composition of the total stock according to the period of construction. The interwar years clearly formed the heyday of the 'suburban semi', with almost half of all dwellings built then being of this type. The semi continued to be the dominant building type during the first two decades of the post-war period, but by the 1980s it was accounting for barely one in eight of dwellings completed.

Dwelling type of the 1991 housing stock, by period of construction, England only, %

Dwelling type	Pre-1919	1919–44	1945–64	1965–80	Post-1980	All periods
Bungalow	1.1	5.5	14.2	13.8	11.9	8.8
Detached house	10.8	11.7	8.9	20.2	33.3	14.7
Semi-detached house	12.9	47.6	39.0	18.4	13.8	26.7
Medium/large terraced	27.5	11.4	8.9	12.1	5.3	14.7
Small terraced	20.9	14.9	8.8	8.5	11.7	13.4
Purpose-built flat	4.1	7.4	19.3	30.1	20.5	14.7
Converted flat	22.7	1.5	0.9	0.7	3.6	6.9
Total dwellings (000s)	5,196	3,891	4,231	4,694	1,713	19,725

Note: 'Converted flat' refers to flats developed in buildings converted from residential or other uses.

Amongst the other types of housing, the terrace accounts for almost half the dwellings in buildings surviving from before 1919, but makes up only one in six of the housing built in the 1980s. Nearly a quarter of the pre-1919 stock comprises flats in converted buildings dating from that time. Purpose-built flats are essentially a post-war phenomenon, associated particularly with the 'high-rise' era but continuing to contribute one in five of new housing units, most of them geared to single people, young couples, the separated and divorced, and the elderly. But the most impressive feature of the post-war period has been the rise of the detached dwelling.

Geographical patterns

The geography of dwelling types across Britain reflects both the local history of urban growth and redevelopment and the environment of areas in terms of the pressure on land and the wealth of residents. Detached housing is most common in more rural areas, as shown by map (a) and the graph. It accounts for 63% of dwellings in the Scottish Islands and 47% in Powys, but only 1% in Inner London and 6% in Tyne and Wear. At the other extreme, purpose-built flats, shown in map (d), are particularly a feature of the major cities and the Scottish housing scene, led by Inner London (48%) and Strathclyde (46%).

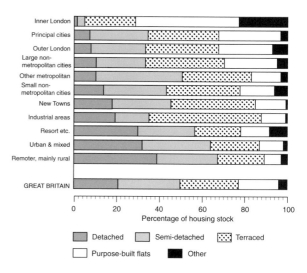

The largest concentrations of both semi-detached and terraced housing are to be found in localities with industrial and mining traditions. The leading counties on map (b) are South Yorkshire and Staffordshire, both with over 40% in semis, while the top district is Scunthorpe with 56%. Almost half (48%) of Mid Glamorgan's housing is in the form of terraces (map (c)), followed by County Durham and Gwent, and the figure for Rhondda district is as high as 78%. As the graph shows, however, terraced housing is not just a pre-1919 phenomenon: amongst the district types, it is in the New Towns that terraced housing features most prominently, with the leading district there being Stevenage at 60%.

(a)

Detached (%)
1991

n	
9	37.0 or over
15	29.0 to 37.0
17	21.0 to 29.0
13	13.0 to 21.0
10	under 13.0

0   50 miles
0   80 km

(b)

Semi-detached (%)
1991

n	
9	36.0 or over
16	32.0 to 36.0
15	28.0 to 32.0
11	24.0 to 28.0
13	under 24.0

0   50 miles
0   80 km

(c)

Terraced (%)
1991

n	
11	34.0 or over
15	29.0 to 34.0
16	25.0 to 29.0
14	21.0 to 25.0
8	under 21.0

0   50 miles
0   80 km

(d)

Purpose-built flats (%)
1991

n	
12	16.0 or over
13	12.0 to 16.0
10	10.0 to 12.0
16	8.0 to 10.0
13	under 8.0

0   50 miles
0   80 km

97

Housing choice

One of the most commonplace claims made about an area, when it is being promoted as an attractive location for mobile industry and people, is that it has a 'wide variety' of housing available. This map shows the results of one way of measuring this variety, and the diagram illustrates the differences which lie behind the very different results obtained for those places which score highest and lowest on this measure of housing choice.

Clearly, there are several different types of housing choice which can be highlighted in order to compare the diversity of housing which is available in each area. Among the types of choice which are *not* considered here are the sizes and ages of housing—both factors which could be included in a more complex study. Instead, the emphasis here is placed on housing tenure (i.e. whether it is rented, and if so from whom), and type of building (e.g. whether a terrace house). The headings of the diagram show the eight categories which have been derived from these two factors so that each one includes a substantial share of Britain's housing.

The eight categories form the basis for a classification of the housing in each area, and by using this data a 'diversity' index was computed (see notes). The value for Britain as a whole was 81.3%—reflecting the findings of the previous page that the label *Semi-detached Britain* is a strong over-simplification of a more diverse pattern in reality. Even so, the fact that the national value is quite a long way away from a diversity 'score' of 100% indicates that housing is by no means equally divided across the eight categories.

It would be possible for diversity at the *national* level to be the combined effect of numerous contrasting *local* areas, in each of which housing was concentrated in just one or two categories. In fact, the map shows that across Britain there is a range of local diversity values: the number of places where the housing stock is more diverse than that of the country as a whole roughly equals the number where there is less housing choice. The map shows quite an unusual pattern, with similarly high values to be found not only in the traditionally poorer areas of Scotland and the major northern cities but also in some affluent areas of southern England and Outer London (in the inset).

The explanation for the map's pattern is hinted at by the diagram, and especially the information shown in the lower part. It can be seen that the places

with low housing choice are most notable for having little housing in the 'social rented' sector (i.e. owned by local authorities, housing associations, New Towns, or Scottish Homes). Given the 1990s 'crash' in house prices across much of Britain, areas which can offer a wide range of alternatives to owner occupation may well be at an advantage when trying to attract mobile young people in particular.

PLACES WITH THE MOST HOUSING CHOICE	Owner occupied				Private rented	Public rented		
	detached	semi-detached	terrace	flat		(semi-)detached	terrace	flat
Berwick	▲	+	+	+	▲	+	+	+
Kirkcaldy	+	+	▲	+	=	=	▲	▲
Dunfermline	▲	▲	▲	+	=	=	▲	▲
Ayr	▲	+	+	=	=	+	▲	+
Aberdeen	▲	+	=	+	+	=	+	▲
Kilmarnock	+	▲	+	+	=	+	▲	▲
Dumbarton	▲	+	+	▲	=	=	+	▲
Edinburgh	+	+	+	▲	=	=	+	▲
Irvine	+	+	+	+	=	+	▲	+
Stirling	●	+	+	+	=	+	+	+
Dumfries	▲	▲	+	=	+	=	+	+
Alloa	+	▲	+	=	=	+	▲	▲
South Shields	=	▲	▲	=	=	▲	▲	+
Newcastle upon Tyne	▲	▲	▲	=	=	+	+	+
Falkirk	+	▲	+	+	=	+	▲	▲
Harlow	▲	▲	▲	=	=	=	+	+

PLACES WITH THE LEAST HOUSING CHOICE								
King's Lynn	◆	▲	+	=	+	+	=	=
St Austell	◆	▲	+	=	+	=	=	=
Brecon	◆	▲	+	=	+	=	=	=
Halifax	=	▲	◆	=	=	=	=	+
Rhyl	◆	▲	+	=	+	=	=	=
Medway towns	+	●	◆	=	=	=	=	=
Merthyr Tydfil	=	=	◆	=	=	+	+	=
Ebbw Vale	=	+	◆	=	=	+	▲	=
Bournemouth	▲	+	+	+	+	=	=	=
Flint	●	●	+	=	=	+	=	=
Aberystwyth	◆	+	+	=	+	=	=	=
Boston	◆	▲	=	=	+	=	=	=
Burnley	+	▲	◆	=	=	=	=	=
Rhondda	+	▲	◆	=	=	=	=	=
Accrington	=	▲	◆	=	=	=	=	=
Colne	+	▲	■	=	=	=	=	=

Percentage of place's housing stock

■ 50% or over	◆ 33 up to 50%	● 25 up to 33%
▲ 15 up to 25%	+ 8.3 up to 15%	= below 8.3 %

Some of the values in the diagram are quite remarkable—the extreme case being that over half of *all* housing in and around Colne (Lancashire) is both terraced and owner-occupied. The other types of place with low housing choice include rural or seaside areas with unusually large numbers of detached houses. At the top of the diagram are the places with the most diverse housing stock: it is a mix of public and private which gives the highest levels of housing choice, and these are to be found mostly in northern Britain.

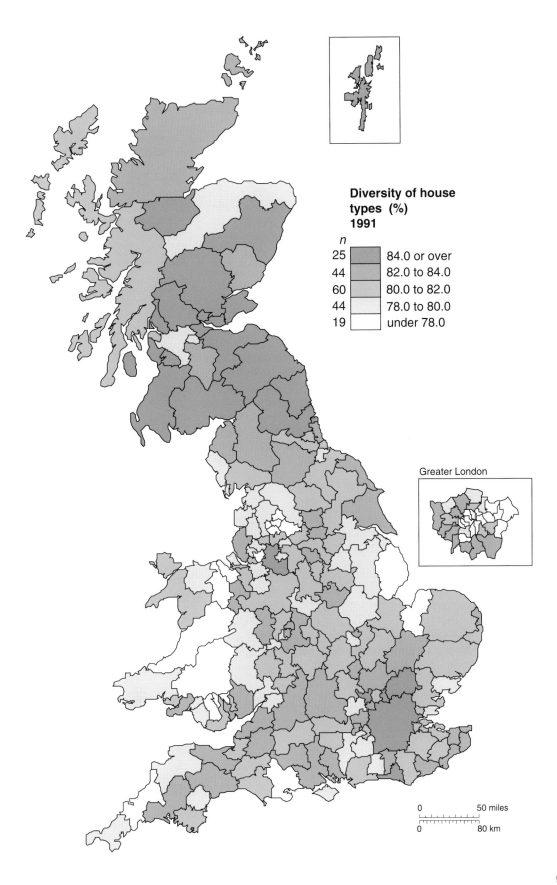

Diversity of house
types (%)
1991

n		
25		84.0 or over
44		82.0 to 84.0
60		80.0 to 82.0
44		78.0 to 80.0
19		under 78.0

Greater London

0   50 miles

0   80 km

Housing tenure

The term 'housing tenure' refers to whether households own or rent the accommodation that they occupy and, if renting, who the provider is. The overall picture of housing tenure in 1991 is shown in the table. Two out of every three households were owner-occupiers. Of these, just over a third owned their homes outright, while nearly two-thirds were 'buying' their homes in the sense that they were borrowing money in order to obtain the dwelling. The remaining third of Britain's households were renting their homes at this time, mainly in the form of 'social housing' rented from local authorities, New Town corporations, Scottish Homes, and housing associations. Private landlords accounted for 7% of households in 1991, with a further 2% being occupied by virtue of people's job or business.

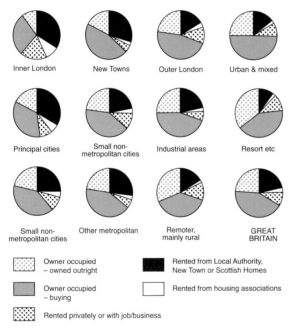

Inner London   New Towns   Outer London   Urban & mixed

Principal cities   Small non-metropolitan cities   Industrial areas   Resort etc

Small non-metropolitan cities   Other metropolitan   Remoter, mainly rural   GREAT BRITAIN

- Owner occupied – owned outright
- Owner occupied – buying
- Rented privately or with job/business
- Rented from Local Authority, New Town or Scottish Homes
- Rented from housing associations

This picture represents a major change from the beginning of the century, when over 90% of households rented from private landlords, but it is also significantly different from the situation just ten years earlier. As the table shows, the proportion of owner-occupiers rose by some 10 percentage points between 1981 and 1991. This partly resulted from the continued contraction of the private-rented sector and the generally strong level of new housebuilding for sale, but primarily it reflects the Conservative Government's policy of publicly subsidizing council tenants to buy their dwellings under the 'Right to Buy' initiative.

Map (b) shows how widespread was the reduction in the size of public-sector stock over the decade. Only a few areas saw it contract by less than 20%, several of these being metropolitan counties with a relatively high proportion of flats which proved less attractive for tenants to buy.

The proportion of households still living in the public-rented sector in 1991 can be seen from the graph and map (a) to be highest in the main metropolitan areas and in northern Britain. It was highest for Strathclyde region (45%), which also accounted for the two highest districts, Monklands and Motherwell (both 63%). At the other extreme came the Isle of Wight (3.6%), Dorset (10%), and the three least urbanized district types, notably the Resort, port, and retirement category.

The picture is more mixed for the other two renting tenures shown. Map (c) reflects the patchiness of housing association activity, though as a rule this has been more important in the larger cities and least in evidence in the remoter rural areas. Private renting, including accommodation provided with job or business, is most common in London, notably in the City of Westminster and the Borough of Kensington and Chelsea, where it accounts for one-third of all housing. Otherwise, as shown in map (d), it is primarily a feature of more rural areas, related to tied farm cottages, military bases, holiday accommodation, and retired people.

Housing tenure in Great Britain 1981–1991

Tenure type	1991	1981	1981–91	
	(%)	(%)	% point (a)	%(b)
Owner-occupied	66.4	55.9	10.5	34.0
Owned outright	23.9	n.a.	n.a.	n.a.
Buying	42.4	n.a.	n.a.	n.a.
Rented privately	7.1	8.7	−1.6	−6.8
Furnished	3.5	2.8	0.7	43.9
Unfurnished	3.6	5.9	−2.3	−30.6
Rented with job or business	2.0	2.2	−0.2	0.0
Rented from a local authority, New Town, or Scottish Homes	21.4	31.3	−9.9	−22.7
Rented from housing associations	3.1	2.0	1.1	76.1
All households	100.0	100.0	0.0	12.8

%(a) = change in tenure's share; %(b)= change in number of households.
n.a. = not available.

(a)

Renting from Local
Authorities, New Towns,
Scottish Homes (%) 1991

n	
8	30.0 or over
13	22.0 to 30.0
15	17.0 to 22.0
19	13.0 to 17.0
9	under 13.0

0   50 miles
0   80 km

(b)

Reduction in number of
households renting from
Local Authorities, New Towns,
Scottish Homes (%) 1981–91

n	
13	28.0 or over
13	25.0 to 28.0
13	22.5 to 25.0
14	20.0 to 22.5
11	under 20.0

0   50 miles
0   80 km

(c)

Renting from housing
associations (%)
1991

n	
14	3.6 or over
13	2.6 to 3.6
12	2.1 to 2.6
13	1.6 to 2.1
12	under 1.6

0   50 miles
0   80 km

(d)

Renting from private
landlords (%)
1991

n	
9	12.0 or over
16	10.0 to 12.0
14	8.0 to 10.0
18	6.0 to 8.0
7	under 6.0

0   50 miles
0   80 km

Buying and owning

The pattern of owner-occupation in 1991, by definition, forms the mirror image of the picture of renting covered in *Housing tenure*. There the graph shows the district types with the strongest representation of owner-occupying households as being the Resort, port, and retirement and Urban and mixed urban–rural categories, both with around three out of every four households. At the other extreme, less than two in every five of Inner London's households were owner-occupiers, and the level is only just over one-half for the Principal metropolitan cities. At district level, the lowest proportion in 1991 is for Tower Hamlets, with only 23% of households being owner-occupiers, despite the building of new private housing in the Docklands.

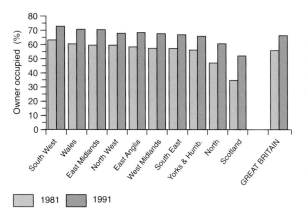

■ 1981   ■ 1991

The most conspicuous feature of map (a) opposite and the graph on this page, however, is the position of Scotland and, to a lesser extent, north-east England, both with well below-average levels of owner-occupation in 1991. But this does not rule out the existence of local pockets where very high proportions of the houses are owner-occupied. Two districts of suburban Clydeside—Eastwood and Bearsden and Milngavie—share with Castle Point and Rochford (both part of the western suburbs of Southend in Essex) the distinction of having the highest proportions of owner-occupation of Britain's 459 districts (see table).

The rise in owner-occupation 1981–1991

Map (b) and the graph confirm how widespread across Britain was the rise of owner-occupation between 1981 and 1991. Most regions saw the proportion of owner-occupying households increase by around 10 percentage points over the decade. The fact that the two principal exceptions are Scotland and the North, with still greater increases, indicates a narrowing of regional differences in this respect.

A narrowing of between-area differences is also evident at district level (see panel (a) of table). The five districts which recorded the biggest increases in owner-occupation were in Scotland and/or included New Towns—none with more than 30% of households being owner-occupiers in 1981. The districts with the lowest increases already had at least three-quarters of households owner-occupying at the start of the 1980s. Significantly, not one district saw a fall in its proportion of owner-occupiers over the decade.

Households with mortgages

Finally, there is a clear geography to the process of 'buying' a home with borrowed finance, as opposed to owning outright. Map (c) shows that the proportion of all households in this form of debt is particularly high in the South East, where housing is at its most expensive, and in the 'suburban' counties of the Midlands and north-west England, which are similar to the South East in containing above-average proportions of younger households, as opposed to older people who have paid off their mortgages.

As panel (b) of the table shows, suburban districts contain the highest proportions of households buying, while New Towns and London Docklands dominate in terms of the proportion of owner-occupiers who are borrowing to buy. These are amongst the areas which were worst affected by problems of 'negative equity' during the early 1990s recession.

Top five districts on selected aspects of owner-occupation

(a)

% Owner-occupied 1991		Change in % 1981–91	
Eastwood	89.4	East Kilbride	33.0
Castle Point	89.4	Cumbernauld	30.2
Bearsden and Milngavie	86.8	Dunfermline	27.4
Rochford	86.4	Corby	27.0
Fareham	86.0	West Lothian	26.5

(b)

Buying as % all households		Buying as % owner-occupiers	
Wokingham	64.3	Cumbernauld	86.4
Surrey Heath	61.0	Tower Hamlets	83.5
Hart	60.1	West Lothian	83.5
Northavon	59.2	Milton Keynes	81.9
Eastwood	58.8	Harlow	81.5

(a) Owner occupiers as proportion of all households (%) 1991

n	
5	75.0 or over
28	70.0 to 75.0
13	65.0 to 70.0
8	60.0 to 65.0
10	under 60.0

0   50 miles
0   80 km

(b) Change in proportion of owner occupiers (% point) 1981–91

n	
5	16.5 or over
8	13.5 to 16.5
12	10.5 to 13.5
33	7.5 to 10.5
6	under 7.5

0   50 miles
0   80 km

(c) Owner occupiers buying as proportion of all households (%) 1991

n	
12	47.0 or over
10	44.0 to 47.0
14	41.0 to 44.0
16	38.0 to 41.0
12	under 38.0

0   50 miles
0   80 km

(d) Owner occupiers buying as proportion of all owner occupiers (%) 1991

n	
11	67.0 or over
11	65.0 to 67.0
16	62.0 to 65.0
12	57.0 to 62.0
14	under 57.0

0   50 miles
0   80 km

House prices and negative equity

Average house prices vary greatly across the country. They have also changed in different ways in different places over recent years. The map opposite illustrates both these trends. Nationally, house prices rose steadily during the early 1980s and then accelerated to reach a peak in 1989. After that, the national average price fell steadily. These falls did not occur everywhere, but where they did take place they had a dramatic effect on the financial security of the many people who bought property which is now worth less than the money they borrowed to buy it.

Average house prices are estimated here using a constant mix of different types of properties that conforms to the national mix of properties for the period being studied. If this were not done, the price of housing in London would appear much cheaper than it really is because so many flats are sold there.

The pattern of price changes in London can be seen to have been similar to the national pattern. However, in many of the counties around London prices rose earlier and much faster than nationally, as the map opposite shows. Cambridgeshire is a peculiar example where prices rose fast, fell sharply, and then rose again. Further out from the Home Counties prices can be seen to have risen much less and to have declined very little since. In north-east England and in Scotland prices were still rising slightly in some counties in 1993.

Negative equity

Where prices have fallen and home-buyers had tended to borrow relatively large mortgages many of these buyers found that their home was worth less than their mortgage. These people are said to have negative equity (where the term 'equity' refers to the positive gap between what a home-owner could sell their home for and how much money they have to pay back to their mortgage lender).

The map on this page shows the 1993 geographical distribution of recent buyers with negative equity. The pattern generally follows the distribution of house-price falls shown opposite. However, in areas such as Surrey where home-buyers tend to be more affluent and borrow smaller mortgages (see *Wealth*), the proportions of people holding this debt tends to be lower.

During the 1980s rising house prices were thought by many people to be a good thing, good in particular for the south of England where the economy was booming and home-owners felt they were becoming richer. In the early 1990s all this changed and many recent home-buyers in the South were, in housing finance terms, worse off than their counterparts living in the north of England, in Scotland, and in Wales.

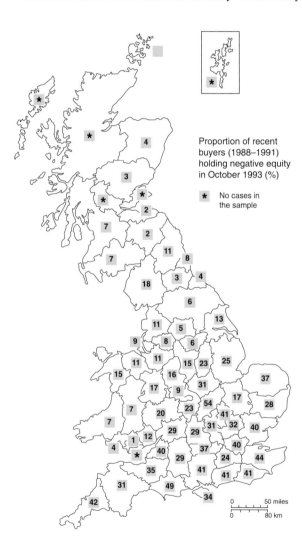

Proportion of recent buyers (1988–1991) holding negative equity in October 1993 (%)

★ No cases in the sample

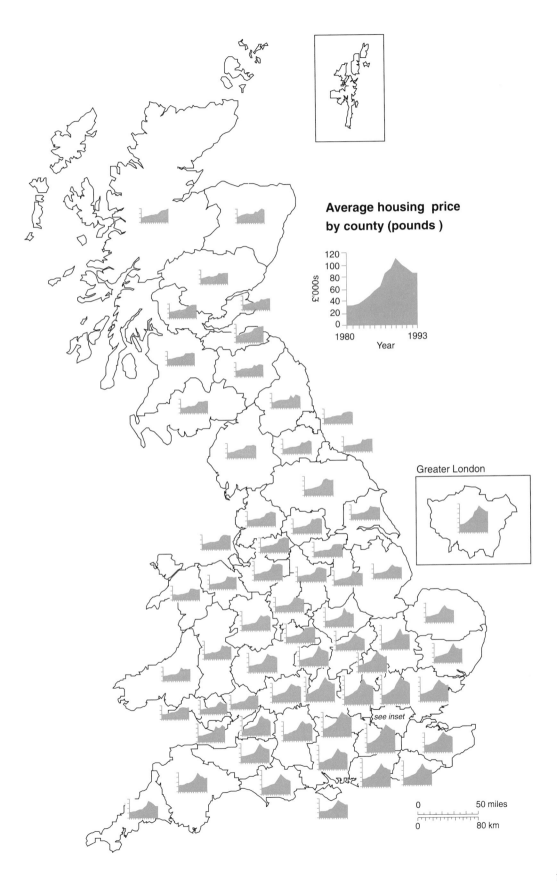

Average housing price by county (pounds)

The future of private housing

Given the turbulence of the British housing-market in the 1980s, how can it be possible to predict what will happen in the next decade and beyond? There are clearly many factors that could affect the price of private housing; mortgage rates, changes in employment, and changes in mortgage-tax relief are a few. Any attempt to encapsulate these into some model to predict house prices would be fraught with difficulty. However, it is possible to apply simpler 'what-if?' scenarios, and to compare these in order to gain an understanding of the range of possible outcomes that may occur. An example of this is illustrated here.

House-price inflation 1982–91

In this analysis, house-price inflation is examined on a county basis between 1982 and 1991. In this period the South East experienced great inflation in housing cost in the later 1980s, which was followed by a downturn. Just at the end of this period, housing in northern England also increased in value, reducing the differences between North and South—one example of the so-called 'North–South Divide'.

The relationship is exemplified by the graph. It can be seen here that throughout the period up to 1991 houses in Greater London have been consistently more expensive than those in Greater Manchester, and that over this period, the average price of housing has increased. However, it should also be noted that the trends shown by the two counties have differed greatly. Whilst the curve for Greater Manchester shows a steady growth, Greater London

shows faster growth over most of the period and then a decline in the latter part.

Clearly the pattern of house prices over space and time is a complex one. Housing booms in one part of Britain do not necessarily imply equivalent patterns in another. However, ignoring complex events that may have happened during the nine-year period, it is possible to compute average levels of house-price inflation that have been experienced by each area.

Map (a) shows the situation in 1982. With the exception of housing around Aberdeen (possibly due to the North Sea oil industry), the most expensive housing centres on London and the South East. By 1991, map (b) demonstrates that, although the South East still has the most expensive housing, there have been some changes; for instance, note that the 'Aberdeen effect' is no longer evident. In map (c), the average yearly levels of inflation taken over the nine-year period are shown. This demonstrates a quite different geographical pattern, with greater average inflation occurring in northern England and the Midlands. Thus, at the end of the 'boom and bust cycle', although the geographical ranking of areas is largely unaltered, the relative level of change has been higher in some of the lower-priced areas.

House-price projection for the year 2000

One possible 'what if?' scenario is to assume that a similar cycle of house-price inflation occurs over the next nine-year period beginning in 1991, with the same geographical differences in inflation as those shown in map (c). The price levels for the year 2000, estimated on this basis, are shown in map (d). It can be seen that, although there are still relatively high prices around London and the South East, cities in the Midlands and northern England stand out as also having relatively high prices. It seems that if the relatively high levels of inflation that occurred in these areas over the period 1982–91 were to occur again, the effect would be to reduce the price difference between the North and the South.

The big question is how valid is the main assumption of this projection exercise compared with alternative ways of viewing the housing-market, particularly given that the housing-market in the first half of the 1990s was even less buoyant than in the early 1980s.

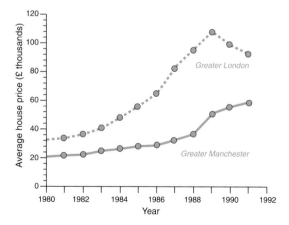

(a)

Average house prices
1982

n	
9	£30,000 or over
18	£25,000 to £30,000
21	£22,000 to £25,000
10	£20,000 to £22,000
6	under £20,000

0   50 miles
0   80 km

(b)

Average house prices
1991

n	
5	£80,000 or over
17	£60,000 to £80,000
26	£50,000 to £60,000
15	£40,000 to £50,000
1	under £40,000

0   50 miles
0   80 km

(c)

Average annual
inflation

n	
13	11.0 or over
20	10.0 to 11.0
20	9.0 to 10.0
5	8.0 to 9.0
5	under 8.0

0   50 miles
0   80 km

(d)

Predicted house prices
2000

n	
5	£200,000 or over
16	£150,000 to £200,000
22	£120,000 to £150,000
13	£100,000 to £120,000
8	under £100,000

0   50 miles
0   80 km

Access to Facilities

Availability and use of cars

The availability of, and access to, transport is a vital ingredient of people's well-being, because work opportunities and facilities for shopping, education, sport, and entertainment are not situated directly outside everyone's front door. Over time, people have become increasingly mobile in terms of both distance travelled and choice of patterns of movement, largely due to the greater availability of private cars. There are, however, considerable variations in car availability and usage between people, which are reflected in geographical differences at regional and local scale.

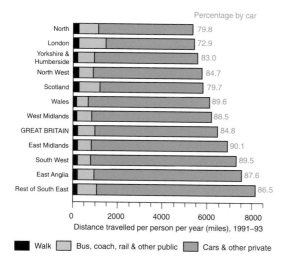

Distance travelled per person per year (miles), 1991–93

■ Walk ▨ Bus, coach, rail & other public ▨ Cars & other private

In the early 1990s, people in Britain travelled just under 6,500 miles per year on average, with almost 85% of this travel being by car (see graph). This represents a substantial increase from 1985–7, when the distance travelled averaged 5,300 miles and 81% was by car. Some two-fifths of this travelling is for leisure of various kinds, one-fifth for commuting, one-eighth for shopping, one-tenth on business, and 3% travelling to and from school.

The average distance travelled and the mode of transport vary considerably according to region of residence (see graph). The most mobile people in 1991–3 were the residents of the South East outside London, followed by those in East Anglia and the South West. Least mobile were the residents of the

northern half of Britain, but also London (where there may be less need to travel far to reach facilities). The proportion of travel accounted for by the car (the percentages in the graph at the end of the bars) ranges from around 90% for residents of the East Midlands, Wales, and the South West to under 80% for those of the North and Scotland, and under 73% for Londoners.

These patterns largely reflect variations across Britain in the availability of cars. As shown in the map opposite, the proportion of households without access to a car is particularly high in metropolitan counties and those areas with industrial and mining traditions, and is generally lowest in the suburban and rural South. The proportions of households with two or more cars is highest in the shire counties of south-east England.

Fuller details for the two extremes are shown in the table. Surrey clearly possesses the highest level of car availability, with an average of 1.3 cars per household and with two-fifths of its households having at least two cars and under one-fifth with no car. This is followed by several other counties in south-east England.

In contrast, average car availability in Tyne and Wear is less than half the figure for Surrey, and over half of all households there have no car, compared to one third for Britain as a whole. Strathclyde's proportion is not much less, followed by Merseyside, Lothian, and South Yorkshire. In none of these areas does as many as one in six households have access to two or more cars.

Car availability 1991: highest and lowest areas

Area	Cars per household	% Households by number of cars			
		0	1	2	3+
Surrey	1.31	17.8	41.4	32.1	8.6
Buckinghamshire	1.27	19.4	41.7	31.2	7.7
Berkshire	1.22	21.0	42.7	29.6	6.7
Hertfordshire	1.19	22.2	43.1	28.0	6.7
Oxfordshire	1.17	22.0	45.2	26.6	6.1
Great Britain	0.94	33.4	43.5	19.1	4.0
South Yorkshire	0.77	41.6	42.2	13.9	2.4
Lothian	0.75	42.4	42.0	13.6	2.0
Merseyside	0.73	45.0	39.4	13.4	2.2
Strathclyde	0.66	49.2	37.3	11.7	1.9
Tyne and Wear	0.62	51.1	37.7	10.0	1.3

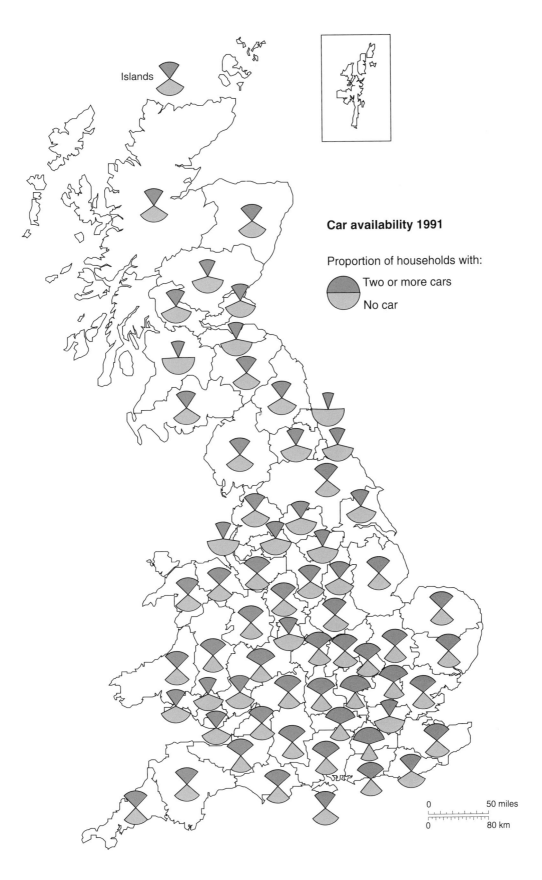

Islands

Car availability 1991

Proportion of households with:

Two or more cars
No car

0   50 miles

0   80 km

Change in car availability

For Britain as a whole, the level of car availability has increased enormously over the past two decades. As shown in the table, almost half of all households had no car in 1971, compared to only one-third twenty years later. The decline in carlessness in the 1980s, though smaller than in the 1970s, nevertheless amounted to a shift of 6% of households, and the proportion of households with at least two cars rose by 7.7 percentage points. Perhaps most impressive of all, between the 1981 and 1991 Censuses the total numbers of cars available to private households rose by fully a third, providing considerably greater mobility as well as increasing the pressure on roads and parking space, and generating greater pollution.

Car availability, 1971–1991, by region

Region % Change (ranked by cars per household)	Cars per house- hold, 1991	% Households with no car				holds with 2+ cars 1981–91	House- in nos. of cars 1981–91
		1971	1981	1991	1981–91		
East Anglia	1.07	39.5	30.7	24.8	−5.9	9.4	42.8
South West	1.07	39.9	30.9	25.0	−5.9	8.9	39.8
South East	1.01	45.5	35.9	30.6	−5.3	8.1	33.9
East Midlands	0.99	46.9	37.2	30.1	−7.1	9.2	39.5
West Midlands	0.96	46.0	37.9	32.6	−5.3	8.0	30.7
Great Britain	0.94	49.0	39.5	33.4	−6.1	7.7	34.5
Wales	0.93	46.8	38.0	32.3	−5.7	7.3	33.5
North West	0.86	54.6	44.5	37.9	−6.6	7.1	30.4
Yorkshire and Humberside	0.84	56.2	45.5	37.8	−7.7	7.2	35.4
North	0.76	58.4	48.3	42.2	−6.1	5.6	30.8
Scotland	0.76	57.6	48.7	42.6	−6.1	5.1	34.2

The table also summarizes the regional variations in car availability and how it has changed over time. The North–South contrast in overall car availability is marked, and clearly is a long-established feature. There is some evidence of a 'catching-up' process between 1981 and 1991, with the proportion of households without cars generally falling most rapidly in regions with lower levels of availability. At the same time, however, the proportion of households with at least two cars rose more steeply in the South and Midlands, and it is remarkable that the proportion of no-car households in Scotland and the North in 1991 was still below the 1971 level for East Anglia and the South West despite the former regions' increases over this period.

These general points are also visible in the sub-regional geography. Comparison of maps (a) and (b) provides much evidence of convergence in the proportion of households with no car, with most of the largest reductions in the 1980s taking place in the areas that were least well-served in 1981, such as the more urban parts of the East Midlands and much of northern England. Conversely, some of the smallest reductions occurred in rural Wales and parts of the South East (notably excluding East Sussex and Kent). Even so, major metropolitan and urban areas like London, West Midlands county, Merseyside, Cleveland, Tyne and Wear, and Strathclyde were further below the national average in 1991 than they had been ten years before.

At the same time, as shown in map (c), the proportion of households with three or more cars grew most strongly in the areas already with most cars in 1981, reflecting the general pattern of economic growth associated with the 'Thatcher decade'. The increase was greatest for Surrey and Buckinghamshire, and least for Tyne and Wear and the Scottish regions of Scotland, Dumfries and Galloway, Borders and Lothian.

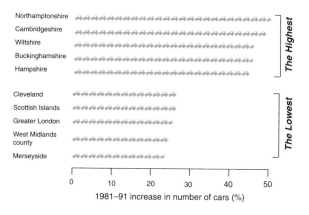

The impact on the total number of cars reflects population change as well as trends in car availability, though the most impressive aspect is the nationwide extent of increases. The table, graph, and map (d) all show a major contrast between the non-metropolitan South and the urban North of Britain. Even so, in Merseyside and West Midlands county the number of cars went up by over 20% between 1981 and 1991, with the lowest increases at regional level being around 30%. At the other extreme, the number rose by nearly 43% in East Anglia and by almost half in Northamptonshire.

(a)

Proportion of households
with no car (%)
1981

n
14 43.5 or over
12 38.0 to 43.5
12 33.5 to 38.0
12 30.0 to 33.5
14 under 30.0

0 ___ 50 miles
0 ___ 80 km

(b)

Reduction in proportion
with no car (% point)
1981–91

n
13 6.8 or over
12 6.1 to 6.8
14 5.5 to 6.1
12 5.0 to 5.5
13 under 5.0

0 ___ 50 miles
0 ___ 80 km

(c)

Change in proportion with
3 or more cars (% point)
1981–91

n
10 2.5 or over
16 2.0 to 2.5
12 1.5 to 2.0
12 1.0 to 1.5
14 under 1.0

0 ___ 50 miles
0 ___ 80 km

(d)

Estimated change in total
number of cars (%)
1981–91

n
12 41.0 or over
13 38.0 to 41.0
13 35.0 to 38.0
14 32.0 to 35.0
12 under 32.0

0 ___ 50 miles
0 ___ 80 km

Access to cars

Variations in car availability, and in trends over time, are even more marked at the scale of Britain's 192 'places' (see Appendix 2) than at regional and county levels, and analyses at this scale reveal very consistent patterns.

Variations between places in 1991

The table identifies the places which had the highest and lowest proportions of households with two or more cars in 1991. At one extreme, around 45% of households in Chiltern and Wycombe fall in this category, and indeed one in ten households there had access to at least three cars. The other four top places are in similar locations round the southern and western edges of the London area.

Top and bottom five places ranked by proportion of households with two or more cars 1991

Place	% Households with 2+ cars	% Households by number of cars			
		3+	2	1	0
Top five places					
Chiltern and Wycombe	44.5	9.5	35.0	38.5	17.0
Aldershot	43.6	8.8	34.8	41.0	15.4
Horsham	40.3	7.9	32.4	43.0	16.7
Guildford	39.9	8.5	31.4	41.2	18.9
Aylesbury	38.9	7.3	31.6	42.5	18.5
Bottom five places					
Sunderland	12.3	1.6	10.7	39.5	48.2
Glasgow	12.2	1.6	10.6	34.0	53.7
Monklands	12.1	1.7	10.4	38.0	49.9
Inverclyde	12.0	1.7	10.3	35.2	52.8
South Tyneside	10.0	1.2	8.8	36.4	53.6

By contrast, barely 10% of households in South Tyneside had access to two or more cars, and very few to three cars. Along with north-east England, Scottish areas feature strongly in the table. For these five 'lowest' places, one in two households had no car at all in 1991, around three times as many as for the five 'highest' places.

Two factors can be considered primarily responsible for these patterns. One is the urban-suburban/rural element, in that whereas cars are more difficult to keep and use in larger cities and may be less necessary because of alternative forms of transport, the absence of a car in suburban areas and the countryside poses severe restrictions on personal mobility.

More important, however, is the nature of the household, particularly in terms of demographic and social characteristics. As the table shows, less well-off groups such as the elderly, unskilled manual workers, Black people, and council tenants have well-below-average levels of access to a car.

1981–1991 trends

The geographical differentials in the proportions of households with at least two cars have been growing more marked in recent years, according to the map opposite. The places with the strongest increases between 1981 and 1991 are very largely concentrated in England south and east of a line between the Severn estuary and the Wash, led by Basingstoke (a 14.6 percentage point increase), Aldershot, Bracknell, Aylesbury, and Milton Keynes. The smallest increases are found in Scotland and north-east England: only 3.2 points up over the decade at South Tyneside and also under 4.0 for Hartlepool, Glasgow, and Inverclyde.

The change in total number of cars between 1981 and 1991 is also considerably wider for these places compared to the broader county pattern shown on the previous page. Milton Keynes led the field in this respect with a 99% increase, i.e. almost a doubling in its number of cars over the decade. Next were Basingstoke, Bracknell, Teignbridge, and Northampton, with increases in the range 51–5%. At the other extreme, the Liverpool area recorded an increase of just under 22%, with Manchester, Hartlepool, Inverclyde, and Walsall around the 24% mark.

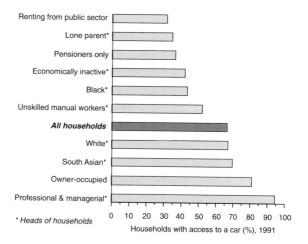

* Heads of households

Households with access to a car (%), 1991

(Categories, top to bottom: Renting from public sector; Lone parent*; Pensioners only; Economically inactive*; Black*; Unskilled manual workers*; **All households**; White*; South Asian*; Owner-occupied; Professional & managerial*)

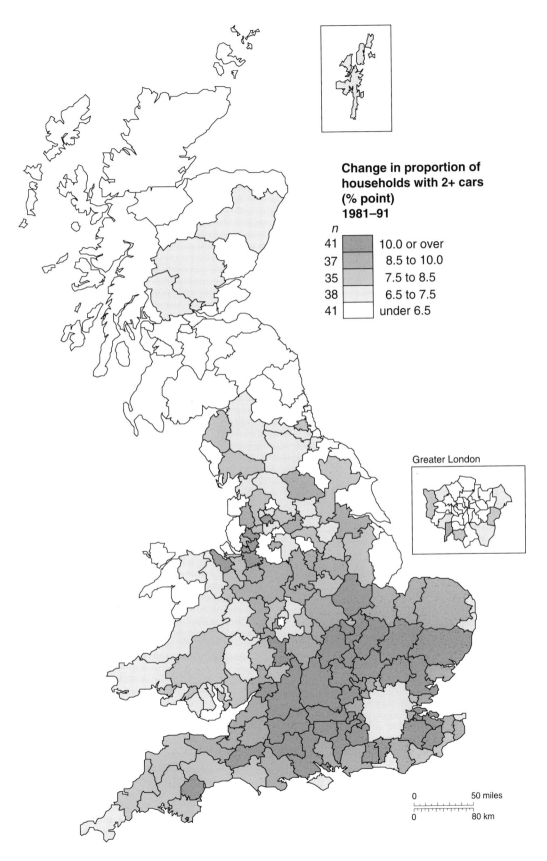

Change in proportion of
households with 2+ cars
(% point)
1981–91

n		
41		10.0 or over
37		8.5 to 10.0
35		7.5 to 8.5
38		6.5 to 7.5
41		under 6.5

Greater London

0   50 miles
0   80 km

Leaving the car at home

The upsurge of environmental concerns in recent years has led to a renewed interest in public transport. Most notably, the increasing prevalence of asthma among Britain's children has been linked, in part, with pollution caused by cars in cities. Yet all predictions suggest that there will be ever more cars owned and so liable to be used in future years. The key challenge, therefore, has become to persuade car owners to use public transport. The map shows the proportion of workers living in car-owning households who do use public transport for their journeys to work.

Where is public transport used?

Although environmental concerns about car use have often concentrated on the cities, the map shows that it is only in the cities where high levels of public transport usage for commuting are to be found. In most regions, it is the principal city or cities which stand out as having the highest levels (e.g. Leeds and Sheffield in Yorkshire, and Birmingham in the Midlands). In some cases, the 'regional capital' is joined in having a high rate by one or more adjacent areas from which numerous workers commute to the centre by public transport (e.g. Greenock and Dumbarton to Glasgow, South Shields to Newcastle). The extreme case of this pattern is, of course, London which is joined both by the relatively prosperous St. Albans and the less affluent 'Thames Corridor' towns in Kent (e.g. Gravesend) and Essex (e.g. Basildon).

To some extent, the map is simply reflecting the availability of public transport services. It can certainly be argued that people who do have access to a car will only use public transport if the local facilities offer a reliable and attractive service at a reasonable cost. From this point of view, it is not surprising that the lowest levels of public transport use are to be found in the more rural areas where service provision is minimal. Yet it is notable that in the Highlands and Islands—where services will be effectively non-existent in several areas—no area falls into the lowest category of public transport usage shown on the map.

Who uses cars?

One of the reasons for some areas showing higher levels of car use than their neighbours is that they are areas which have higher proportions of those groups who are likely to use cars *wherever* they live. One dramatic contrast in levels of car use is that between men and women: over two-thirds of men (67%) commute by car, compared with just 52% of women. Yet this wide gap shown by the 1991 data is, in fact, markedly less than that which was found in the 1981 Census (when the figures were 59% and 37% respectively). It can be seen that car use is increasing for both genders, but that there is a 'catching up' effect due to a faster shift to car use among women. Even so, it is usually the man who uses the car to commute where a couple both work but have only one car.

The major change since 1981 in commuting by public transport has been the rapid decline in travel by bus. This period has seen the deregulation of the bus industry: bus usage has been in long-term decline, but the policy changes certainly seem to have done nothing to turn this around. Adoption of similar policies for the rail industry in the 1990s is thus understandably controversial.

The areas where distinctive public transport policies have been tried are concentrated among the major cities. Centred on Newcastle, the Tyne and Wear Metro was hailed in the early 1980s as a 'new dawn' for urban light railways, although usage has declined in more recent years. In the 1990s trams have been reintroduced in Manchester and Sheffield, but there is little sign yet of these new services attracting as many users as did traditional buses in Sheffield (and the rest of South Yorkshire) in the early 1980s when there were heavily subsidized cheap fares.

London probably offers the best prospect for a strategy to promote the use of public transport. The traffic problems are so great that car travel can never provide a high level of mobility for the whole population. Car ownership among Londoners has grown only modestly (from 57% in 1981 to 60% in 1991). However, a survey in and around London found that ownership rises to over 90% among higher-earning groups. One key question, then, is how to attract car owners to public transport. In fact, if shown separately on the map, every London borough would be placed in the top category—but there is still a huge contrast between the residents of an area like Hillingdon (where under 19% of car owners commute by public transport), and their west London neighbours in Hammersmith and Fulham where over 45% of car owners already commute by public transport.

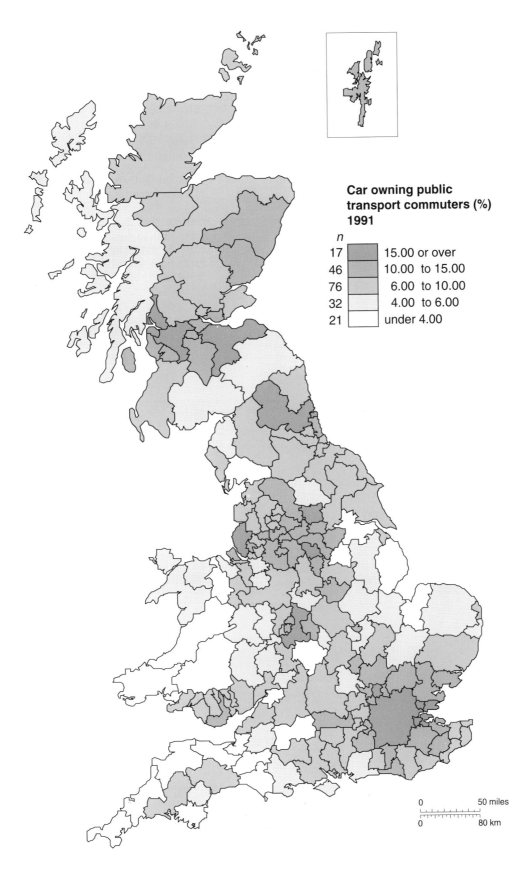

Car owning public
transport commuters (%)
1991

n		
17		15.00 or over
46		10.00 to 15.00
76		6.00 to 10.00
32		4.00 to 6.00
21		under 4.00

0   50 miles

0   80 km

Patterns of commuting

The pattern of commuting in any area strongly reflects the way in which the local towns or cities form the basic 'urban structure' of that region. Large flows can be seen between residential districts and nearby commercial or industrial centres. Viewed from a distance, as on the national map here, the major urban centres appear as clusters of large flows. Most of these flows are still in the 'traditional' direction—swelling the cities' daytime population with commuters from surrounding smaller towns and rural areas.

The table compares the commuting distances of women and men, and also those of women who work no more than fifteen hours per week. It can be seen that, perhaps surprisingly, about one in twenty of both men and women work at home. At the same time, the table also shows that men are by far the more likely to have 'no fixed workplace' (for example, by selling door-to-door).

The main feature of the table is the greater emphasis on short-distance commuting among women, and especially those with part-time work. Adding those who work at home to the group commuting less than 2 kms, it can be seen that over half of women part-time workers—who make up the vast majority of part-time workers—work in or very near their homes. Taking all women together, this proportion is over a third, while for men it is less than a quarter. Part of the explanation lies with women who choose part-time work to fit in with family commitments, and this working pattern goes along with needing to avoid longer-distance commuting away from the home and, perhaps, the children's schools. At the same time, part-time workers earn far less than full-timers on average, and more long-distance commuters are found among groups of workers who earn more.

The map provides a summary picture which cuts across these contrasts in the commuting behaviour of different groups of workers. It shows only the very largest flows, and these are so substantial that they will be made up from many different subgroups, and certainly of women as well as men commuters. It is possible for the longer-distance flows to catch the eye on a map, but here the emphasis is on the clusters of numerous flows, most of which are of shorter or medium length. It is notable that around London, which does attract more long-distance commuters than anywhere else, the map suggests that the complex of flows entirely within the Greater London boundary is relatively separate and distinct from the flows in the adjacent areas (just beyond the M25). The principal exception is in the west where the many jobs in and around Heathrow attract many large flows from adjacent Home Counties towns.

Place of work and commuting distance, 1991 (percentages)

	All men	All women	(Part-time*)
Work at home	5.0	5.2	(8.0)
Less than 2 kms from home	17.7	31.2	(45.8)
2–4 kms from home	20.1	25.0	(22.1)
5–9 kms from home	18.6	18.1	(11.5)
10–29 kms from home	21.3	14.6	(5.9)
At least 30 kms from home	7.8	3.1	(1.6)
No fixed workplace	9.4	2.8	(5.0)

* Women who work no more than 15 hours per week.

It is interesting to look at the other conurbations to see how far the areas within the metropolitan county boundaries are dominated by their principal cities. For example, within West Midlands county the flows between Coventry and Birmingham are very limited. Manchester is, on the other hand, very clearly dominant across most of its county, while Liverpool has only sparse links with its hinterland. Similar contrasts can be made between the 'estuarine' counties which, despite being newly created in the 1970s in the expectation that conurbations would emerge there by the end of this century, are scheduled for dismantling in the 1990s. Avon shows only a sparse link between Bristol and Bath—with the two centres continuing to have their own, largely distinct, commuting hinterlands. This pattern is even clearer for Hull and the southern Humberside towns (Scunthorpe and Grimsby). In contrast, Cleveland appears to have been a stronger candidate for integration because the Teesside towns of Stockton and Middlesbrough have become knitted together with commuting flows, although Hartlepool in the north of the county remains a distinct cluster in its own right.

Away from the cities, local centres can be seen in many areas. Even the Western Isles' main town of Stornoway is shown as a local cluster of commuting flows. Some of the most noticeable smaller complexes of flows are centred on county towns: for example, Ayr, Carlisle, Carmarthen, and Truro stand out down the western half of the country. One or two commuting clusters reflect the location of very large localized industrial sites. In particular, the complex of flows shown near the west Cumbrian coast is largely plotting the hinterland of the Sellafield nuclear plant. In most cases, however, the map's portrayal of major commuting flows is a fair reflection of the general disposition of Britain's towns and cities, and also of their respective commuting hinterlands—and also thereby of the areas which remain rather remote from these concentrations of job opportunities and other facilities.

Patterns of commuting

—— Major flows

| 0 | | | | 50 miles |
| 0 | | | | 80 km |

Railways and motorways

The opening of the Channel Tunnel not only completes over a century of hesitant steps towards the ultimate 'international gateway' for Britain, it may also mark the end of a long period of decline in the fortunes of rail transport. Thirty years ago the Beeching Report led to huge reductions in the rail network and since then nearly all the major additions to Britain's transport route system have been motorways or other major roads. Shifting emphasis back to the railways may also now be encouraged by 'green' arguments against over-reliance on road transport, with the increasingly clear evidence that new roads stimulate still more traffic and so often actually *increase* congestion. These recent developments are set in a historical context by the map, which compares existing networks with the situation 150 years ago when the railways were first extending across the country.

The 1990s are seeing a return of one aspect of the nineteenth-century heyday of railways—the re-creation of separate companies with names like Great Western (plus the operator of the less prestigious services, known as Regional Railways). The map shows the Principal Places on the British Rail maps of the 1990s, complete with the routes which currently make up the two top categories of main-line services. It is notable that no current route towards the Channel Tunnel qualifies as part of this elite section of the network, in stark contrast to the situation in France where new lines were built *well in advance* of the Tunnel opening.

The map also indicates which of the current main railway centres were linked together over 150 years ago when the separate railway companies were beginning to connect into a first national network—which *did* then include a link to Dover! Almost all of the 1840s links which are not main lines in the 1990s are cross-country, in the sense that they are unlikely to be used by many travellers to and from London. Most of these lines *are* still used today, but their provincial role has relegated them from the national main-line network.

The table lists a selection of links in Britain's inter-city network which have developed very differently over the years. The first railway was from Darlington to Stockton: Regional Railways now operates this local line in and around the area's new main centre of Middlesbrough. The next major railway was between Liverpool and Manchester, and although it too is excluded from the modern main-line network, these two large cities are now also connected by motorway. The third major railway project was

Contrasting inter-city links

	1840s railway?	1990s main line?	Motorway?
Darlington–Stockton/ Middlesbrough	Yes	No	No
Liverpool–Manchester	Yes	No	Yes
London–Birmingham	Yes	Yes	Yes
York–Darlington	Yes	Yes	No
Glasgow/Motherwell–Carlisle	No	Yes	No
Cardiff–Swansea	No	Yes	Yes
London–Cambridge	No	No	Yes
Sheffield–Stoke	No	No	No

between London and Birmingham, a route which has come to feature a full range of modern transport infrastructure. The table's final example from the early railway era is the York–Darlington route which remains a main line today but is not paralleled by a motorway.

The map shows that the early railways system has an echo in the current motorway network in that the routes in central Scotland are completely detached from those in England. The table notes the example of Glasgow–Carlisle as a route which is now a main line without a parallel motorway—and which has no parallel in early railway history. The map shows that routes such as this are a feature of peripheral Britain, not only elsewhere in Scotland, but also in north and west Wales and in south-west England. In contrast, routes with newer main lines *and* motorways—represented by Cardiff and Swansea in the table—can be seen on the map to be mostly in more central areas of Britain.

The motorway-only category, typified in the table by the London–Cambridge route, is largely to be found near London (and includes the M25—such ring routes have never been a part of the British railway system). The final category in the table covers adjacent centres with no link shown on the map: the example of Sheffield and Stoke typifies the cross-country nature of most of these 'missing' links.

For all the differences in emphases between the three transport networks shown on the map, there are some notable common features. The influence of Britain's landscape is clear: mountain ranges in Scotland are only crossed by the later railways, and few major routes span the Pennines or the Downs (south of London). Wales has been particularly affected in this way, with no major infrastructure links between the north and south—except via Birmingham—and so the map shows no provision in Mid Wales at all.

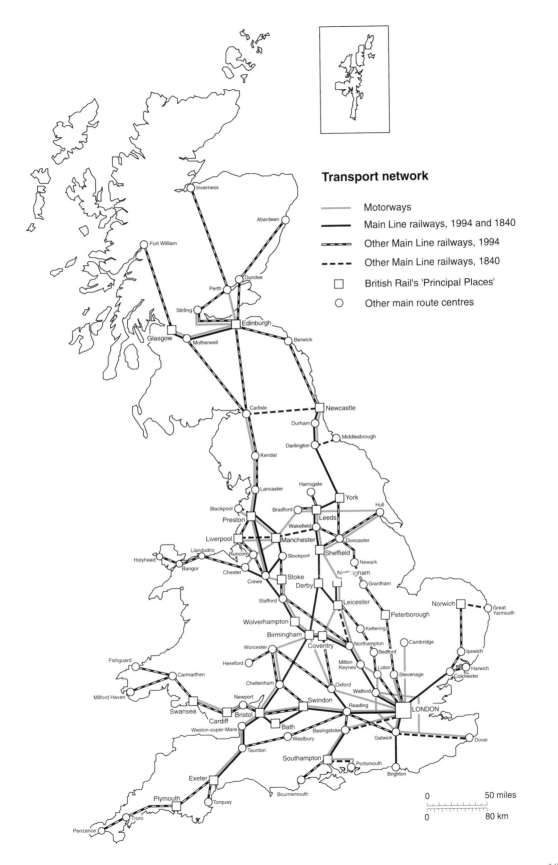

Transport network

Motorways

Main Line railways, 1994 and 1840

Other Main Line railways, 1994

Other Main Line railways, 1840

☐ British Rail's 'Principal Places'

○ Other main route centres

Inverness

Aberdeen

Fort William

Perth
Dundee
Stirling
Glasgow
Motherwell
Edinburgh
Berwick

Carlisle
Newcastle
Durham
Middlesbrough
Darlington
Kendal

Lancaster
Harrogate
Blackpool
Bradford
York
Hull
Preston
Leeds
Wakefield
Liverpool
Manchester
Doncaster
Runcorn
Stockport
Sheffield
Llandudno
Newark
Holyhead
Chester
Crewe
Nottingham
Bangor
Stoke
Derby
Stafford
Grantham
Leicester
Norwich
Wolverhampton
Peterborough
Great Yarmouth
Birmingham
Kettering
Worcester
Coventry
Cambridge
Hereford
Northampton
Ipswich
Fishguard
Bedford
Harwich
Milton Keynes
Luton
Colchester
Carmarthen
Cheltenham
Stevenage
Milford Haven
Oxford
Newport
Watford
Swansea
Swindon
Reading
LONDON
Cardiff
Bristol
Bath
Dover
Weston-super-Mare
Basingstoke
Westbury
Gatwick
Taunton
Southampton
Portsmouth
Brighton
Exeter
Bournemouth
Plymouth
Torquay
Truro
Penzance

0   50 miles
0   80 km

121

International gateways

As an island nation, access to other countries has always been important for Britain. In recent years the emphasis for exporters has been shifting from seaports to airports—at first for their own travel, as passengers, but now increasingly for some types of freight too. The map shows the relative accessibility of each part of Britain to airports with international flights, and the table shows some contrasts between airport and seaport locations.

Airport accessibility

The table shows that there are twenty-two airports with scheduled flights to overseas destinations. The map is produced from a computerized analysis which first 'weights' each airport by the number of overseas flights per month (a number which varies from six for Plymouth to over 3,300 for Heathrow). The analysis then considers each part of the country in turn, and divides each airport's number of flights by its distance from the district under examination. The overall level of accessibility of that district, then, is the sum of these values for all the twenty-two airports.

International accessibility and the regions

	Airports (no.)	Flights* (% of GB)	Seaports (no.)	Sea freight* (% of GB)
Scotland	3	5.3	9	6.4
Wales	1	0.9	10	10.0
North England	2	1.7	7	10.4
Yorks. and Humb.	2	1.5	6	17.4
North West	2	8.6	4	6.4
West Midlands	1	5.2	0	0.0
East Midlands	1	0.8	2	1.1
East Anglia	1	0.4	5	13.1
South West	3	1.6	7	3.9
South East	6	74.0	13	31.4

* See text and notes for definitions.

The map shows these accessibility values in terms of a 'surface'—a set of contours. The highest value is in the south-west of London, on the Gatwick side of Heathrow. The contours show how dramatically the generalized level of access to international airports declines beyond south-east England. There is a small local 'peak' centred on Manchester airport, but otherwise the surface continues to decline with distance from London, showing only a slight levelling off near to those regional airports (such as those in central Scotland) which have numerous international flights.

Sea and air

The table confirms the dominance of south-east England for air transport, with almost three-quarters of overseas flights using one of the region's six international airports. In contrast, less than a third of international sea freight (excluding petrochemicals) uses the South East's ports. The main reason is probably that sea freight concentrates on bulk products so it is far more likely to be sent via the nearest port. In contrast, the mobility of air passengers means that it is viable for most services to be provided from one of London's 'hub' airports, because people will travel across Britain to make the connection.

The table's high value for East Anglia is partly due to Felixstowe's role as the main port for European trade for the industrial West Midlands—a region with no coastline and so no ports of its own. The importance of trade with Europe is underlined by Britain's busiest port areas now being the Haven ports (including Felixstowe), the Humber ports (e.g. Immingham and Hull), London, the Tees ports, and Dover. Liverpool and the Clyde have suffered from the declining Atlantic and 'Empire' trade flows, while the Welsh ports' values in the table are kept high by the volume of traffic generated by the steel industry.

The widespread provision of port facilities around Britain's coast means that few areas' firms suffer from difficulties of importing and exporting goods. There are also many airports, so there are also relatively few problems of accessibility for the high-value freight which goes by air. However, the map and table show that the provision of international air-passenger services is very much concentrated on London's airports. Recent developments have reinforced this favoured position, because London gained a new airport in the Docklands at the same time as the region was being provided with the Channel Tunnel as an alternative facility for international travel. Whilst it is inevitable that northern and western regions are always likely to be disadvantaged by their 'peripherality' from the European mainland, it is widely acknowledged that problems of remoteness will be much less severe in their impact where the regional centre is strongly linked into the international air-transport networks which, in turn, means being 'on the map' for key decision-makers in multinational firms and international organizations.

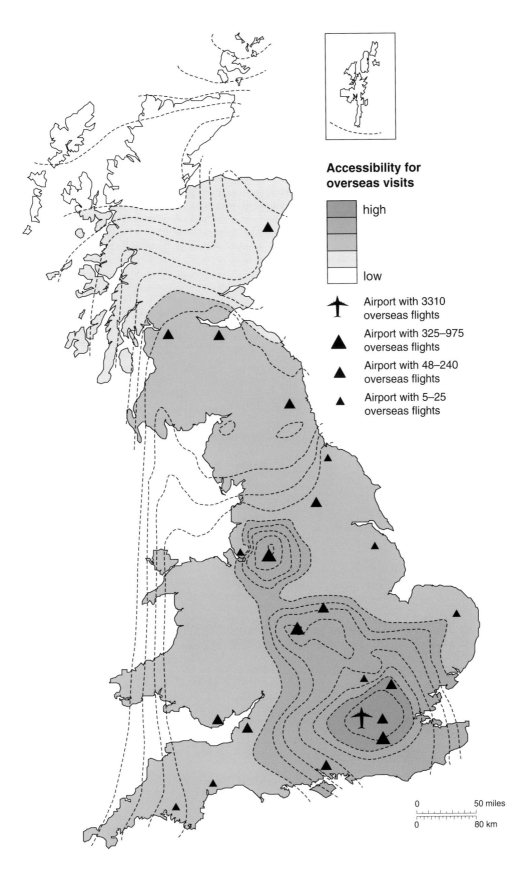

Accessibility for overseas visits

high

low

✈ Airport with 3310 overseas flights

▲ Airport with 325–975 overseas flights

▲ Airport with 48–240 overseas flights

▲ Airport with 5–25 overseas flights

0   50 miles

0   80 km

Places to visit

The number of museums, 'heritage' features, and other attractions has grown consistently over recent years. Some of these sites aim to attract tourists rather than local visitors, but all are having to compete increasingly intensely for visitor numbers which have remained at a fairly stable level. One result is that some attractions bring in visitors over a long distance, whilst many less spectacular sites struggle to attract even the local population. The table shows the towns and cities which have thus become 'honeypots' for visitors, alongside those areas with few popular attractions (which can therefore be assumed to be providing a large proportion of the trip-makers to the country's top places to visit).

It is impossible to measure fully the numbers of leisure visits and outings—because these can extend from a drive in the country to a day in a sports centre. The most comprehensive source of information is the British Tourist Authority survey of sites which can count or estimate the numbers of visitors each year. Open areas are inevitably excluded (e.g. attractive landscapes, such as the Lake District, or beaches), although there *is* information on the numbers attracted to some visitor centres, for example in certain National Parks.

This dataset provides visitor numbers to at least one such attraction in every area shown on the map (the 'places' which have been defined for this atlas—see the note to *Ethnicity and opportunity*). Summing the numbers of visitors to all the attractions in an area gives an indication of its overall attractiveness, and this can be divided by that place's population to produce the ratio value shown on the map and illustrated in the table.

These ratio values can be interpreted by bearing in mind that, on average, people made around five trips each in 1991 to attractions covered by this dataset. Surveys suggest that the variation between areas in the numbers of trips made by people is not great, so an area showing a much higher value is likely to be attracting these 'extra' visitors from other areas. For example, the ratio value for London as a whole is not *very* much above the national average, despite the capital's concentration of major attractions. However, the inset map shows how strongly visits are clustered in the central boroughs—in fact some boroughs have no measured attractions whatsoever. These adjacent high and low ratio values are thus produced by people travelling to visit attractions in nearby areas.

The table shows the fifteen highest and the fifteen lowest values for places on this ratio measure of visitors per resident. The top three places are long-familiar holiday destinations, and several similar areas are also included a little lower down in the top part of the ranking. However, the next three places are cathedral cities, closely followed by areas covering the castles of Caernarvon and Stirling. The mix of main attractions continues down the list, because the vast majority of visitors to the Motherwell area were counted at Britain's busiest Country Park. Next come South Lakeland and Inverness, whose attractions have been developed in response to the flows of visitors to their scenic landscape. Clearly, these are all areas which attract visitors from some distance, on day trips or for breaks and holidays.

Places with highest/lowest numbers of leisure visitors per resident

Highest		Lowest	
Gt. Yarmouth	36.99	Wycombe and Chiltern	0.85
Isle of Wight	32.40	Wrexham and Oswestry	0.81
Blackpool	28.68	Warrington	0.75
York	28.61	Oldham	0.71
Canterbury	24.84	Chesterfield	0.70
Chester	22.16	Wolverhampton	0.62
Bangor and Anglesey	18.59	Hemel Hempstead	0.57
Motherwell and Hamilton	18.53	Rossendale	0.53
Stirling	18.15	Milton Keynes	0.42
South Lakeland	17.68	Falkirk	0.35
Inverness	17.43	St. Helens	0.31
Eastbourne	17.35	Pontypridd and Rhondda	0.25
Lancaster and Morecambe	16.74	Rugby	0.25
Truro and Penzance	16.66	Accrington	0.24
Torbay	16.47	Watford	0.21

The right-hand side of the table shows the places with the lowest values, which will be providing a fair number of the visitors to the highest ranked areas. These areas are not scattered across the country but are concentrated on the edge of the main conurbations of the North West, West Midlands, and South East. Slightly fewer trips per person may be made by the residents of a town like St. Helens due to their lower average incomes, but they will also provide many of the visitors to the nearby attractions. These areas' history of rapid growth in late Victorian times—and the similar growth surge in the period of post-war affluence which was experienced by the low-valued places near London such as Watford—seems to have left them with few attractions for their modern residents to visit locally.

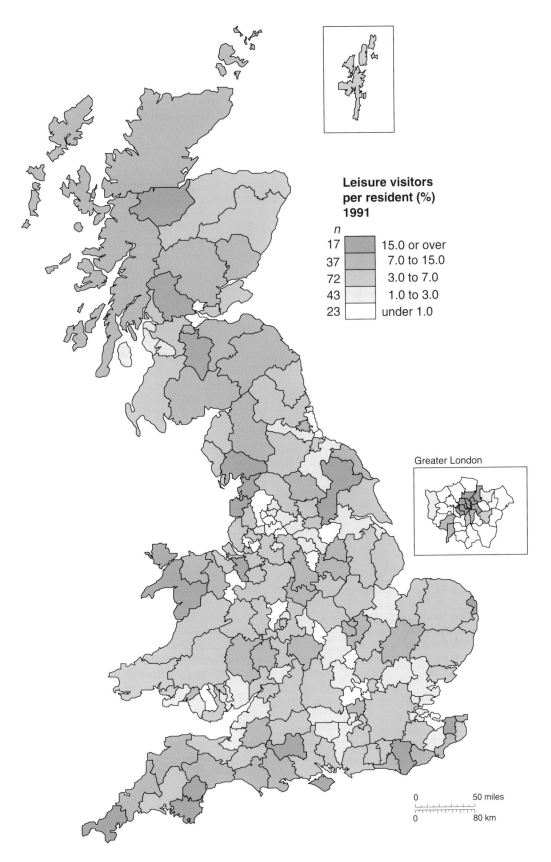

Leisure visitors
per resident (%)
1991

n		
17		15.0 or over
37		7.0 to 15.0
72		3.0 to 7.0
43		1.0 to 3.0
23		under 1.0

Greater London

0   50 miles

0   80 km

Major tourist attractions

Tourism is now one of Britain's major industries. The decline of traditional seaside holidays—and the flow of holiday-makers to warmer and more exotic locations—has been accompanied by a growth in day trips and short breaks. One consequence has been increasing numbers of visitors to a variety of tourist attractions, most of which are located away from traditional seaside resorts.

The map shows the distribution of major tourist attractions, categorized within six broad categories (e.g. museums and galleries). The information is derived from a survey of visitor numbers, so any attraction which cannot provide an annual count, or even an estimate, is excluded. The major problem category here covers outdoor attractions, such as 'honey-pot' sites in National Parks, so country parks have also been excluded for consistency. Conspicuous among these is Strathclyde Country Park near Glasgow, which reported over 4 million visitors in 1991.

Scotland in fact provides a dramatic example of the point which the map brings to the fore. Large cities now house a large share of the most visited attractions: the only exception north of the Border is in fact only just north of the Border because it is the Old Blacksmith's at Gretna Green. There is a notable contrast between Scotland and Wales on the map. Wales has just two attractions shown and these are both amusement park complexes in small seaside resorts, whereas Scotland's major attractions are in Edinburgh and Glasgow and are mainly museums or galleries.

Tourism and cities

Clearly, it is easier to attract many visitors if the attraction is in or near a city containing many people who will be looking for places to visit. Different cities have benefited to very different degrees, with some large centres like Sheffield and Bristol including no major attractions. However, tourism has been very actively developed by cities like Bradford and Liverpool—confounding the doubts which their initial efforts prompted, and going on to attract so many visitors that many other cities are now trying to follow their example.

Interest in 'heritage' features such as historic buildings has grown steadily, while the presentation of artefacts and information in museums has been transformed to attract very many more visitors. York has become a major centre for this type of attraction, complementing its Minster with the Jorvik Centre

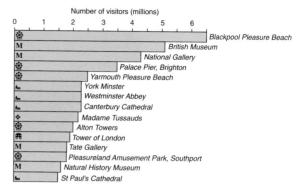

'state-of-the-art' presentation of the city's Viking past. York and Bradford have also gained branches of the National Science Museum—the Railway and the Photography, Film, and Television Museums respectively. Plans for other 'branch plants' of national collections are only restrained by the funding needed, because there are many provincial cities which are eager to develop these attractions, and most national museums and galleries can display only a small portion of their collections at their London sites at any one time. The map shows that from London to Glasgow the museum category is the most common feature in large cities.

The diagram shows the fifteen attractions which had the most visitors in 1991. Blackpool Pleasure Beach leads the way, but there are five more attractions from the 'theme park' category in this elite list. Taken together with Madame Tussauds, nearly half of the top fifteen are thus private-sector attractions. Of the other eight top attractions, half belong to the Church of England and the others are run by government agencies. There is no simple relationship between the numbers of visitors attracted and the question of whether there is a charge for admission—although the apparently surprising fact that free admission sites do not dominate the list of top attractions is partly due to many free tourist attractions not counting their visitor numbers. For example, it is not known how many people go to look at Big Ben or Buckingham Palace (from the outside), or go for a walk on the Malvern Hills or Chester's city walls.

The important role which museums and galleries play for cities is illustrated by the fact that all the museums and galleries in the diagram are in London, whereas half of the most visited cathedrals are outside the capital—and all the busiest theme parks are in rural or seaside locations.

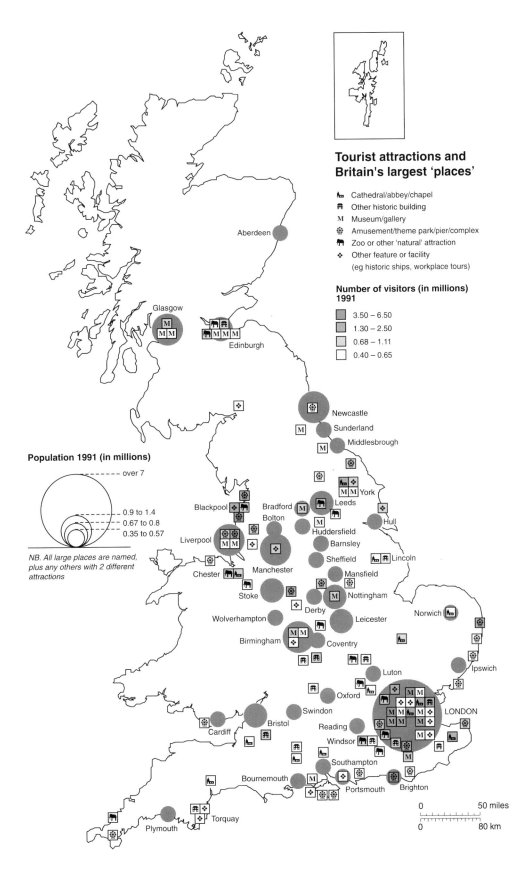

Tourist attractions and Britain's largest 'places'

🏛 Cathedral/abbey/chapel
🏛 Other historic building
M Museum/gallery
❀ Amusement/theme park/pier/complex
🐘 Zoo or other 'natural' attraction
❖ Other feature or facility
(eg historic ships, workplace tours)

Number of visitors (in millions) 1991

▨	3.50 – 6.50
▨	1.30 – 2.50
▢	0.68 – 1.11
▢	0.40 – 0.65

Population 1991 (in millions)

- – – over 7
- – – 0.9 to 1.4
- – – 0.67 to 0.8
- – – 0.35 to 0.57

NB. All large places are named, plus any others with 2 different attractions

Aberdeen

Glasgow

Edinburgh

Newcastle
Sunderland
Middlesbrough

York
Leeds
Hull
Bradford
Bolton
Blackpool
Huddersfield
Liverpool
Barnsley
Sheffield
Chester
Mansfield
Manchester
Nottingham
Stoke
Derby
Wolverhampton
Leicester
Norwich
Birmingham
Coventry
Luton
Ipswich
Oxford
Swindon
LONDON
Cardiff
Bristol
Reading
Windsor
Southampton
Bournemouth
Portsmouth
Brighton
Torquay
Plymouth

0   50 miles
0   80 km

Information cities

Cities are the major centres for the collection and distribution of information. Historically, information was the preserve of a privileged minority. For example, a medieval city's cathedral would include among its clergy the majority of those who could read. Nowadays access to information is widespread, but cities remain as the key focal points in the various networks through which information is made available.

Postcodes and newspapers

The map shows the participation of various cities and towns in two forms of service information which have developed over a long period—newspapers and the postal system. Over the latter part of this century, postal services have been organized by postcodes. Towns not allocated their own postcode area felt that they were not 'on the map'—for example Grimsby was assigned 'DN' postcodes and resented this 'takeover' by Doncaster. The map also shows that Grimsby, unlike Doncaster, has retained a local evening newspaper. Evening papers can reflect and reinforce a distinct local economy and civic pride. It is very notable that in many parts of the country there is a pattern of towns and cities in which the evening paper publishing centres match 'one for one' the postcode area centres.

TV regions

The other information on the map is a set of boundaries which roughly divide up Britain between ITV Channel 3 regions. These regions overlap in many places—and major overlaps are hinted at on the map by showing a boundary passing through, rather than around, a city (e.g. Peterborough). In these cases, different viewers in the city were found to watch different Channel 3 regions.

The modern media often display *hierarchies* in their distribution in Britain. For example, below the ITV regions are the centres of local radio stations. Similarly, weekly newspapers are published in a much wider set of towns than those which support daily evening papers.

Metropolitan cities

The table shifts attention to the 'first eleven' cities of Britain. The first column suggests that a single-digit

Britain's 'first eleven' cities

	Single-digit postcode?	Four-digit STD code?	Regional ITV centre?
London	E N W	0171, 0181	LWT, Carlton
Birmingham	B	0121	—
Manchester	M	0161	Granada
Glasgow	G	0141	Scottish
Newcastle	—	0191	TyneTees
Liverpool	L	0151	—
Leeds	—	—	Yorkshire
Edinburgh	—	0131	—
Sheffield	S	—	—
Nottingham	—	—	Central
Bristol	—	—	HTV

postcode will be seen as 'more metropolitan' than a two-digit code. London's pre-eminence is witnessed by it housing three of these codes, with the next three cities (by size) each being the centre of one single-digit code area. There are only two other single-digit postcodes and these both appear among the 'first eleven' cities, Liverpool and Sheffield. An even clearer example of the influence of a city's size upon its role as an information centre is given by the second column in the table. This list of four-digit STD codes almost exactly matches the size ordering of cities. Interestingly, the 1994/5 code changes retained the distinction between these major cities and all others (which became the five-digit centres). In fact, the other four 'first eleven' cities, together with Britain's twelfth largest city (Leicester), were the subject of the only other major 1994/5 changes to STD codes.

The final column in the table echoes the map by documenting which cities are ITV regional-broadcasting centres. This is the one column in the table which is not exhaustive, in that there are other, smaller, cities which also have broadcasting centres (e.g. Carlisle is the centre of Border TV). The notable absentee in this list is Birmingham, which *had* been the centre for ATV but that company did not have its franchise renewed, being replaced by Central ITV which is based in Nottingham.

In detail then, the table shows that only a very few cities join London in possessing all three attributes of metropolitan status. In contrast, the map suggests that most larger cities and towns are both 'on the national network' as centres of postcode areas, and also locally significant as the homes of an evening newspaper.

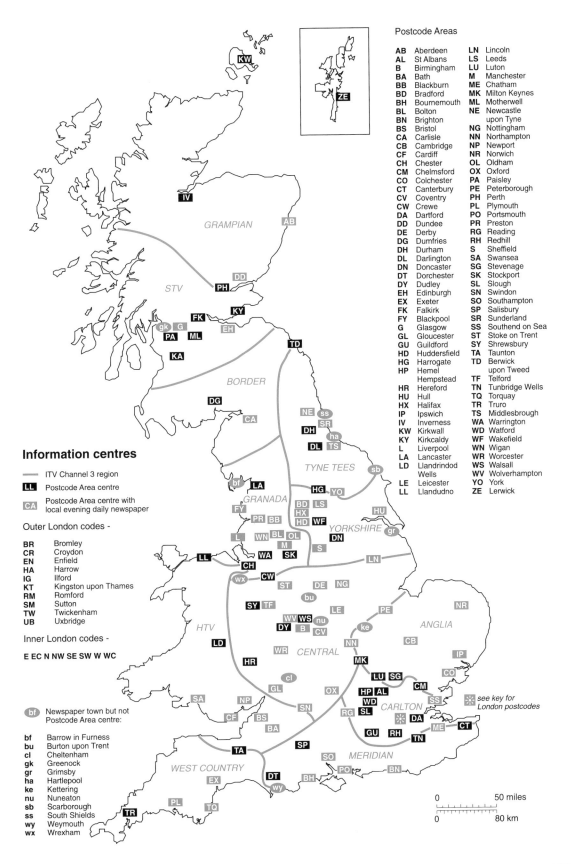

Postcode Areas

AB	Aberdeen	**LN**	Lincoln
AL	St Albans	**LS**	Leeds
B	Birmingham	**LU**	Luton
BA	Bath	**M**	Manchester
BB	Blackburn	**ME**	Chatham
BD	Bradford	**MK**	Milton Keynes
BH	Bournemouth	**ML**	Motherwell
BL	Bolton	**NE**	Newcastle
BN	Brighton		upon Tyne
BS	Bristol	**NG**	Nottingham
CA	Carlisle	**NN**	Northampton
CB	Cambridge	**NP**	Newport
CF	Cardiff	**NR**	Norwich
CH	Chester	**OL**	Oldham
CM	Chelmsford	**OX**	Oxford
CO	Colchester	**PA**	Paisley
CT	Canterbury	**PE**	Peterborough
CV	Coventry	**PH**	Perth
CW	Crewe	**PL**	Plymouth
DA	Dartford	**PO**	Portsmouth
DD	Dundee	**PR**	Preston
DE	Derby	**RG**	Reading
DG	Dumfries	**RH**	Redhill
DH	Durham	**S**	Sheffield
DL	Darlington	**SA**	Swansea
DN	Doncaster	**SG**	Stevenage
DT	Dorchester	**SK**	Stockport
DY	Dudley	**SL**	Slough
EH	Edinburgh	**SN**	Swindon
EX	Exeter	**SO**	Southampton
FK	Falkirk	**SP**	Salisbury
FY	Blackpool	**SR**	Sunderland
G	Glasgow	**SS**	Southend on Sea
GL	Gloucester	**ST**	Stoke on Trent
GU	Guildford	**SY**	Shrewsbury
HD	Huddersfield	**TA**	Taunton
HG	Harrogate	**TD**	Berwick
HP	Hemel		upon Tweed
	Hempstead	**TF**	Telford
HR	Hereford	**TN**	Tunbridge Wells
HU	Hull	**TQ**	Torquay
HX	Halifax	**TR**	Truro
IP	Ipswich	**TS**	Middlesbrough
IV	Inverness	**WA**	Warrington
KW	Kirkwall	**WD**	Watford
KY	Kirkcaldy	**WF**	Wakefield
L	Liverpool	**WN**	Wigan
LA	Lancaster	**WR**	Worcester
LD	Llandrindod	**WS**	Walsall
	Wells	**WV**	Wolverhampton
LE	Leicester	**YO**	York
LL	Llandudno	**ZE**	Lerwick

Information centres

— ITV Channel 3 region

LL Postcode Area centre

CA Postcode Area centre with local evening daily newspaper

Outer London codes –

BR Bromley
CR Croydon
EN Enfield
HA Harrow
IG Ilford
KT Kingston upon Thames
RM Romford
SM Sutton
TW Twickenham
UB Uxbridge

Inner London codes –

E EC N NW SE SW W WC

bf Newspaper town but not Postcode Area centre:

bf Barrow in Furness
bu Burton upon Trent
cl Cheltenham
gk Greenock
gr Grimsby
ha Hartlepool
ke Kettering
nu Nuneaton
sb Scarborough
ss South Shields
wy Weymouth
wx Wrexham

see key for London postcodes

0   50 miles
0   80 km

Sporting cities

The map highlights Britain's largest cities and towns—the 'places' which were introduced in *Ethnicity and opportunity*. The theme for the map is the distribution of 'major league' sports clubs. The four sports shown are those which operate leagues which aim to be national in coverage, and whose clubs can also expect attendances of several thousand people. The table begins to extend the number of sports considered.

Once 'major league' sports have been defined by attendance figures, as here, it's not surprising that larger towns and cities emerge as the main sporting centres. Football ('soccer') is by far Britain's major spectator sport; the map is restricted to showing clubs in the 1993/4 Premier Leagues (north and south of the Scottish Border) plus Division 1 of the Football League in England. Almost all the larger places are then represented, with most of the exceptions in southern England. A town such as Bournemouth has less of a 'football culture' than Dundee—a smaller city which has two well-established clubs.

Rugby Union in England is similarly dominated by clubs based in the larger cities, although this would not be obvious from a glance at the English league tables. The reason is that these big city clubs show their origins by being named after relatively affluent pre-war suburbs such as Richmond (London), Moseley (Birmingham), and Sale (Manchester). Newcastle Gosforth is so far the only such club which has added the wider city name to try to widen the club's appeal.

The exceptions to the cities' dominance are most evident on the map in Scotland and Wales. Each country has a 'heartland' cluster of Rugby Union clubs, in the smaller towns of the Borders (e.g. Kelso), and industrial south Wales (e.g. Pontypridd) respectively. A similarly distinctive history underlies the distribution of Rugby League clubs across the Pennines (where, in smaller towns like Castleford or Leigh, Rugby League was better able than football to survive financially on lower attendances).

The map shows that ice hockey is another sport which based many of its clubs where there was less competition from football. Several less spectator-orientated sports have thrived mainly in the smaller southern towns which have less of a football 'culture'—for example, the national league for field hockey features Slough and East Grinstead among its elite.

The table further stresses the cities' dominance for the major sports by focusing on just the very largest centres. Indeed, of the sixteen British football clubs

Britain's 'first eleven' cities as sporting centres

	'Major league'		European winner clubs	Test grounds	Other major-event venues (a selection of 'famous name' facilities)
	clubs	sports			
London	14	2	4	2	Wembley, Twickenham, Wimbledon, Crystal Palace
Birmingham	3	2	1	1	National Exhibition Centre
Glasgow	4	2	2	0	Hampden
Manchester	4	3	2	1	New stadium?
Newcastle	3	3	1	0	Gateshead
Liverpool	3	2	2	0	Aintree
Bristol	2	2	0	0	Badminton
Leeds	3	3	1	1	—
Nottingham	4	3	1	1	—
Edinburgh	9	3	0	0	Murrayfield
Sheffield	4	3	0	0	Crucible

which have won one of the three European football trophies, only Aberdeen and Ipswich are not from one of the nine biggest cities. This dominance of the big city clubs seems certain to increase with recent trends for the sport's income to be further concentrated in the more successful clubs. The table shows that even the very traditional sport of cricket has all the grounds for Test Matches—the only grounds which attract substantial attendances—in the biggest cities.

The final column mentions some other major venues, and so finally extends the analysis beyond those male team games which regularly attract the most paying spectators. Some of the very largest attendances are at single annual events, such as the Grand National at Aintree, the Badminton horse trials (near Bristol), or the British Grand Prix. The last of these is usually at Silverstone, which is near Northampton and so not near one of the largest cities. Of course, the largest audiences are on television, with snooker from Sheffield's Crucible providing a classic example: it is notable that many of these 'other' sports are for individual players, rather than teams.

Several new venues—such as Manchester's stadium for a future Olympiad or similar event—are largely justified as economic development schemes for those areas. In contrast, traditional local pride fuels the support, and hence the stadium redevelopment, at a football club like Middlesbrough. The footballers can truly 'represent' the town to both locals and people elsewhere—but the hosting of a major event (such as the recent World Student Games at Sheffield) may also offer the chance of bringing the city's name to national or international attention.

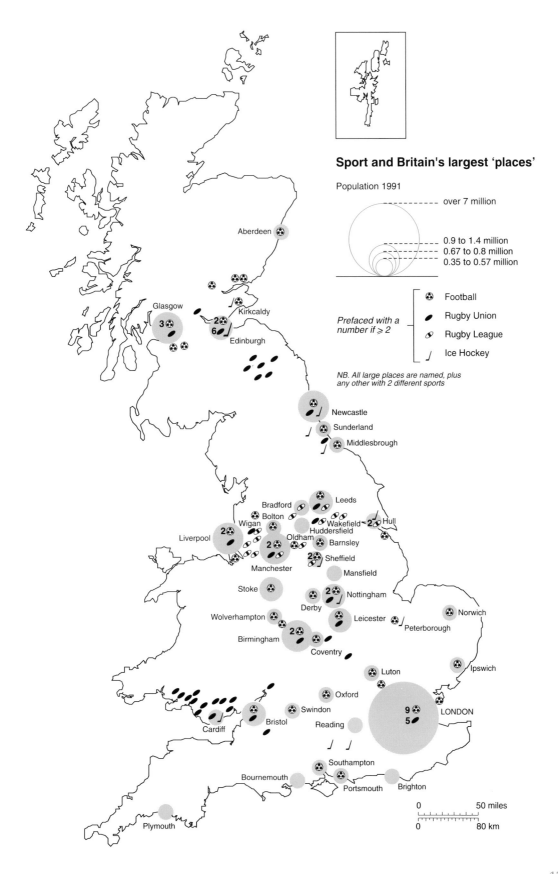

Sport and Britain's largest 'places'

Population 1991

- over 7 million
- 0.9 to 1.4 million
- 0.67 to 0.8 million
- 0.35 to 0.57 million

Prefaced with a number if ≥ 2

- Football
- Rugby Union
- Rugby League
- Ice Hockey

NB. All large places are named, plus any other with 2 different sports

Aberdeen

Glasgow

Kirkcaldy

Edinburgh

Newcastle
Sunderland
Middlesbrough

Bradford
Leeds
Bolton
Wigan
Wakefield
Hull
Liverpool
Huddersfield
Oldham
Barnsley
Manchester
Sheffield
Mansfield
Stoke
Nottingham
Derby
Wolverhampton
Leicester
Norwich
Birmingham
Peterborough
Coventry
Luton
Ipswich
Oxford
LONDON
Swindon
Bristol
Reading
Cardiff
Southampton
Bournemouth
Portsmouth
Brighton
Plymouth

| 0 | 50 miles |
| 0 | 80 km |

Voting

Voters' apathy

A general election, or even the threat of one, leads to unparalleled interest and speculation in newspapers and on television. The faces of Members of Parliament and issues surrounding the Palace of Westminster dominate the news in Britain most weeks. When people complain about issues such as the building of roads near their homes, the taxes they pay, or the lack of available work, they are invariably told that, if they are not happy with the state of the country, then they should vote for a change of government at the next general election. Given all this, it may seem surprising that one adult in four chooses not to vote at such elections. Why is this? Who is not voting?

Among the elections in the last decade, the proportion of the electorate not voting was highest in 1983 when, in fact, more people chose not to vote at all than voted for either of the two main opposition parties. One possible reason for this is that the outcome of the General Election of that year was quite predictable, the government being very strong in the aftermath of the Falklands War, so many people saw little reason to vote.

Geography of abstention

However, the level of abstentions varies far more over space than it does over time. The map opposite uses a population cartogram of the constituencies of Britain as its base. On the cartogram each constituency is drawn as a circle, positioned in an area equal to its electorate. The size and shade of the circles indicates the proportion of the electorate not voting in each constituency. A key to this map is given in Appendix 2. The map shows that people are most likely to abstain when they live near the centres of large cities.

All non-voters

More than 9 million people on the electoral register chose not to vote at the 1992 General Election. These were not the only people who did not vote. A further million potentially eligible people (i.e. aged over 18 and resident in the UK) could not have voted even if they wished to, because they had not registered to vote.

Part of the explanation for this state of affairs is believed to lie with the introduction of the Community Charge by the government in the late 1980s—a tax which was levied on virtually the same people as were eligible to vote, hence it becoming known as the 'Poll Tax'. One result of this tax was that increasing numbers of people stopped registering to vote, lest they were identified by the Community Charge officer. These numbers have now begun to reduce following the abolition of this tax in 1990.

Regional patterns of voting and non-voting

The bar graph shows how the proportions of adults who register and vote varies substantially between regions. Those not registered to vote were most likely to be living in London, whereas those on the register who chose not to vote were most numerous in the South Yorkshire Metropolitan County. The areas in the graph are arranged according to the popularity of the Conservative government at that General Election. Even in their strongest subregion (the South East outside London) only two out of five adults voted to support the incumbent party then— but they still won.

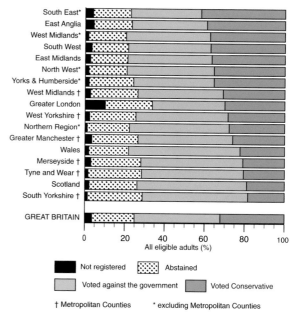

**Electorate not voting
1992 (%)**

over 35.00

28.00 to 35.00

21.00 to 28.00

18.00 to 21.00

7.00 to 18.00

*Circle radius in proportion to percentage
(on an equal population projection of
constituencies)*

Election results 1992

The map on the previous page showed the numbers of people that were registered in each area in 1992 and whether they chose to vote or not, using a population cartogram to give a fair impression of the geographical distribution of voting activity. Here we turn to look at the patterns of political support recorded by the votes cast.

Conservative and Labour constituencies

At the 1992 General Election the Conservative party managed to secure an overall majority of the 651 parliamentary constituencies (or 'seats') which existed at that time. On the cartogram opposite, the 336 seats which they won on the British mainland are those in the two shades of blue (there are also 17 seats in Northern Ireland which are not shown here). The dense southern concentration of support for this party of government is clear on the cartogram as the blue circles, which fill the Home Counties, form a ring around London.

The pattern for Labour is very much the mirror image of Conservative support. This main opposition party is strongest in the cities of the North, Wales, Scotland, and East London as indicated by the black circles on the map. The Labour party secured 271 seats at this General Election—55 short of a majority and thus a long way from victory.

Liberal Democrats and other parties

The reason for this large gap between the two main parties is that a number of smaller parties also contest general elections, most notably the Liberal Democrats. The constituencies which the latter won are coloured grey on the cartogram and also show distinct geographical clustering in the 'Celtic Fringe'. However it is misleading to see this small number of seats as a measure of support for the Liberal Democrats across Britain. In terms of the number of votes cast for this party they secured half of the support which Labour achieved, but won only 7% of Labour's number of seats.

The reason the Liberal Democrat party does so badly at general elections is that their support is very evenly spread across the country. The cartogram shows this by highlighting those seats in which they came second to the government candidate. A better way to visualize this is to use an 'electoral triangle' as

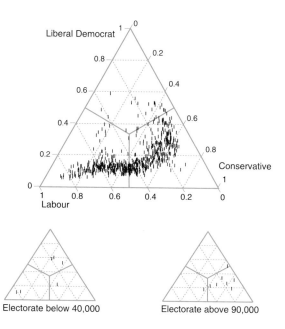

Electorate below 40,000   Electorate above 90,000

on this page. In this triangle each seat is drawn as a dash, positioned according to the share of the vote won by each of the three main parties. The sickle shape to the pattern of seats is a result of a recent upsurge in 'tactical voting' (where voters vote for the opposition party most likely to beat the government candidate in their area).

A number of other parties also contest general elections and win seats. Most important here are the various nationalist and loyalist parties of Northern Ireland which win all of that province's constituencies. On the British mainland, nationalist parties in Scotland and Wales won only seven seats at the last election (shown as white circles), but if the result of the next election is very close, then even these parties could make a difference to the formation of a new government.

Geography can be seen to play a key role in the politics of Britain through the divisive patterns of regional support for the various political parties. One final point worth remembering is that this geography is always changing, not just in the changing patterns of support from voters but also in changing patterns of seats. The next general election will not be fought on the same boundaries as in 1992. However, the overall pattern of support is unlikely to change radically.

Winner of seat in 1992 General Election

- ⬤ Conservative win, Liberal second
- ⬤ Conservative win, Labour second
- ⬤ Labour
- ⬤ Liberal Democrats
- ◯ Nationalists

Projecting voting patterns

It is tempting to try and project voting patterns into the future. Before doing so, however, it is useful to study recent patterns of British voting. For both these purposes, counties (and Scottish regions) are used as the units of analysis, instead of the constituencies shown in *Election results 1992*, for although the outcome of any general election will depend on majorities in constituencies rather than counties, mapping patterns at this level helps in identifying regional trends in voting behaviour. In particular, one should examine maps demonstrating which parties obtain the majority of votes in each county.

Voting in 1992 and trends since 1987

Map (a) shows the voting patterns for the 1992 General Election. All the counties in the south of England then had a majority of Conservative voters, as did most of the Midlands and some of those elsewhere in Britain. Areas in which Labour was in the majority in 1992 are concentrated primarily in the industrial Midlands and North, including all the metropolitan counties together with central Scotland, north-east England, and south Wales. Although the Conservative party may have won the 1992 Election, there are clear regional variations in the level of their support.

The patterns for the 1992 'runners-up' at county level are shown in map (b). In south-west and central southern England, Liberal Democrats obtained the second largest number of votes, whereas further east it was usually Labour following the Conservatives. Not only are there strong regional pockets of opposition-party voters, but there are also notable regional variations in the nature of the fight for power.

The changes in voting patterns since the 1987 Election are shown in the triangular diagram. The circles (1992 voting) generally lie closer to the Labour region of the triangle than the symbols for 1987, suggesting swings in voting trends towards Labour, although many of the points are still located in the Conservative-held part of the diagram. Although the Conservatives were in the majority in 1992, trends seem to have been moving away from this.

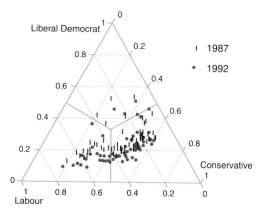

Forecasting the outcome of a future election

From this information on voting at the 1987 and 1992 General Elections, it is possible to produce forecasts of the outcome of a future election. Like all forms of prediction, this must be treated with some caution, and will depend heavily on any assumptions made about the behaviour of the electorate. Here it is assumed that the changes in voting seen between 1987 and 1992 in each county (in percentage terms) will occur again before the next election.

Applying this 'simple swing' model, and assuming the above trend continues until the next election, gives the prediction shown in map (c). Here the map illustrates the margin (as a percentage of all votes cast) by which the Conservatives beat the runner-up, in those counties where they hold a majority. The tightness of the majority in Greater London is notable. Also of note are the Conservative losses in various parts of the country under this model: Cornwall, Somerset, Isle of Wight, Cheshire, and Lancashire fall to the Liberal Democrats, while Humberside and Staffordshire become Labour. Map (d) shows the pattern projected for the Labour party under this model. See *Tactical voting and a future political map* for the results of a more sophisticated model.

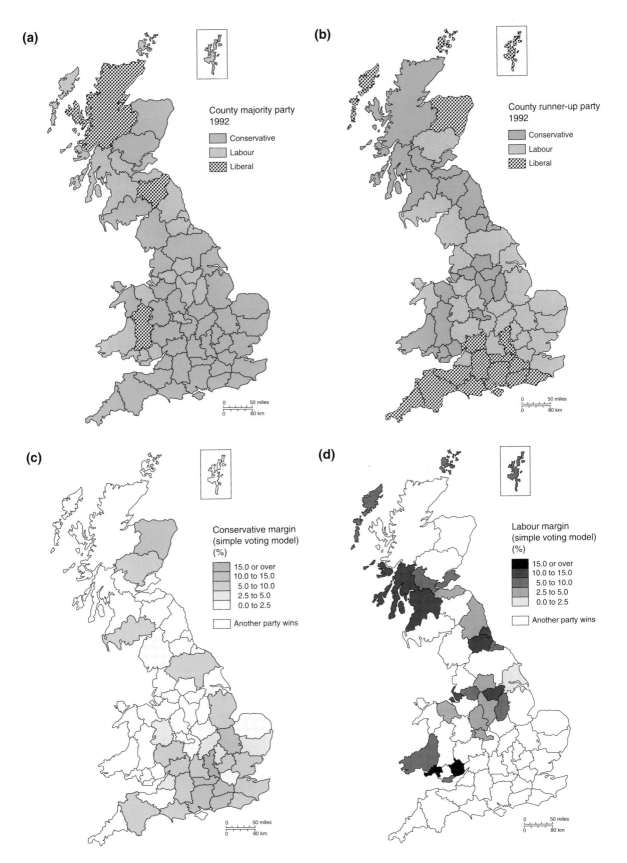

139

Tactical voting and a future political map

On the previous two pages, a simple model for *Projecting voting patterns* was illustrated, based on the repetition of swings observed between the 1987 and 1992 General Elections. However, this may not be a reasonable assumption. One important aspect of voting behaviour that this overlooks is that of tactical voting. If voters are reasonably aware of other people's voting intentions within their constituency, they may feel that their party has little chance of being elected and, in a three-party system, they may have a preference for one of the remaining two parties. By transferring their vote, a compromise may be reached whereby people vote for their second choice of party in order to block their least-favoured party.

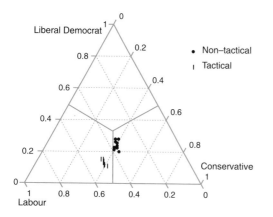

In the forecasts used to obtain the maps opposite, tactical voting against the Conservatives is considered. In counties where they are in the majority by a margin of 10% or less, half of those intending to vote for the least popular party decide to vote for the runner-up. For this model, tactical voting against the Labour party will not be modelled.

These 'tactical swings' are illustrated in the triangular diagram. The level of swing is similar in all cases, and causes the Conservative/Labour boundary to be crossed, so that the circles (based on a simple voting model) are marginal Conservative victories, whilst the dashes (tactical voting model) are Labour

victories. Map (a) shows the winning party in each county predicted on the basis of the tactical voting model, and map (b) shows the runner-up. Map (c) shows the Conservative margin in counties with a Conservative majority, and map (d) shows the same for Labour margins.

Under this tactical voting model, the Conservatives lose their narrow majority in Greater London. Also worth noting is the disappearance of the strong spatial trends in the runner-up, as seen in the 1992 voting analysis on the previous page. In the South West, a mixture of both Liberal Democrat and Labour counties have displaced the Conservatives, although this would have happened to some extent with the simple voting model.

Within the south-eastern core, it is seen from map (c) that many of the counties have a Conservative majority of less than 10%, although there is a stronghold 'core within a core' comprising Buckinghamshire, Berkshire, Hampshire, Surrey, and West Sussex where there is a margin of more than 10% between the Conservatives and the runner-up party, and Cambridge also remains Conservative. If the assumptions about marginal voters adopted in these forecasts were to underestimate the degree of swing (and tactical voting) against the Conservatives the south-eastern core could be reduced to just these counties.

Looking at the margins for the Labour party in map (d), it can be seen that the swing for Greater London due to tactical voting has been quite dramatic. From being a Conservative county (albeit with a very close margin), tactical voting could make it become one of the strongest Labour counties in Great Britain, alongside South Yorkshire, Gwent, and West Glamorgan.

Thus, if trends in voting continue in the way they did between the elections of 1987 and 1992, and if there is some degree of tactical voting, the political map of Britain could strongly challenge many preconceptions of the geography of British voting. In particular, as shown in map (d), the idea that the Labour party has all its strongholds in northern England could well be contradicted.

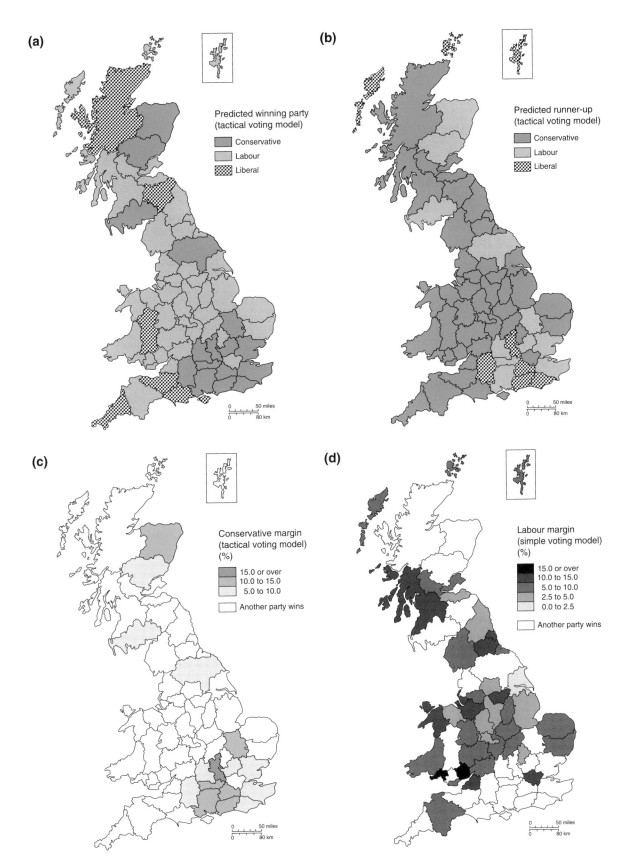

(a)

Predicted winning party
(tactical voting model)

- Conservative
- Labour
- Liberal

0   50 miles
0   80 km

(b)

Predicted runner-up
(tactical voting model)

- Conservative
- Labour
- Liberal

0   50 miles
0   80 km

(c)

Conservative margin
(tactical voting model)
(%)

- 15.0 or over
- 10.0 to 15.0
- 5.0 to 10.0

- Another party wins

0   50 miles
0   80 km

(d)

Labour margin
(simple voting model)
(%)

- 15.0 or over
- 10.0 to 15.0
- 5.0 to 10.0
- 2.5 to 5.0
- 0.0 to 2.5

- Another party wins

0   50 miles
0   80 km

141

Appendix 1: Technical notes

These notes should be read alongside the separate topics in the atlas. They provide information about the sources of the data presented in the maps, graphs, and tables, together with more technical details about how the measures have been derived. Where appropriate, potential weaknesses of the data source or method of calculation are also indicated.

People and places

Where people live: The population statistics for the county map and district-types table are the final versions of the 1991 estimates produced by OPCS and GRO(S), adjusted in the light of the 1991 Census results and subsequent checks. The district-level map of population-weighted densities uses census data because the method of calculation requires ward-level data (see below). The county-level map shows overall population density: population divided by area for each county and Scottish region. The district map shows population-weighted densities: for each district, the density of each census ward is calculated and multiplied by its total population, and the sum for the district is divided by the total population of the district, to give the mean ward density at which people in the district live.

The district types used in the table comprise a modified version of the classification used by OPCS for England and Wales, itself derived from the work of Richard Webber and John Craig, 'Which Local Authorities are Alike?', *Population Trends*, 5 (1976), 13–19. Extended to Scotland, it defines the area of the former Central Clydeside Conurbation as metropolitan, with Glasgow treated as a Principal City.

Patterns of population change: The population data is calculated from the official mid-year estimates produced by OPCS and GRO(S), adjusted for boundary changes. In map (b) the conventional measure of overall density is used: total population divided by total area at county level. In map (d) and the table the 'shift' is calculated by subtracting the 1971–81 rate of population change from the 1981–91 rate.

Births, deaths, and migration: The population data in the table, graph, and maps (a) and (b) is calculated from the official mid-year estimates, adjusted for boundary changes. The data for maps (c) and (d) is collected by the Registrar General, as published in *Regional Trends*, 27 (HMSO, 1992), ch. 14. The district classification is a modified version of the OPCS district typology (see note on *Where people live*).

People on the move: All material here is based on data yielded by the 1991 Census question on usual residence a year ago, as presented in the *National Migration* topic volumes, the *Small Area Statistics*, and the *Special Migration Statistics*.

The results should be interpreted with caution because the data is known to underestimate the number of residential moves made. This is because this source excludes people who emigrated from Britain, people who died after moving, children under 1 year old on Census night, people who moved away and then returned to their former address within the period, and any other intermediate moves made by people over the period, as well as a significant number of people who wrongly failed to answer this question on the Census form or did not get entered on to a Census form at all.

Map (a) is based on all resident migrants, irrespective of place of origin, including local moves and immigration from overseas, but the other exhibits relate only to migration taking place within Britain or to elements of this, as specified.

Migration between regions: The data is derived via the OPCS from the National Health Service Central Register and is based on re-registrations of doctors' patients that involve them in a change of Family Health Service Authority. In the graph showing net migration between North and South, the South is defined in terms of East Anglia, East Midlands, South East, and South West, with the North comprising the rest of Great Britain.

Age of newcomers: This is based on calculations from the *Local Base Statistics* of the 1991 Census. The Census identified 5.35 million people who had been living at a different address one year before Census night, accounting for 9.9% of Britain's total number of residents. The line on the graph shows how the proportion varies between five-year age groups, and the first row of the table shows this for four broader age groups. The remainder of the table gives the age composition of in-migrants to five selected counties and demonstrates how the relative importance of each age group can be compared between counties through subtracting the national proportions. It is these deviations that are presented in the map for all areas.

Age structure: The age 'pyramid' is based on the mid-1991 population estimate produced by the Registrar General. The four county maps and district-type table are based on the 1991 Census and should be treated with some caution because of the under-enumeration problem, which is believed to have been particularly severe for people aged 18–29, particularly males, and for people aged 85+ (though numerically this latter is a small element of the total population). For information about the district types, see the note on *Where people live*.

The elderly: The nation-level statistics mentioned in the commentary are based on mid-year estimates, but the rest of the analysis uses 1991 Census data and should be treated with caution (see the note on *Age structure*), though the patterns are so clear that the general conclusions must be valid. The analysis is based on 458 districts, with the City of London being excluded because of its small and highly distinctive population. In the bar graph the highest and lowest districts for each age group are named, and the median and interquartile range are identified by ranking all the districts and dividing them into four (approximately) equal groups.

An ageing population: The data for the table and graph is taken from the official mid-year estimates and 1992-based population projections for the UK. The four maps are based on data taken from the 1991 Census *County Monitors*, which provide in table E age breakdowns for both 1981 and 1991 on a consistent basis (1981 definition of residents, ignoring wholly absent households). Caution is, however, required in interpreting these results because of the under-enumeration problem in 1991: though the maps avoid the worst affected ages (18–29), the age groups shown here are not immune because there were problems with those aged under 1 and those aged 85 and over, and there is the indirect effect of the 'missing million' on the proportions calculated for 1991 (see the note on *Age structure*).

Multicultural Britain

Three nations: The data is derived from the 1991 Census. The questions on ability to speak Welsh and Gaelic were asked only of people enumerated in Wales and Scotland respectively. The historical data for the graph is taken from the relevant topic volumes: *Welsh Language, Wales*, table 1, and *Gaelic Language, Scotland*, table 2.

The information in the table should be interpreted as follows: County Durham has a higher proportion of England-born in its population than any other county in England, and Greater London the lowest; of all the Scottish regions, Borders has the highest proportion of England-born; and in Wales Clwyd is the county with the highest proportion of England-born. As regards the Scotland-born, in England these are most common in Northamptonshire; and so on.

Born overseas: The data relates to immigrants, in the strict sense of being born outside Great Britain, and is derived from answers to the 1991 Census question on birthplace. Care is needed in interpreting the information, as noted in the commentary. A further

example is that the numbers of those born in the New Commonwealth include children born there to British people in the colonial service, armed forces, etc. This aspect is explored further in the next topic.

Immigrants and non-whites: All the statistics are taken from the 1991 Census. The graph is drawn in such a way that the area of each section is proportional to the number of people in that age/birthplace category.

Ethnic-minority population growth: The data on numbers born in the New Commonwealth is taken from the respective Censuses. The national estimates of the non-white population for 1951–81 are those of the OPCS, published in *Population Trends*, 46 (1986), p. 18. The 1971 regional and subregional statistics for non-whites are purely estimates, in the sense that they are deemed to be equivalent to the number of people whose parents were both born in the New Commonwealth. The 1991 data on non-whites for all geographical scales is taken from the 1991 Census.

As regards the last point in the commentary, it can be seen that for the five bottom regions in the table the proportion of people born in the New Commonwealth in 1971 was higher than the estimate of the non-white population, which for that year refers to people with both parents born in the New Commonwealth, whereas for the top five regions the proportion was lower in every case. There are at least two possible explanations for this pattern. The bottom five regions may be home to more of the 'white settler' descendants who have moved to the UK, and they may contain more people of mixed ancestry, where only one parent was born in the New Commonwealth.

The ethnic-minority groups: All the statistics on ethnic-group populations are taken from the 1991 Census. The answers indicate 'self-ascribed' ethnicity, i.e. respondents allocate themselves to the group to which they feel that they belong, or write in their own answer which is subsequently coded by the Census authorities. The reliability of this data is affected by some non-response (which is treated as White) as well as by the problem of under-enumeration which is known to have been larger among non-whites.

Black and white Britain: All the statistics used here are taken from the 1991 Census.

Ethnicity and the labour-market: All the data used here is taken from the 1991 Census, drawing from the section which refers to 'economic position' of residents aged 16 and over. Caution needs to be exercised in interpreting the maps for the three ethnic-minority groupings, because the rates in many areas (especially the more rural) are based on small numbers. Note that those who consider themselves as available for work and/or who are actively seeking a job are considered as 'economically active' and thus part of the labour-force — a definition which differs from the Employment Department's claimant-based count of unemployed persons.

Ethnicity and opportunity: Apart from the inset, which shows London boroughs individually, the map uses a set of areas which have been specially devised for this atlas (see the Key Map of 'places' in Appendix 2). They are based on the Local Labour Market Areas (LLMAs) which form part of the Functional Regionalisation created in CURDS (Centre for Urban and Regional Development Studies) see the paper by M.G. Coombes, J.S. Dixon, J.B. Goddard, S. Openshaw, and P.J. Taylor (1982), 'Functional Regions for the Population Census of Great Britain', in D.T. Herbert and R.J. Johnston (eds.), *Geography and the Urban Environment 5: Progress in Research and Applications* (Wiley, London). The areas used here are given the informal title of 'places' to reflect the fact that they are pseudo-LLMAs produced by grouping local authority districts (whereas accurately defined LLMAs are groupings of much smaller 'building block' areas such as wards). The 'best fit' of districts to LLMAs was guided by the requirement that the match between any LLMA and its corresponding pseudo-LLMA (i.e. 'place') should not be less than 70% of the population concerned. In other words, the population which is included *both* in the original LLMA boundary *and* in the (grouping of) district(s) which are to represent it must be *at least* 70% of the total LLMA population *and* of the (grouping of) district(s). The boundaries of a few individual LLMAs are so incompatible with the district boundaries in their area as to make it impossible to define a 'place' which can represent the LLMA to this degree of accuracy. In these cases, the LLMA has been combined with an adjacent one and then the 70% test is applied again to the (grouping of) district(s) which are now identified as the approximation to the *combined* LLMAs. This procedure continues until all districts are included within places which meet these statistical requirements.

The map presents data from the 1991 Census *Local Base Statistics*, using the same definitions of 'non-white' and 'unemployed' as elsewhere in this atlas. The data for the diagram, on the other hand, is derived from the Labour Force Survey (via tabulations which appear in *Employment Gazette*). A point to bear in mind when considering the diagram and the map is that there has been no 'standardization' for the possible influence on non-white unemployment levels of these groups including higher proportions of the unskilled, of young people, and of males—all categories of the labour-force who tend to have higher unemployment rates *whatever* their ethnic group.

Ethnicity and unemployment: See note on *Ethnicity and the labour-market*. The figures for unemployment

include those who are 'on a Government Scheme'. Unemployment rate is expressed as a percentage of the labour-force, i.e. all those who are in work or seeking a job. Full-time and part-time employment refers to those who work for others, the latter being termed as 'self-employed'.

Education and employment

Men without work: Data from the 1991 Census is used for both the map and the graph. Apart from the London boroughs in the map's inset, the areas used are 'places' (see *Ethnicity and opportunity* notes). In the graph, the 'South' refers to the standard regions of South West, East Anglia and South East (which includes London). The analysis of unemployment needs to be put in a wider context, which includes related categories of people such as the prematurely retired. The following table is from the Labour Force Survey (as reported annually in *Employment Gazette*):

Economic activity of those aged over 15 in 1994 (million)

Employed:		
Full-time	16.1	(0.7 in temporary jobs)
Part-time	5.4	(0.7 in temporary jobs)
Self-employed:		
Full-time	2.6	
Part-time	0.6	
TOTAL IN PAID WORK	24.7	(1.2 with a second job)
Unpaid family workers	0.2	
On Government Schemes	0.3	
TOTAL OCCUPIED	25.2	
Seeking work	2.7	(0.9 not on unemployment benefit)
Others wanting work	2.3	(0.5 long-term sick/disabled)
Economically inactive (e.g. retired)	14.1	
TOTAL PERSONS AGED OVER 15	44.3	

Lacking skills and jobs: The 1991 Census data used here is limited to the manual socio-economic groups covering agricultural, semi-skilled and unskilled workers. The data is analysed for individual London boroughs, and also for the 'places' which were defined in the Notes to *Ethnicity and opportunity*. In the graph, 'northern England' includes not only the three northernmost standard regions but also the East and West Midlands. 'Northern metropolitan areas' are those places which lie within the metropolitan counties of those regions.

Young people and work: All the figures are calculated from the 1991 Census, specifically *Local Base Statistics*, table 37 on young adults. The labour-force comprises the employed, the unemployed, and those on a Government Scheme, with everyone else being treated as '(economically) inactive'. The 'unemployment rate' refers to the proportion of the labour-force that is unemployed or on a Government Scheme.

Staying on at school: Both the diagram and the map here draw on information from the 1991 Population Census, with the diagram also using 1981 data. The 'units of analysis' throughout are the 'places' which were described in the *Ethnicity and opportunity* notes. In addition, data is presented on individual London boroughs (all of which have been separate education authorities since the abolition of the Inner London Education Authority). In the graph, the places are grouped into three broad regional categories, with the two Midland standard regions joining Wales in a single swathe which thereby also demarcates the north and south groups either side of its borders. The graph is based on a simple two-way division of 1981 rates, so that places where over 55% were staying on at school are represented in the upper half of the graph. The measurement used for the figure is the percentage of places in each region (so that each column sums to 100%). The measure of change here is the percentage point increase—that is, the number of percentage points by which the percentage staying on in education in 1991 was higher than the 1981 per cent rate.

Exam results and qualifications: The data for the map comes from *Regional Trends*, 28 (1993), table 14.2. The graph is based on data in *Social Trends*, 25 (1995), ch. 3, and information on 1951 comes from the 1951 Census reports.

Going to school: The data for the table and diagram comes from *Social Trends*, 25 (1995), tables 3.2 and 3.3, and for the maps is from *Regional Trends*, 29 (1994), table 14.2. The data for Scottish regions in map (a) refers to local authority provision only. In map (b) the percentages are calculated with reference to the total number of 3- and 4-year-olds.

New and old universities: The academic staff numbers are full-time equivalent values (i.e. two part-timers are counted as equal to one full-timer) and are from the 1991–2 data provided by the Higher Education Funding Council for England (Analytical Services Division). The 'enumeration' issue which is set out in the text—for example, the decision whether London University is a single institution or is only a loose liaison of colleges which should be treated here as individual units—not only affects the size of the symbols shown but also their distribution (e.g. the single Durham University symbol could have been split to show its new separate college in Stockton-on-Tees). The principle applied here is that there is a separate symbol for each institution which possesses a separate charter—and it is the charters which are used to date the universities' foundation. The map uses county (and Scottish region) boundaries for its background.

Matching ability to responsibility: This analysis is concerned with a labour-market 'matching' process and so it is appropriate to use 'places' (see notes to *Ethnicity and opportunity*) as its analytical units. However, individual London boroughs are shown too, by way of comparison. In the graph, the places are grouped in the same way as in the parallel graph on *Lacking skills and jobs* (see notes to that topic). The graph presents percentages for which the denominator is the economically active population below pensionable age who have degrees or equivalent qualifications: the values which were calculated were percentages of these well-qualified people who are unemployed or on government training schemes. The map is based on a different analysis which uses as its numerator an extended version of the graph's denominator (having added in the well-qualified who are *not* economically active, because they are part of the *potential* labour-force of the area): this wider measure is then divided by the size of the (semi-)professional/managerial work-force.

Projecting future employment patterns: The employment data for 1991 comes from the Census of Employment via NOMIS at the University of Durham. The national projections of sectoral change come from *Review of the Economy and Employment*, i: *Occupational Assessment* (1992) (University of Warwick: Institute for Employment Research).

Contrasting employment sectors: Sources are the same as for *Projecting future employment patterns*. The definition of 'production sector' which is used here focuses on core industries—including those facing the most rapid job loss—but excluding the Other manufacturing and Construction industries.

Life chances

New enterprise: The opening paragraph and the graph use information from the seasonally adjusted time-series on levels of employment which are tabulated within the 1980 Standard Industrial Classification (in the September 1995 edition of *Employment Gazette* and, for the earlier years' data, in the *Historical Supplement 4* to the October 1994 edition). The graph reports on Britain as a whole, whereas the map presents district-level data which has been grouped (apart from in the inset where London boroughs are shown individually) to the 'places' which—as explained in the notes to *Ethnicity and opportunity*—approximate to the local labour-market areas which are the most appropriate units for this analysis. Socio-economic group data from the 1991 Census provides the denominator for the analysis, while the numerator is the count of firms newly registering for VAT and, as such, comes from the VAT dataset which is made available by the

NOMIS computerized labour-market information system.

Wealth: The information on share ownership was made available for analysis by the NorthEast Regional Research Laboratory (NE.RRL) by International Communications and Data Ltd. Despite the dearth of official statistics against which to check it, it appears to provide a reasonable estimate of the distribution of share-ownership in Britain. The Gini Curve is prepared by adding the values for districts in cumulative fashion, starting with the country's poorest district.

Social class: The data is from the 1991 Census *Local Base Statistics*, table 90 (for heads of households) and table 91 (for men and women). The percentages are calculated by reference to the total number allocated a social class, with the denominator excluding members of the Armed Forces, those on a Government Scheme, and the 'inadequately described', as well as the retired and others not in the labour-force.

Waged and unwaged: This map shows, in the inset, individual London boroughs and, elsewhere, the 'places' which have been devised for sections in this atlas dealing with local socio-economic patterns (see the notes to *Ethnicity and opportunity*). The data is taken from the 1991 Census and is analysed in the way described in the text. The diagram, on the other hand, drew upon *Regional Trends 28* for Eurostat Labour Force Survey 1990 measures.

Growing up in poverty: This map follows on the previous one by using 'places' as its areas of analysis (apart from the separate London boroughs in the inset). All the data here is taken from the 1991 Census, with the diagram being derived from an analysis of the new SAR (Sample of Anonymised Records) dataset. The forms of analysis used are described below, or in the text. Incidentally, the fact that few one-parent households are deemed to be overcrowded is largely because the SAR data can only support a simple measure of overcrowding which will tend to 'count against' households with only one adult in the main bedroom.

To produce the diagram, a sample of individual Census records has been analysed in a new way. Every child (aged under 16) in the sample is 'scored' according to whether their household has any of three problems—no earner, no car, or being overcrowded. The diagram shows the percentage of all children who fall into each of the eight categories which are produced by cross-classifying these three binary (i.e. 0/1) measures. It can be seen, then, that two-thirds (67%) of children live in households with none of these problems. Nearly a fifth (8% + 6% + 5%) have a single problem, of which the most common is not having a car. Because the values in the diagram are all distinct 'shares' of the national total,

they can be added together in different way to answer different questions. For example, adding all the shaded cells shows that only 11% of Britain's children live in overcrowded conditions.

Finally, the diagram is designed to draw attention to the number of problems faced by children: the highest cell shows that just 2% of children faced all three problems simultaneously, but the three cells immediately below this (2% + 9% + 1%) show that around one in eight of all children are faced with two of the three problems. The two 'at risk' groups (which will *both* include those ethnic minority children who live with a single parent) are analysed in the same way as all children were in the upper part of the diagram. The results show that both risk factors are associated with higher levels of deprivation. It is noteworthy that the rather basic method of calculating overcrowding which has to be used here (due to the way the data is coded) means that few lone-parent households are likely to be deemed to be overcrowded.

Born outside marriage: The information for the table and graph is taken from OPCS's *Birth Statistics, series FM1*, no. 21 (1992). The data for the map comes from *Regional Trends*, 29 (1994), table 14.1. 'Births' refers to live births only. For background reading on demographic developments, see: J. McLoughlin (1991) *The Demographic Revolution* (Faber & Faber, London), and D.J. van de Kaa (1991), 'Europe's Second Demographic Transition', *Population Bulletin*, 42, 1–57.

Who lives with whom: The information for the table and graph comes from the *General Household Survey*, and the maps are calculated from the 1991 Census *Local Base Statistics*, table 22 (for number of persons in household) and table 40 (for 'lone-parent' households). Note that in the 1991 Census a 'lone-parent' household refers to a household comprising one adult aged 16 and over and one or more persons aged 0–15.

Limiting long-term illness: The data comes from the 1991 Census, specifically tables 12 and 13 of the *Local Base Statistics*. Note that the Census requires the form-filler to be the judge of the severity of an ailment rather than this deriving from any kind of assessment. The background to the district typology is given in the notes for the first topic *Where people live*.

Who the ill are: The maps and the table are prepared from 1991 Census data: see the note on *Limiting long-term illness*. The graph showing 'limiting long-standing illness' is based on data from the *General Household Survey*, which appears to have a broader definition of illness than the 1991 Census.

Death chances: Standardized mortality ratios (SMRs) are such a commonly used statistic that it is well worth knowing how they are constructed. The first step is to calculate national mortality rates for groups of people subdivided by age and sex. Thus you might have a national mortality rate of 10% for women aged over 85 (if one in ten died a year). In this example the nation is Britain, but a much larger population could be used such as that of Europe. The second step is to take these national rates and multiply them by the number of people living in a small area to calculate the number of people you would expect to die there in a year if the local mortality rates were equal to the national rates. The final step is to take this expected figure away from the actual observed number of deaths in that area to see how many more or less deaths occurred there than might be expected (given people's ages and sexes). This figure is then divided by the expected number of deaths to standardize it and multiplied by 100 to produce an SMR. Thus an SMR of 100 is normal, an SMR of 120 implies that an additional 20 people died for every 100 you would have expected to die and so on. This is also known as the 'indirect' method of standardization.

The data on standardized mortality ratios by district is published by OPCS in *Regional Trends*. It applies to all deaths in the year to 31 December 1991. Note, however, that standardized mortality ratios are not necessarily an ideal measure of people's chance of dying; for instance, see N.E. Breslow and N.E. Day (1987), *Statistical Methods in Cancer Research,* ii: *The Design and Analysis of Cohort Studies* (Lyon: International Agency for Research on Cancer).

Offenders and crimes: All the statistics are derived from *Home Office Official Crime Statistics for England and Wales* (HMSO, 1992).

Housing

Overcrowding and underoccupancy: All the statistics are derived from the 1991 Census *Local Base Statistics*, mostly from table 22 on rooms and household size but with density of occupancy (persons per room) from table 23. Note that the room count covers the main living-rooms including bedrooms, but excludes small kitchens, bathrooms, toilets, etc. For 1991 the definition was standardized across the whole of Great Britain, having previously been different in Scotland from the rest of the country. In this analysis, overcrowding is taken to be where there are more than 1.0 persons per room.

Amenities and gadgets: The regional data in the table is taken from *Regional Trends*, 29 (1994), table 8.13. The information for the maps and graph is derived from the 1991 Census *Local Base Statistics*, table 20 and, for the comparable 1971 position on amenities, from the 1971 Census *Small Area Statistics*, table 18.

The 1991 Census was the first to ask about central heating.

Vacant and vacation housing: All the information is derived from the 1991 Census *Local Base Statistics*, table 54. Vacation housing is all accommodation not used as a main residence, except for vacant housing and household spaces defined as 'student accommodation'. 'Second homes' refers to household spaces identified as 'second residences' by Census enumerators, together with owner-occupied household spaces where persons were present but no residents. 'Holiday accommodation' is what is normally called 'holiday lets', including rented household spaces where there were people present on Census night for whom this was not their usual address.

Second homes and holiday lets: see the comments on vacation housing in the note on *Vacant and vacation housing*. See the note on *Where people live* for background to the district typology.

Semi-detached Britain?: The table is derived from information collected by the English House Condition Survey, 1991. The maps and graph are prepared from 1991 Census *Local Base Statistics*, table 56 on household space type in permanent buildings. Note that there are some differences between the two sources in the classification of housing types, as well as the fact that the former source relates to England only.

Housing Choice: Apart from the individual London boroughs which are shown in the map's inset, the analysis here is presented for 'places'—the areas devised by selectively grouping districts until they approximate local labour-market areas (see the notes to *Ethnicity and opportunity*). The basic data is provided by the 1991 Census and is a classification of all dwellings by building type and tenure. Privately rented dwellings are not subdivided by type here because this tenure category covers only a small proportion of the total. The most common tenure is now owner-occupation so these dwellings are divided into four categories: detached houses, semi-detached, terraced, and other (largely flats). There are few detached houses in the public sector (i.e. rented from a local authority or a housing association) so they are grouped into the same category as semi-detached here. The proportion (i.e. from 0.0 to 1.0) of dwellings in each 'place' which fall within each category is first calculated, and then a 'monopoly index' is computed by squaring each separate proportion, and then summing these. Finally this index value is multiplied by 100 to give it the form of a percentage, which is subtracted from 100.0 to reveal the 'diversity index' for each area.

Housing tenure: The data is from the 1991 Census *Local Base Statistics*, table 20 and the 1981 Census

Small Area Statistics, table 10, and refers to households in permanent buildings.

Buying and owning: See the note for *Housing tenure*.

House prices and negative equity: Both maps have been produced using unpublished data provided by the Nationwide Building Society. County-level statistics, published quarterly by the Halifax Building Society, have been used to update the series for the most recent years.

The future of private housing: source of original data is as for *House prices and negative equity*.

Access to facilities

Availability and use of cars: The information on distance travelled in the graph is taken from *Regional Trends*, 30 (1995), table 10.8. The map and table are prepared from the 1991 Census *Local Base Statistics*, table 21. The Census data includes vans where these are normally available for private use.

Change in numbers of cars: The data is calculated from the 1991 Census *Local Base Statistics*, table 21 and the 1981 Census *Small Area Statistics*, table 12. The calculated rates of change in total number of cars 1981–91 are only approximate because in both Censuses households with three or more cars are counted as having three cars.

Access to cars: See the note on *Change in numbers of cars* for the sources. The information in the graph is drawn from several different tables in the *Local Base Statistics*.

Leaving the car at home: The map presents data for 'places' (see the notes to *Ethnicity and opportunity*). The data is from the 1991 Census and shows, for each place, the percentage of non-homeworking employed residents in car-owning households who use public transport for (the main part of) their journey to work. Other statistics from the 1991 and 1981 Censuses are quoted in the text, along with one measure taken from the 1991 London Area Transport Survey—quoted in the London Research Centre's *Research News* (Sept. 1993).

Patterns of commuting: The map draws upon the ward-level *Special Workplace Statistics* of the 1991 Census. A line is drawn between the central points of each pair of wards which had a flow of at least fifteen in either direction (note: a single line is drawn even if there is such a flow in both directions). The dataset is a 10% sample, so each line represents a minimum of approximately 150 people commuting. The probability of any pair of wards having a flow of this size between them is greater in metropolitan areas because the wards there tend to contain larger populations and numbers of jobs. On the other hand, the workplaces of large cities are more likely to be scattered across a wide area—and hence many different wards—than they are in more rural areas. The data for the table is taken from the same source, but was tabulated in the 1991 Census workplace report.

Railways and motorways: The identification of 1994 'Main Lines' and 'Principal Places' is taken from the corporate publicity (e.g. timetables and maps) of British Rail InterCity in 1994—when the network had been reviewed and readied for the franchising or privatization of services. Motorways were also taken from 1994 maps, although there is more subjective judgement involved in assigning them to a city-based network (e.g. it is not self-evident whether the M1 should be deemed to go from Sheffield to Leicester via Derby or Nottingham or, indeed, via neither of them). The 1840 railway network was taken from M. Freeman and D.H. Aldcroft (1985), *The Atlas of British Railway History* (Croom Helm, London).

International gateways: The map is based on the number of scheduled international flights from each airport in Britain in the first week of May 1993 (as listed in the British Airports Authority directory). This week was chosen to avoid the extremes of either summer or winter schedules. The accessibility 'surface' was calculated as described in the text, using GIS techniques—see D. Martin (1991) *Geographic Information Systems and Their Socio-economic Applications* (Routledge, London). The table presents the basic data, on numbers of airport and flights, by standard region; it also presents equivalent sea-freight data from *Port Statistics 1991* (Dept. of Transport STB Division, London). The freight flows analysed here exclude liquid bulk, which is primarily oil, and all domestic traffic: imports and exports were combined together, then any port with less than 125,000 tonnes in the year was ignored.

Places to visit: The inset on the map shows individual London boroughs, but 'places' are the areas shown elsewhere on the map and diagram: see the notes to *Ethnicity and opportunity* for a description of these areas. The data used, and the form of analysis carried out, are specified in the text. The British Tourist Authority publishes tabulations from this data source in its annual publication *Sightseeing in the UK* (this analysis is based on the 1991 dataset).

Major tourist attractions: This map and graph draws upon the same British Tourist Authority dataset as did the map for *Places to visit*. Here the data is analysed by individual attraction, rather than combining together the number of visitors to all the attractions in an area. Even so, the symbols on the map are presented against a background which shows whether or not they fall within major cities. It is not simple to obtain accurate measures of the size of British cities: for example, a coherent definition of London would clearly include the whole of the Greater London county—and probably more—but this could not be sensibly compared with Birmingham if that city was similarly represented by the whole of the West Midlands county, because that area also includes Coventry, Wolverhampton, and several other major centres. For this reason, the map measures the 1991 population size of 'places' (see the notes to *Ethnicity and opportunity*). The caption on the left-hand side of the map shows the size ranges into which the large cities are grouped for the map. Even this careful approach produces some surprising results, however, such as Sheffield's greater size not being quite enough to lift it into a larger size band than its neighbour Barnsley (largely because the latter has to be combined with Rotherham as a single 'place').

Information cities: The table's definition of Britain's 'first eleven' cities is derived from the size ranking of 'places' which is described in the notes to *Major tourist attractions*. The listing of daily evening newspaper publishing centres was taken from *Benn's Media 1993, i: United Kingdom* (Benn Business Information Services, Tonbridge). The boundaries of the ITV Channel 3 regions are a simplified version of those mapped by the Independent Television Commission: in some areas two or even three regions overlap, and where an overlap is large enough to include one or more of the towns or cities shown on the map this is represented by the border passing through, rather than round, those places; e.g. the overlap between Central and Anglia includes not only Peterborough, Kettering, and Northampton,

but also Milton Keynes (which is in the Carlton region as well).

Sporting cities: This map uses as its background the same large 'places' as were introduced for the map of *Major tourist attractions* (see the respective notes above). The decisions taken on which sporting centres to include on the map are documented and—so far as is possible—justified in the text.

Voting

Voters' apathy: The data on non-registration used to produce this graph was provided by Steve Simpson. Note that people who are not Commonwealth or Irish citizens cannot vote at general elections. It was Margaret Thatcher who argued that the Community Charge resulted in fewer adults registering to vote.

Election results 1992: The source of the 1992 General Election data is *The Times* newspaper. The data is also available in *Dod's Guide to the House of Commons 1992* (London: Dod's Parliamentary Companion Ltd.).

Predicting future voting patterns: The voting data has been extracted from the ESRC Data Archive at Essex University, and aggregated to the level of counties and Scottish regions.

Tactical voting and a future political map: The source of the voting data is as for *Predicting future voting patterns*.

Appendix 2: Key maps

Counties, Scottish regions, Islands areas and districts

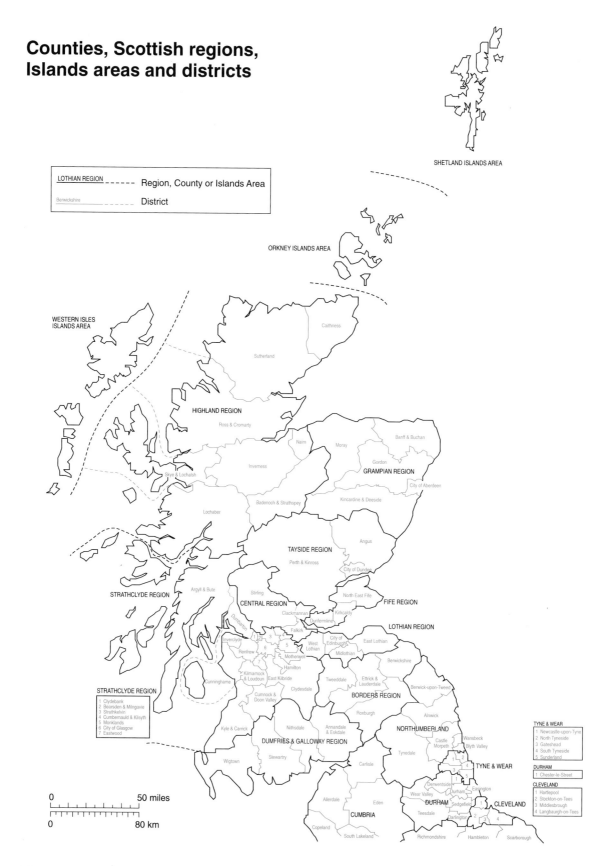

SHETLAND ISLANDS AREA

LOTHIAN REGION — — — — Region, County or Islands Area

Berwickshire — — — — District

ORKNEY ISLANDS AREA

WESTERN ISLES
ISLANDS AREA

Caithness

Sutherland

HIGHLAND REGION

Ross & Cromarty

Nairn

Moray

Banff & Buchan

Gordon

GRAMPIAN REGION

City of Aberdeen

Inverness

Skye & Lochalsh

Badenoch & Strathspey

Kincardine & Deeside

Lochaber

Angus

TAYSIDE REGION

Perth & Kinross

City of Dundee

STRATHCLYDE REGION

Argyll & Bute

Stirling

CENTRAL REGION

North East Fife

FIFE REGION

Clackmannan

Kirkcaldy

Cumbernauld

Dunfermline

LOTHIAN REGION

Inverclyde

Falkirk

City of
Edinburgh

East Lothian

Renfrew

West
Lothian

Midlothian

Motherwell

Berwickshire

Hamilton

Kilmarnock
& Loudoun

East Kilbride

Tweeddale

Ettrick &
Lauderdale

Cunninghame

Clydesdale

Berwick-upon-Tweed

BORDERS REGION

Cumnock &
Doon Valley

Roxburgh

Alnwick

STRATHCLYDE REGION
1 Clydebank
2 Bearsden & Milngavie
3 Strathkelvin
4 Cumbernauld & Kilsyth
5 Monklands
6 City of Glasgow
7 Eastwood

Nithsdale

NORTHUMBERLAND

Wansbeck

Kyle & Carrick

Annandale
& Eskdale

Castle
Morpeth

Blyth Valley

Tynedale

TYNE & WEAR

DUMFRIES & GALLOWAY REGION

Stewartry

TYNE & WEAR
1 Newcastle-upon-Tyne
2 North Tyneside
3 Gateshead
4 South Tyneside
5 Sunderland

Wigtown

Carlisle

DURHAM
1 Chester-le-Street

0 ————— 50 miles

0 ————— 80 km

Allerdale

Eden

Wear Valley

Derwentside

Durham

Easington

CLEVELAND
1 Hartlepool
2 Stockton-on-Tees
3 Middlesbrough
4 Langbaurgh-on-Tees

DURHAM

Sedgefield

CLEVELAND

CUMBRIA

Teesdale

Darlington

Copeland

South Lakeland

Richmondshire

Hambleton

Scarborough

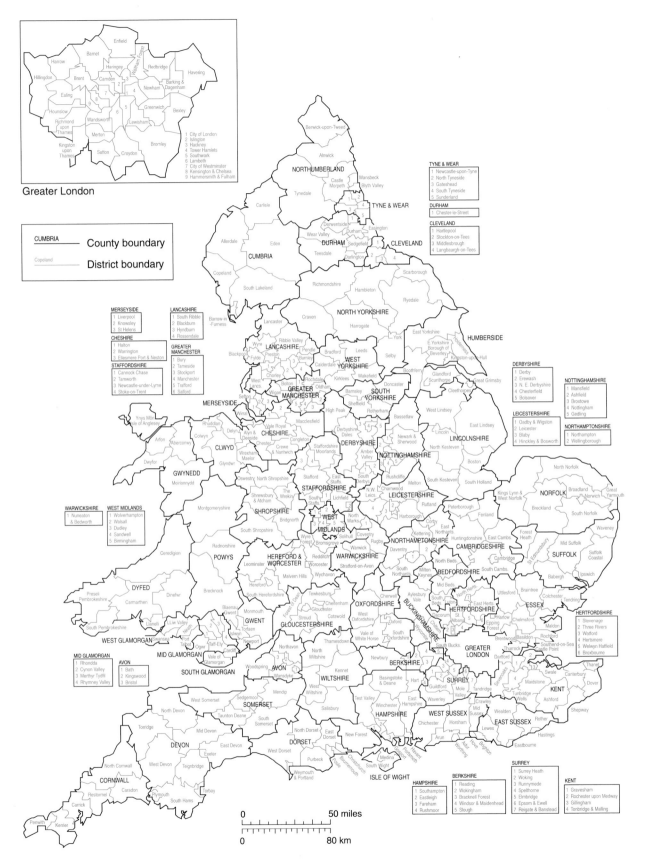

Greater London

1 City of London
2 Islington
3 Hackney
4 Tower Hamlets
5 Southwark
6 Lambeth
7 City of Westminster
8 Kensington & Chelsea
9 Hammersmith & Fulham

CUMBRIA ——— County boundary
Copeland ——— District boundary

MERSEYSIDE
1 Liverpool
2 Knowsley
3 St Helens

CHESHIRE
1 Halton
2 Warrington
3 Ellesmere Port & Neston

STAFFORDSHIRE
1 Cannock Chase
2 Tamworth
3 Newcastle-under-Lyme
4 Stoke-on-Trent

LANCASHIRE
1 South Ribble
2 Blackburn
3 Hyndburn
4 Rossendale

GREATER MANCHESTER
1 Bury
2 Tameside
3 Stockport
4 Manchester
5 Trafford
6 Salford

TYNE & WEAR
1 Newcastle-upon-Tyne
2 North Tyneside
3 Gateshead
4 South Tyneside
5 Sunderland

DURHAM
1 Chester-le-Street

CLEVELAND
1 Hartlepool
2 Stockton-on-Tees
3 Middlesbrough
4 Langbaurgh-on-Tees

DERBYSHIRE
1 Derby
2 Erewash
3 N. E. Derbyshire
4 Chesterfield
5 Bolsover

LEICESTERSHIRE
1 Oadby & Wigston
2 Leicester
3 Blaby
4 Hinckley & Bosworth

NOTTINGHAMSHIRE
1 Mansfield
2 Ashfield
3 Broxtowe
4 Nottingham
5 Gedling

NORTHAMPTONSHIRE
1 Northampton
2 Wellingborough

WARWICKSHIRE
1 Nuneaton & Bedworth

WEST MIDLANDS
1 Wolverhampton
2 Walsall
3 Dudley
4 Sandwell
5 Birmingham

MID GLAMORGAN
1 Rhondda
2 Cynon Valley
3 Merthyr Tydfil
4 Rhymney Valley

AVON
1 Bath
2 Kingswood
3 Bristol

HERTFORDSHIRE
1 Stevenage
2 Three Rivers
3 Watford
4 Hertsmere
5 Welwyn Hatfield
6 Broxbourne

SURREY
1 Surrey Heath
2 Woking
3 Runnymede
4 Spelthorne
5 Elmbridge
6 Epsom & Ewell
7 Reigate & Banstead

HAMPSHIRE
1 Southampton
2 Eastleigh
3 Fareham
4 Rushmoor

BERKSHIRE
1 Reading
2 Wokingham
3 Bracknell Forest
4 Windsor & Maidenhead
5 Slough

KENT
1 Gravesham
2 Rochester upon Medway
3 Gillingham
4 Tonbridge & Malling

0 ———— 50 miles

0 ———— 80 km

153

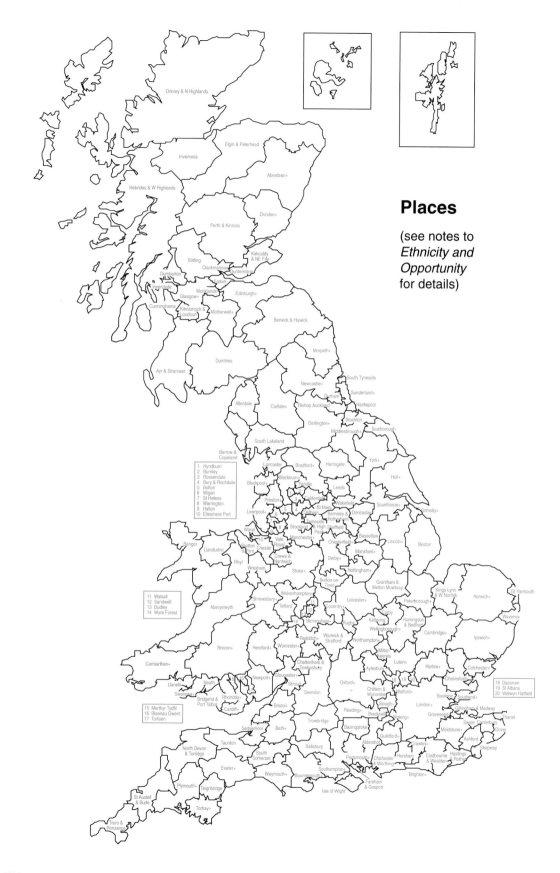

Places

(see notes to
*Ethnicity and
Opportunity*
for details)

Orkney & N Highlands

Elgin & Peterhead

Inverness

Hebrides & W Highlands

Aberdeen+

Dundee+

Perth & Kinross

Kirkcaldy
& NE Fife

Stirling
Clackmannan Dunfermline
Dumbarton Falkirk
Inverclyde Monklands Edinburgh+
Glasgow+
Cunninghame Kilmarnock &
Loudoun Motherwell+

Berwick & Hawick

Ayr & Stranraer

Dumfries

Morpeth+

Newcastle+ South Tyneside
Durham+ Sunderland+
Bishop Auckland Hartlepool

Allerdale
Carlisle+ Stockton
Darlington+ Middlesbrough+ Scarborough

Barrow &
Copeland South Lakeland
York+

Lancaster Bradford+ Harrogate
1 Hyndburn
2 Burnley Blackpool+ Blackburn Pendle Hull+
3 Rossendale Leeds
4 Bury & Rochdale Preston+ Calderdale Wakefield+
5 Bolton Kirklees Scunthorpe+ Grimsby+
6 Wigan Liverpool+ Oldham Barnsley & Doncaster
7 St Helens Tameside Rotherham
8 Warrington Wirral Stockport High Sheffield+ Bassetlaw
9 Halton Manchester Peak Lincoln+ Boston
10 Ellesmere Port Vale Chesterfield+
Flint Royal Mansfield+
Chester Crewe & Derby+
Bangor Nantwich Nottingham+
Llandudno Stoke+
Burton-on- Grantham &
Rhyl Trent Melton Mowbray Kings Lynn
Wrexham & W Norfolk Gt Yarmouth
Shrewsbury+ Telford Leicester+ Peterborough+ Norwich+
11 Walsall Coventry Waveney
12 Sandwell Aberystwyth Rugby Huntingdon
13 Dudley Birmingham Kettering & Bedford
14 Wyre Forest Redditch Wellingborough Cambridge+ Ipswich+
Warwick & Northampton+
Brecon+ Worcester+ Stratford
Hereford+ Milton
Carmarthen Keynes Colchester+
Cheltenham & Luton+ Harlow+ 18 Dacorum
Llanelli Tewkesbury Aylesbury 19 St Albans
Neath Gloucester+ Chelmsford 20 Welwyn Hatfield
Newport+ Stroud Chiltern & Watford London+ Southend+
Swansea Oxford+ Wycombe Basildon
15 Merthyr Tydfil Bridgend & Rhondda+ Swindon Slough Gillingham & Medway
16 Blaenau Gwent Port Talbot Cardiff+ Reading+ Bracknell Woking+ Gravesend Thanet
17 Torfaen Trowbridge Basingstoke London+ Maidstone Swale Canterbury
Sedgemoor Bath+ Guildford Ashford Shepway
North Devon South Salisbury Aldershot Crawley+
& Torridge Taunton Somerset Portsmouth+ Chichester Horsham Hastings
Southampton+ Worthing Eastbourne Rother
Exeter+ Weymouth+ Bournemouth+ Fareham & Wealden
Plymouth+ Teignbridge & Gosport Brighton+
Isle of Wight
Torbay+

St Austell
& Bude

Truro &
Penzance

Cartogram of parliamentary constituencies

(see *Voters' Apathy* for details)

Orkney & Shetland
Banff & Buchan
Western Isles
Aberdeen
Inverness, Nairn & Lochaber
Argyll & Bute
Dundee

SCOTLAND

Falkirk
Glasgow
Edinburgh
Midlothian
Cunninghame
Motherwell
Ayr
Dumfries

Berwick-upon-Tweed
Blyth Valley
Newcastle upon Tyne
NORTH
Hexham
Gateshead East
Tyne Bridge
Carlisle
Sunderland
Durham
Hartlepool
Workington
Bishop Auckland
Stockton
Copeland
Harrogate
Blackpool
Lancaster
York
Bridlington
Burnley
YORKSHIRE AND HUMBERSIDE
NORTH WEST
Blackburn
Leeds
Bradford
Southport
Bury
Kingston-upon-Hull
Bolton
Huddersfield
Wigan
Barnsley
Manchester
Liverpool
St Helens
Hazel Grove
Sheffield
Bassetlaw
Wirral
EAST MIDLANDS
Grantham
Warrington
Stoke-on-Trent
Derby
Nottingham
EAST ANGLIA
Caernarfon
Wrexham
Erewash
Leicester
Great Yarmouth
Walsall
Huntingdon
Norwich
Wolverhampton
Bury St Edmunds
Shrewsbury & Atcham
WEST MIDLANDS
Coventry
Cambridge
WALES
Dudley
Birmingham
Luton
Leominster
Northampton
St Albans
Enfield
Chingford
Warwick
Chesham & Amersham
Carmarthen
Chelmsford
Cheltenham
Finchley
LONDON
Ilford
Blaenau Gwent
Oxford
Brent
Basildon
Rhondda
Islington
Newham
Swansea
Gloucester
Windsor
City of London
Southend
Cardiff
Bristol
Bath
Ealing
Chelsea
Thurrock
Reading
Bexley Heath
Putney
Lewisham
Canterbury
Westbury
Spelthorne
Dartford
Dover
Taunton
Winchester
Twickenham
Mid Kent
SOUTH WEST
Yeovil
Woking
Croydon
Orpington
Tiverton
Christchurch
Guildford
Tunbridge Wells
Exeter
Horsham
Hastings & Rye
Truro
Bournemouth
REST OF SOUTH EAST
Torbay
St Ives
Plymouth
Isle of Wight
Portsmouth
Worthing
Brighton

GP